CARRY THE ROCK

CARRY THE ROCK

RACE, FOOTBALL,
AND THE SOUL
OF AN AMERICAN CITY

JAY JENNINGS

RODALE

© 2010 by Jay Jennings

All rights reserved. No part of this publication may be reproduced or transmitted in any form or by any means, electronic or mechanical, including photocopying, recording, or any other information storage and retrieval system, without the written permission of the publisher.

Rodale books may be purchased for business or promotional use or for special sales. For information, please write to: Special Markets Department, Rodale Inc., 733 Third Avenue, New York, NY 10017.

Printed in the United States of America

Rodale Inc. makes every effort to use acid-free ∞, recycled paper ♲.

Book design by Christopher Rhoads

Map on page viii–ix by Erin Greb Cartography

Library of Congress Cataloging-in-Publication Data

Jennings, Jay.
    Carry the rock : race, football, and the soul of an American city / Jay Jennings.
       p.   cm.
    Includes bibliographical references and index.
    ISBN-13: 978–1–60529–637–1   hardcover
    ISBN-10: 1–60529–637–6   hardcover
    1. Central High School (Little Rock, Ark.)—Football. 2. Football—Arkansas—Little Rock. 3. Central High School (Little Rock, Ark.)—History. 4. Little Rock (Ark.)—Race relations—History. I. Title.
    GV958.C44J46 2010
    796.332'620976773—dc22   2010013327

Distributed to the trade by Macmillan

2 4 6 8 10 9 7 5 3 1   hardcover

We inspire and enable people to improve their lives and the world around them

For more of our products visit **rodalestore.com** or call 800-848-4735

For my father, **WALTER**,
and in memory of my mother, **MEDORA**,
and brother, **WALT**

CONTENTS

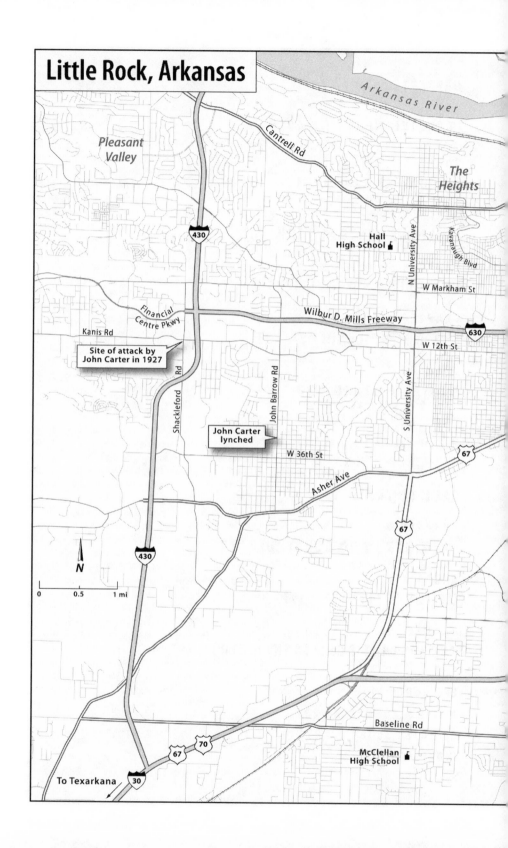

Little Rock, Arkansas

Arkansas River

Pleasant
Valley

Cantrell Rd

The
Heights

430

Hall
High School

N University Ave

Kavanaugh Blvd

W Markham St

Financial
Centre Pkwy

Wilbur D. Mills Freeway

630

Kanis Rd

W 12th St

**Site of attack by
John Carter in 1927**

Shackleford Rd

John Barrow Rd

S University Ave

**John Carter
lynched**

W 36th St

67

Asher Ave

67

N

0   0.5   1 mi

430

67 70

Baseline Rd

McClellan
High School

To Texarkana 30

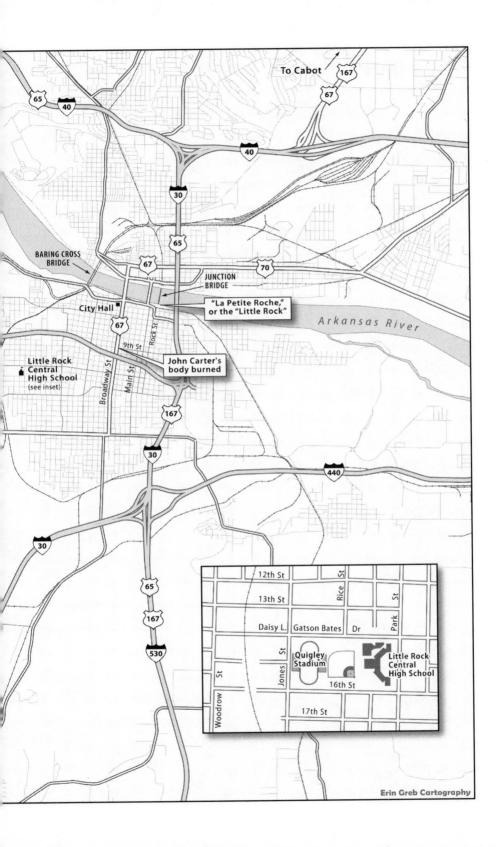

UPON THIS ROCK

THE ACTUAL "LITTLE ROCK," AN ORDINARY-LOOKING chunk of sandstone sticking out from the southern bank of the Arkansas River, hardly seems prepossessing enough to name a city after. French explorer Jean-Baptiste Bénard de La Harpe only noticed it because, as he navigated up the Arkansas from the Mississippi in 1722, it was the first rock he saw, the very point at which the Mississippi Delta plains rise into the foothills of the Ouachita Mountains to the west. La Harpe didn't think it so distinctive that it deserved an official name. Farther on, when he came to a bluff (*"un grand rocher"*—the big rock) on the north side of the river, he called it, with Gallic ego, *"le Rocher Français."* Only later, in comparison to the geology upstream, did the smaller outcropping gain the name *"le Petit Rocher,"* as it first appeared on a map in 1799. (The Indians, of course, were already there, the Quapaw tribe having established the point as being the easiest spot to cross the river.)

Some two decades later, after the territory had been acquired in the Louisiana Purchase, Thomas Nuttall, a British botanist, recorded the appeal of the area's rolling, verdant landscape following his slog through the Delta: "After emerging as it were from so vast a tract of alluvial lands, as that through which I had now been travelling for more than three months, it is almost impossible to describe the pleasure which these romantic prospects again afforded me." The scene still delights. A road-tripper from Pennsylvania recently wrote to the *New York Times* letters page, "Who outside of Arkansas knew Little Rock was so beautiful?"

Some early landholders tried to ennoble the nascent town by rechristen-
ing it Arkopolis, but the name didn't stick. So since 1821, it has been Little
Rock, a modest name for a modest frontier town. Then, only forty families
lived there. They did not all get along with each other, but the place had
promise. In 1834, shortly after Little Rock was incorporated and two years
before Arkansas would be admitted to the Union as a slave state, George
Featherstonhaugh, an English geologist touring the South, commented on
the disputatious nature of Little Rock's "young bucks and bloods" armed
"with pistols or large hunting knives," but he finally concluded, "in virtue of
its being the seat of government, it may in time become a respectable small
town, have good seminaries for the education of the youth of the territory,
and afford agreeable society."

It would be a while. An early mayor was discovered to head a band of
counterfeiters. Violence ruled politics. Duels were common. Little Rockians
even seemed more likely to fight among themselves than against outsiders.
Union general Frederick Steele took the town without much resistance in
1863, but during Reconstruction some ten years later, a gun battle in the
streets outside the State House over the rightful holder of the governorship
left two hundred people dead. As one historian put it in 1887, the conflicts
among the citizens "bore much bloody fruit, and gave Arkansas an unenviable name abroad, from which she has not entirely recovered to this day."

Toward the end of the nineteenth century, the spot was booming, nearly
doubling its population during the 1880s to 25,874. Up sprang a couple of
the "good seminaries" that Featherstonhaugh had predicted, the public Peabody High School (the precursor of Little Rock Central High) and the private Little Rock Academy. The young bucks were now in school and found
in the rugged new sport of football an outlet for their aggression that lacked
the overt and illegal dangers of guns and knives. On Thanksgiving Day in
1894, just three years after Walter Camp had codified the game's differences
from English rugby in his book *American Football*, the two schools met in the
first recorded game involving a public high school in the city. Of the contest's atmosphere, the *Arkansas Gazette* reported that "there is a great deal of
latent football enthusiasm in Little Rock which is wasting away for an oppor-

tunity to turn loose and yell itself hoarse." Neither did the pageantry go unremarked upon: "The teams and their maids of honor arrived in vans shortly after 3 o'clock and were driven around the field several times." Apparently the enthusiasm became more than latent, when Peabody's "O'Hair got around the end for a good gain, but was interfered with by spectators and a possible touchdown missed." Peabody lost that initial game 12–0, but football caught on.

One hundred and thirteen years later, in 2007, a similar scene at the very same spot unfolded on a fall Friday night. The plot of land once called West End Park had been transformed over the decades from a densely wooded public recreation ground into the site of a minor-league baseball field and then into the campus and stadium of a massive high school. The layers of history, writ both large and small, accrue like geologic strata here, each one pressing upon the last. In 1899, a series of assaults near the park by "a negro" victimizing "highly respected white women" put the town so on edge that "the officers will find it difficult to protect their prisoners, should the right men be captured." In 1921, a neighborhood boy named Dee Brown watched a minor-league baseball game through a wire-mesh fence, and the kindness of an American Indian player named Moses Yellow Horse spurred in him a lifetime interest in the West that culminated in his book *Bury My Heart at Wounded Knee*. In 1935, Helen Hayes packed the high school auditorium for her touring show *Mary of Scotland*. And, in 1957, on Park Street in front of the school and in the halls of Little Rock Central High, one of the seminal conflicts of the civil rights era erupted as nine African American students integrated the school. Once again, Little Rock seemed like a frontier town, and the words of the nineteenth-century historian about Arkansas's "unenviable name abroad" echoed again.

Now, more than fifty years later, that event has both receded and reemerged. It has been the defining moment for the city and the one the city hopes to transcend. It has been the old wound reopened by every racial conflict since, and it is distant history to current Central High students.

The process of examining that past in 2007 would be painful, exasperating, and occasionally encouraging. Two years before the integration of

Central High, James Baldwin wrote in *Notes of a Native Son:* "In the context of the Negro problem neither whites nor blacks, for excellent reasons of their own, have the faintest desire to look back; but I think that the past is all that makes the present coherent, and further, that the past will remain horrible for exactly as long as we refuse to assess it honestly." The living present soon becomes the past, and you never know when your own small history will become large, which coach's words will ring in your ears dozens of years later, what personal fight might ascend to the highest court in the land. So the little battles of Little Rock matter. Now, the ordinary politics—the school board races and the local legal actions, the ones that matter most to the people who live here—consume the community. And now, as they have every fall for more than a century, two high school football teams face each other on this same little patch of Little Rock.

As for the "little rock" itself by the river, it was formerly larger than it is now. Showing a practical rather than a romantic turn of mind, the city fathers chipped away at it over the years in favor of industry. In 1872, construction on a proposed but never completed bridge cut away several tons of the rock and dumped them into the river. In a more successful attempt at devising a crossing, some businessmen formed the Little Rock Junction Railway Company and hacked away again at the stone, building right on top of it the foundation of their bridge, which was finished in 1884 and eventually used by the Missouri Pacific Railroad.

In 1932, members of Little Rock's Civitan Club, mindful of history and perhaps regretful that the city's namesake had been so diminished, persuaded the railroad to let them break off a 4,700-pound piece so they could place it on the grounds of City Hall, thus making the little rock even smaller. The monument has sat there for seventy-five years, with a large plaque explaining the city's name affixed to it. Now the orphan rock might be on the move again: The city's center of activity has drifted downstream to the Clinton Presidential Library and the River Market area, and someone advanced a proposal to give the fragment a more prominent display there.

The bridge supported by the remains of the original "little rock" has been recently converted into a pleasant pedestrian walkway, an easy passage to the other side of the river at the same place the Indians had established their ford. A tangential stairway leads down to a small platform under the bridge. There's talk of doing more at the site, of historical markers and lights and plazas and picnicking. But for now, from that spot, a viewer doesn't really know where to look, and his gaze wanders out to follow the brown progress of the river.

CHAPTER 1

THE DISTANT GOAL

AS THE BALL WAS SNAPPED, KE'WON JONES, one of Central's cornerbacks, backpedaled in quick, choppy steps. The Catholic High receiver broke toward the sideline and Jones pivoted off his right foot, turning to run back and looking over his right shoulder to gauge the angle of intersection between ball, receiver, and sideline. The move was second nature by now, the ninth game of the season. He'd been burned once already tonight—Senior Night, his last home game as a Little Rock Central High Tiger football player—and no one was going to get by him again.

Catholic, the Tigers' fiercest in-town rival, had just recovered a fumble at the Central 37 with nine minutes left in the fourth quarter. That mistake, with Catholic leading 27–21, seemed to have ended Central's chances of coming back from a twenty-point second-half deficit. Two running plays gained the Rockets a first down. A few more such plays—Catholic had moved the ball easily for three quarters—would bring the clock closer to zero, and the Rockets closer to a playoff spot that was practically guaranteed to the winner, who would go to 6-3 for the season as the loser dropped to 5-4. Instead, Catholic went for the kill with a long pass down the Central sideline.

The Rockets had thrown for three touchdowns, victimizing the secondary as Russellville High had earlier in the year in a 23–0 shutout, the Tigers' worst loss in a decade. That game had been acutely embarrassing for the players, the coaches, and the parents, one of whom had nearly come to blows

1

with two other fans in the stands. The shame and shock of the loss had stemmed not just from the team's No. 1 ranking in the preseason, but also from the Tigers' history as the reigning dynasty of Arkansas high school football, owners of thirty-two state championships in more than a hundred years of play.

The year 2007 was supposed to be Central's year in any number of ways. A host of starters were returning from a young team that had gone through the conference schedule undefeated the season before and then lost in the first round of the playoffs to the eventual state champion. Moreover, all during the fall, the school had been the focus of attention, both in the community and in the national media, arising from the fiftieth anniversary of its integration. Some of the players proudly wore T-shirts bearing the commemoration logo under their pads. But the promise of achieving some kind of salutary symmetry with the 1957 team, an all-white squad that had produced an undefeated season amid the racial turmoil, hadn't been answered. The 2007 team hadn't lived up to expectations.

After the terrible loss to Russellville, defensive backs coach Darrell Seward had told the secondary, "There's only one way to say it: We have sucked this year." Part of the failing was due to personnel problems. The team's best athlete, safety Kaelon Kelleybrew, had missed several games, including the Russellville loss, and other d-backs had suffered injuries. Even so, the secondary had underperformed. On the Friday of the Catholic game, as Jones and some other football players left their stagecraft class being held behind the auditorium's proscenium—a class in which only nose guard Quinton Brown was applying himself, conceiving a set for *Women of Troy*—Jones glanced at the words he'd lettered earlier in the year on the back of a scenery scrim: "K. Jones #6 'Shutdown.'" The self-awarded nickname had been more of a hope than a reality up to that point.

But on this late October night, as the ball hung in the galaxy of lights above the seventy-one-year-old Quigley Stadium, K. Jones saw that its trajectory was off—the pass was badly overthrown, or perhaps was intended to go out of bounds but had not been thrown far enough. In any case, Jones ignored the receiver and tracked the ball as it descended toward the sideline. At his own 5-yard line, he leapt and caught the ball above his head. His left foot came down on the 3-yard line and his right crossed in front of it, landing inches inbounds at the 2. As he brought the ball into his gut to secure the interception, he stepped out at his own 1-yard line, right in front of the Central student section, which erupted. The players also burst into cheers, some even raising both arms in a gesture that mimicked a touchdown signal. The reality, however, was that the Tigers remained ninety-nine yards away from the goal line, as far away as they could be from a touchdown.

The offense trotted into its own end zone, and the bulbs on the scoreboard at the other end looked distant and dim. Above the numbers reporting the six-point difference, the players could see the painted sign identifying the structure as Quigley Stadium, named for an early Central coach, Earl Quigley, and below it—but for some reason in larger letters—the grass they stood on as Bernie Cox Field. From his position on the sidelines, head coach Bernie Cox himself looked on.

It was a field he sometimes walked and pulled weeds from, as if it were his own well-tended front yard, but if Cox accepted and appreciated such honors, he didn't relish or encourage them. This one had been planned in 2005, the year before he was elected to the Arkansas Sports Hall of Fame, by Kevin Crass, a Little Rock lawyer whose son had played for Cox. Now a brass plaque with his etched likeness, a stern visage one could imagine as Mark Antony, was screwed to a pillar in the stadium's concourse, reading in part: "A man of high moral character, he has been a great teacher of life's lessons to his players. Former players routinely state their gratitude for the impact Coach Cox had upon their lives. Parents of his players see firsthand this impact upon their sons."

The plaque was about the only cosmetic improvement Quigley Stadium had seen in many years. The slightest rain left pools of water on the main-level concession area and in the locker rooms below the east stands. A pigeon infestation among the concrete supports over the concourse kept the cleaning staff occupied. The coaches met in the same one-room office from which Clyde Van Sickle, a former Green Bay Packers guard, had run the team in the brand-new, Works Progress Administration–built stadium after he took over the head coach's job in 1936. At that time, it was a marvel of modernity, the largest football facility in the state. Since Bernie Cox had arrived in 1972 as an assistant, the walls of the office, he estimated, had been painted twice—both times in a Tiger old gold that has since faded to Dijon mustard. When he ascended to head coach in 1975, he moved approximately six feet away from the assistant coaches' table to the room's only desk, next to a big window that looked out into the locker room.

For thirty-two years, his stare had struck fear in the hearts of players tough enough to make it in the NFL and smart enough to become surgeons. Damien Lee, a Division I college prospect at tight end, said that once, during a busy class changeover, Cox tripped going up the school's front steps, his armload of books spilling around him. "It was like time stopped," Lee said. "Nobody moved. I didn't know whether to go help him or not." Cox retrieved his books and went on his way. "Nobody laughed or said anything like they would have with anybody else."

||||||||||||||||||||||||||||||||||||||

Fifty years before, those front steps and their surroundings were the stage upon which one of the country's great civil rights dramas was enacted. The graceful sloping lawn and reflecting pool, the false portico supporting the name LITTLE ROCK CENTRAL HIGH SCHOOL, and the soaring collegiate gothic tower filled television screens, newspaper front pages, and magazine covers, serving as the backdrop for a real-life morality play.

No one had expected that there would be significant problems with desegregation in Little Rock. The city's reputation as a place with moderate views on race relations, especially among its community leaders, seemed to bode well for peaceful adherence to the law decided in *Brown v. Board of Education of Topeka* in 1954. The second *Brown* decision, which came to be known as *Brown* II and was handed down in 1955, added the provision that desegregation should proceed "with all deliberate speed"— four words that have befuddled constitutional scholars for years—but left specific remedies largely to the discretion of local districts. Future cases would determine "whether the action of school authorities constitutes good faith implementation."

After the Supreme Court's first ruling, officials in Little Rock set right to work, resignedly, devising a plan of token compliance. Conceived largely by superintendent of schools Virgil Blossom, a hulking former college football player whose girth and sometimes autocratic manner belied his dainty name, the program originally called for integrating at the elementary school level before gradually moving up to the high schools. Over the year between the two *Brown* decisions, his proposal was turned on its head, starting with one high school, Central High, and trickling down over the next seven years to the lower grades. It also became more restrictively cautious, whittling down, through screening and interviews, the initial list of seventy black candidates requesting transfer into Central to the famous nine. They were the best and brightest, superior students of good character who knew they were taking a moral and political as well as a personal and educational stand: Minnijean Brown, Elizabeth Eckford, Ernest Green, Thelma Mothershed, Melba Pattillo, Gloria Ray, Terrence Roberts, Jefferson Thomas, and Carlotta Walls.

For some black leaders, nine was not enough. The primary voice protesting Blossom's minimalist start came from the Arkansas Council on Human Relations, a biracial organization whose members included the progressive editor Harry Ashmore of the *Arkansas Gazette*; Daisy Bates, then of the NAACP and later the chief mentor of the Little Rock Nine; and a young black attorney named John Walker, the group's associate director. Colbert Cartwright, a Disciples of Christ minister who was the chairman of the board of the organization, contended that under the Blossom plan, "every effort was being made to keep the number of Negroes entering white schools to a minimum."

Though segregationists had held noisy rallies all year, the elite of Little Rock seemed to discount their influence and underestimated the growing class resentment. "Apparently not until August 1957 did city officials formulate even a meager . . . plan for maintaining order in the Central High School area," wrote historian Numan V. Bartley in 1966. The school board members, as well as most of the city's business leaders, lived in the affluent Heights area, and their children would be attending Hall High, to be newly opened, unintegrated, in 1957. That left the burden of desegregation to be imposed on the mostly middle- and lower-class families remaining at Central, groups with whom governor Orval Faubus felt some kinship.

On Labor Day, the day before classes were to begin, Little Rockians returning home from a last gasp of summer at Lake Hamilton or the newly created Lake Ouachita in Hot Springs might have noticed caravans of National Guard troops descending on the city, headed for Central High. Faubus had ordered them there, as he stated in a televised address that night, to "protect the lives and property of citizens," but he added that that might not be possible "if forcible integration is carried out tomorrow." His language was oblique, and he insisted that the matter was still a local one, but his words and actions fired segregationist resistance.

By the next morning, a crowd of four hundred to five hundred people had gathered at the school, along with Little Rock police and 270 soldiers. Concurrently, legal efforts by white groups to stop integration had been brought in several local courts, and, finally, after weighing the potential for trouble, the school board itself had asked for a delay. Under instructions from Blossom, all black students (and black employees) stayed away from Central High on the first day of school, "until this dilemma is legally resolved." Later that day, federal judge Ronald N. Davies, on a temporary appointment from North Dakota to help reduce the caseload in Arkansas, ruled that integration must proceed.

On Wednesday, September 4, the crisis got its iconographic moment. Late Tuesday night, Bates had instructed the nine students to meet before school the next morning at her home, where a phalanx of black and white ministers, whose presence she hoped might shield them from potential trouble, would escort them to the school. The family of fifteen-year-old Elizabeth Eckford didn't have a phone, and, in the confusion of the events of the next morning, she was not informed of the plan. She took a city bus to the corner of Park and Twelfth Streets, two blocks north of the school.

A crowd of two hundred white protesters was waiting for her opposite the school, waving Confederate flags and Nigger Go Home! signs and yelling "Go back where you came from!" If she felt initial comfort at the sight of the National Guard troops, it turned to fear and confusion when she saw the soldiers parting for white students approaching the building but raising their guns and blocking her way as she followed the same path. Barred from entering, she crossed in front of the school toward the bus stop at Sixteenth Street for the return trip home, and photographer Will Counts of the *Arkansas Democrat* caught the stoicism of her face behind her big, tortoiseshell sunglasses as she walked away from the jeering mob, a picture of vulnerability and courage amid apoplectic anger. The image would introduce Little Rock's dilemma to the nation and the world.

"For two months, Little Rock would have a firm grip on page one," wrote the authors of *The Race Beat*, an exploration of press coverage of the civil rights movement. After more legal jockeying, on September 20, Faubus removed the National Guard under court order, and five days later, after the black students faced a mob of some one thousand outside the school with only Little Rock police for protection, president Dwight Eisenhower federalized the Guard and called in the 101st Airborne Division to help ensure the nine students' entrance and future safety.

For the rest of the fall, as the soldiers remained at "Fort Central" and escorted the black students in and out of the building and from class to class, the nine precariously tried to balance the ordinary anxieties and activities of high school with the controversy swirling around them. The security detail could not prevent them from being harassed by a persistent group of tormentors.

Life for the 1,981 white students at Central went on as normally as it could, and "normal" meant having a winning football team. The Tigers were once again proving themselves a national powerhouse, beating some of the best teams from Tennessee, Kentucky, and Louisiana on the way to an undefeated season. The stands of Quigley Stadium were packed all season with new fans as well: the soldiers of the 101st who manned the jeeps and helicopters parked on the Tigers' practice field.

Not allowed in the bleachers were the nine black youths. As a condition of their transfer to Central, they were barred from participating in extracurricular activities.

IIIIIIIIIIIIIIIIIIIIIIIIIIIIIIIIIIIIIII

The same government programs that built Quigley Stadium in 1936 also built Dyess, Arkansas, where Bernie Lynn Cox was born in 1944. In the wake of the Great Depression, the government recruited farmers from all over Arkansas to apply for acceptance to the Dyess Colony, an experimental, cut-from-the-cypress-swamps cooperative farming community in northeast Arkansas, about fifteen miles west of the Mississippi River. The land was available on good terms, but it was tough to farm. You got twenty acres, a house and a barn, a mule and a horse, and groceries until your first crops came in. The fields, however, were "buckshot soil," "rich and lumpy but hard to work in wet weather," according to one source. Every house also kept at least one guinea fowl, Bernie Lynn remembered, to peck around and keep the ticks under control. There were no black farmers; the program excluded them.

Bernie's father, Bernie Lee Cox, had been born in southwest Arkansas, north of Murfreesboro, and had spent his early childhood on his father's farm, where his dad ran a blacksmith shop and raised watermelons, tomatoes, cotton, peanuts, sorghum, anything that would grow. "He'd take a load of stove wood to town," said Bernie Lee, "and maybe pick off a tow sack of peanuts and put it up on that wood, and he'd trade that wood and peanuts for salt, pepper, coffee." When the government came calling with its offer of land in northeast Arkansas in 1936, the family packed up and moved to Dyess. Already there, having made a similar trip from south Arkansas, was a family named Cash, with a three-year-old called J.R., later to be known as Johnny.

Bernie Lee, just into his teens, worked the farm while his dad set up a business selling farmers' insurance and became a middleman between the Dyess community and used furniture stores in Oceola and tractor equipment dealers all over. "He just had his hands in everything," said Bernie Lee, who tended a cultivator at age thirteen with his twin one-year-old siblings on the back of the buggy "so my mama could do the housework." He was married at eighteen, drafted in 1943 at nineteen, and served in the infantry in the Pacific during World War II. He was wounded on Saipan shortly after his oldest son, Bernie Lynn Cox, was born. Shrapnel embedded in Bernie Lee's heart, too dangerous to remove, remained there still. When he returned home and had recovered from his injuries, he worked as a taxi driver and a butcher, but soon moved his young family to Little Rock so he could attend Draughons Business College. After a stint selling women's shoes at the M. M. Cohn department store downtown, he eventually got a job as a purchasing agent for the Arkansas Highway Department, from which he would retire after a thirty-one-year career.

The two oldest boys of five siblings, Bernie Lynn and his brother Donnie, said Bernie Lee, "played ball from sunup to sundown" in a vacant lot on Second Street near their home by the Missouri Pacific train station. All the Cox children "happened to be kind of smart, one way or another," he said with a grin, but Bernie Lynn proved particularly responsible: "I didn't have to tell him to brush his teeth. I didn't have to tell him to get his homework done. He did it all hisself." During one Little League game, the catcher didn't show up, so Bernie Lynn started putting on the protective equipment without any prompting from the coach. "That's the way he was," said his father. "He just took charge."

At the same time Bernie was playing sandlot ball, Little Rock High School, which became Little Rock Central in 1953 with the anticipated 1957 opening of Little Rock Hall High in the western part of the city, was at the height of its football powers. From 1944 through 1957, Central's football team won twelve state championships and was twice honored as the best team in the nation, regularly defeating high schools from states all over the South and Midwest. For big games, Central filled the ten thousand seats at Quigley Stadium, and often drew more than eight thousand fans. The coverage of the Tigers in the newspapers was easily double or triple that given to the University of Arkansas, which would not capture the state's football imagination until 1954, the season the Razorbacks won the Cotton Bowl.

Until the late summer of 1957, if Little Rock High School was known at all nationally, it was for the football team. Growing up in downtown Little Rock, some dozen blocks from the school, Bernie Cox was set to be a part of that history as a player. But when he was in fifth grade, his father's job with the highway department moved the family to Jacksonville, fifteen miles northeast of the city, where the air force base was the main source of employment and culture. There, the military uniform was the leveling agent among all races and colors and religions, though, like those in many towns across Arkansas, Jacksonville's public schools remained segregated while officials waited to see what would transpire in Little Rock and the courts. Bernie would graduate in 1962 from Jacksonville High School, where he was a feisty and skilled quarterback, earning an athletic scholarship to Harding College just up the road in Searcy, a Church of Christ–affiliated school twenty miles to the northeast.

There, the teams were not strong, but he was a leader and knew he wanted to go into coaching. He thought he'd probably spend his career as a college assistant, but then he learned what assistant coaches at colleges do: recruit and travel. You might arrive at 2:00 a.m. in a small town and keep your fingers crossed that the seventeen-year-old athlete who said he would sign with you would actually keep his word. "That's probably not me," he remembered thinking at the time. He decided he'd rather work with what he was given than go chasing down what he needed, so high school coaching seemed like a better fit. He'd teach seventeen-year-old kids to keep their word rather than hope they would.

He landed a job in Conway, Arkansas, in 1968 under Dennis Fulmer, then under Joe Fred Young. It was a tumultuous time in the country, but an idyllic one in a small town in a dry county in Arkansas. The Conway schools (and the town) were predominantly white, but had integrated without incident in 1965. Four years later, when Young left for Central, Cox had a decision to make. He was only twenty-eight, but he'd already so impressed the administration in Conway that the principal said he'd support Cox if he wanted to apply for the head job. Cox wasn't sure he was ready. Young had told Cox that he wanted him to join him at Central, and that he could have whatever side of the ball he wanted, offense or defense. "I agonized" over the decision, said Cox, but the pull of coaching at the state's largest and most dominant high school football program was too much, and he moved with his wife, Myrene, to Little Rock in August 1972, taking up residence in a one-story bungalow on Quebec Drive, near Little Rock University, in a neighborhood where the streets' names are Canada-themed.

Though integration had begun fifteen years earlier, it had proceeded at a glacial pace. In the early '70s, a larger wave, prompted by a federal district court order to institute busing, was just breaking, "demolish[ing] the post-*Brown* tactics of relying on housing patterns to minimize integration," writes historian Ben F. Johnson III in *Arkansas in Modern America, 1930–1999*. Cox found that the Central football team of 1972 had a fifty-fifty makeup of white and black players, but he didn't know why it should be different from coaching any other team. His Christian beliefs had him apply what he thought was a simple rule: Treat everyone the same.

After his arrival from Conway, he soon reacquainted himself with the bleachers at Quigley Stadium, the same ones he'd sat on for the first time, he remembered, as a spectator at a track meet when he was a junior at Jacksonville High. From the field so many years later, his perspective was altered: "When I saw how steep they were, I said, 'That's a motivator.'" And so began the long, painful association of Central High Tiger players with the bleachers of Quigley Stadium.

A simple battle of man—or boy—against gravity, running the bleachers was nevertheless a versatile tool. In the off-season, the regimen was a way to lay down a foundation of fitness that could be built on for the lengthy season ahead. When Cox first instituted it, the minimum a player was required to complete was fifteen ascents of the thirty-nine rows and back in fifteen minutes, or in Tiger shorthand, "fifteen in fifteen." But times had changed, he explained to parents at a meeting in Central's auditorium at the beginning of the 2007 school year. Now he required only ten in ten. If he demanded that this generation run fifteen in fifteen, he said, he wouldn't be able to field a football team because none of them could complete it.

Bleachers were also the currency of Tiger football. A missed practice, excused or not, cost a player ten extra bleachers, not including the daily allotment. Enjoy that late summer trip to Florida with your parents? Good. Now do ten bleachers for every day of that week you missed. A helmet left outside a locker might cost five bleachers for the offender who sheepishly claimed it in the coaches' office. An unflushed toilet—Cox checked—meant ten bleachers for the whole team.

Did you put only one foot, not both, on the top bleacher? "Get up!" Cox cried from halfway up the stands one day during preseason workouts, after the players had assumed they'd finished their daily dose. "Two more. You test me and I'm going to test you! Start with both feet on the bottom and when you get to the top, you put both feet on the top. You tested me and I caught you." By the last one, players were sprawled on the lowest row or doubled over in various states of infirmity.

They hated the bleachers, but some came to understand their benefit. Adam Acklin, who had played at Central and returned in 2007 as an assistant coach, said that he used to picture a championship trophy at the top of the stands in order to get himself there, though none of his teams ultimately won a trophy. "It's all mental," he said. Alumni who returned to visit remarked on the toughness that running the bleachers had engendered in them. Cox told the story of one of his players who went off to pharmacy school and came back to tell him, "Those bleachers right there got me through exams." If he could beat them, the former Tiger said, he could do anything. Cox was also wise and experienced enough to put such comments in perspective. "Sometimes I think they tell me that," he said, "because they think that's what I want to hear. He was a sharp kid anyway. I'm not sure it's true."

On the day before the Catholic game, the bleachers were not fitness tools or currency or character builders. They were punishment.

||||||||||||||||||||||||||||||||||||

From the first day of practice on July 23, 2007, "selfishness" was the word Cox had repeated most often to this group of Tigers. He had tried to instruct it out of them in his daily speeches after practice, cajole it out of them with parables like the one about the tribe with spoons too long to feed themselves so they had to feed each other. He'd tried to condition it out of them by making them run sprints in what was called the fourth quarter at the end of practice every day. Most of all, he'd tried to *coach* it out of them.

Coaching is a nebulous skill, and the personalities on Cox's staff embodied the multiple forms it can take. Where Cox was wiry and terse, Norman Callaway, his assistant head coach, offensive coordinator, and best friend for twenty-five years, possessed the girth and voice of an opera singer. Almost everything connected to his heart had been bypassed (some would say his heart had been bypassed altogether), and he peppered his practice diatribes with sayings like "You couldn't play dead in a Western movie." Originally from Florida, Larry Siegel was the good-natured defensive coordinator, the leader of the Fellowship of Christian Athletes chapter of the team, and a believer in positive reinforcement; his shock of white hair sat atop a youthful face and he sat in a youthful car—his red Mazda Miata stood out in a parking lot filled with trucks and SUVs. Clarence Finley, whose father had been a chef at one of the best barbecue spots in Little Rock, was even larger than Callaway and had a self-deprecating touch, especially with the black players. He was quick to temper criticism with remarks designed to evoke a laugh. "I'm a big black elephant," Finley said one day during practice. "I don't ever forget." No one worked harder or was better prepared than Finley, his portable DVD player always loaded with game footage or instructional videos. Stan Williams had coached for two decades at Pulaski Heights Middle School, one of Central's feeder schools, before coming to the Tigers, and he was full of streetwise stories of staring into drug dealers' guns in his attempts to use athletics to save some of Little Rock's young black men from their tough neighborhoods. Defensive backs coach Darrell Seward was even more meticulous than Cox. He painted the practice-field lines to a fraction of an inch and organized the locker room's bulletin boards and the game films. Keith Richardson and Adam Acklin worked mainly with the ninth graders and junior varsity, but their youth and natural empathy made them willing and open confidants for the players.

These eight men, sometimes joined by volunteer coaches Clyde Horton and Tommy Walker, packed the 270-square-foot office, which also served as a changing room, conference room, confessional, war room, psychologist's office, and comedy club. Even empty of coaches it was crowded, with six wooden desks wedged into a half-finished Tetris game pattern, a full-size refrigerator, and, watching everything from the corner, a chipped plaster statue of a tiger, its roaring mouth holding a coat hanger (for Larry Siegel's rain slicker) and its head piled with hats. The spring-hinged door constantly opened and closed with bus drivers bearing paperwork, maintenance men looking for instructions about what to fix (or looking to shoot the shit), administrators with bad news, parents with cookies, and football players needing everything: advice, shoulder-pad straps, clarification about plays, college-selection guidance, scouting reports, cell phone numbers, statistics, pens, reassurance.

Through most of the season, the 2007 Tigers had frustrated all the coaches' attempts to foster passion and unity in them. Some years it came pretty easily, and the players did most of the work for the coaches. The championship teams of 2003 and 2004 were like that; the players, black and white, had hung out together, spent time at each other's houses, formed deep and lasting friendships. "Any really good team is made up of guys who are friends," Hall of Fame basketball coach Bob Knight once said, "guys who want to help each other and play together." Nancy Rousseau, the principal of Central, remembered the school's atmosphere around those teams as "electric, absolute magic." The excitement during that time, her second and third years as principal, "permeated everything." Those teams had bonded, this one had not.

Those were the years when you collected coaching awards, but those weren't the years when you necessarily did your best coaching. During Cox's worst season, in 1993, gangs were tearing apart the city, and only thirty-five or forty players came out for the team; talent among those who did was thin, and the Tigers went 1-9 (the win coming in overtime, Cox recalled, his access to that fourteen-year-old memory as instantaneous as if he were powered by a computer). Of that season, he said, "I'm not sure we didn't do a pretty good coaching job. We didn't have any size, speed, or skill."

For Cox, the job of a coach was to instill in his players, in proportions dependent on what he thought the team needed, commitment, discipline, leadership, and love. Cox was not afraid of the last word, even as his style so often rewarded aggression. He believed that you could hit hard—that you should hit hard, that that was the only way to play the game—and still abide by the rules and play fair. His big linemen would knock you off your feet, and then a big back would run over you on his way to the end zone. The Central offense under Bernie Cox was all about carrying the rock. "We'll run sixty plays a game," said Callaway, "and fifty of them will be runs off tackle."

On defense, the line of scrimmage would be guarded with ferocity, the Tigers refusing to cede an inch and pursuing the ball like a pride hunting a gazelle. In the fourth quarter, when the other team was gasping with exhaustion, Central's players seemed to get faster and more relentless. That was Bernie Cox football. Then, whether you won or lost, you took your hat off, looked the opponent in the eye, and went down the line slapping his hand and telling him, "Good game," and you meant it.

All fall, the 2007 team had Cox quite literally scratching his head as he surveyed practice from somewhere near center field (the practice field doubled as the baseball team's outfield), the east stands of Quigley rising to one side and the back of the school to the other. Some twelve starters on offense and defense had returned from the 10-1 2006 team and several transfers added depth, so the preseason No. 1 ranking had seemed warranted. The seniors lost from the previous season, though, were the kind of leaders Cox and Central had always counted on, players who, quietly or vocally, were willing to bear the load for the team and inspire confidence in the fragile psyches of doubting teammates. Charles Clay, for instance, was a big tailback who always wanted the ball when a yard or two (or ten) was needed, and he'd moved on to the University of Tulsa in Oklahoma, where he was already a go-to player in his freshman year. Also at Tulsa was Genesis Cole, a big-play receiver who would tenaciously go after any pass. As a junior, quarterback Randy Rankin had flourished with those two playmakers around him. But when it looked as if Rankin himself would have to be one of the clutch contributors this season, his darting mind would often get the better of him. "Randy is going to be Randy" had been a refrain in the coaches' office, meaning eccentricity should be expected. And the player you could least tolerate eccentricity in was your quarterback.

All in all, they were eminently likable guys, these Tigers, but neither Cox nor the other coaches had figured out how to light a flame under them. It felt like a failing as a coach more than any mistake of X's and O's, and it had gnawed at them all year.

Was there something racial in their failure to mesh? There didn't seem to be, even though they rarely chose to intermingle off the field and didn't seem to form strong interracial friendships. That was symptomatic of the school as a whole, and junior tight end Damien Lee chose to blame his peers. "There's plenty of opportunities to get together," he said. "I put it on the students. The school provides things to do. You go to school at lunchtime and you'll see. The white students are sitting together and the black students are together. They don't ever get close or go out or anything. Students have to get together." Perhaps the team's casual habit of separation was a reflection of the current moment in Little Rock, when the old racial grievances of the past fifty years were being revisited. Or maybe it was a symptom of the larger ills that had wedged the city (and the country) apart for decades—neighborhood segregation, electoral power plays, lack of trust between the races. Ken Richardson, a former Central football star, a Stanford graduate, and an elected representative on Little Rock's city board of directors, summarized it in a question posed of the city, the state, and the country as a whole: "Are we really embracing each other or are we just tolerating each other?"

By October, it was late in the year to still be thinking it, but the coaches had to keep trying: What will motivate this team to unite, to clench into a single fist? They were still pondering it the Thursday before the Catholic game, when Cox finally reached his breaking point.

Thursday was always a light day of practice, a day to tighten the nuts and bolts of the week's lessons, to line up the personnel for special teams, to kick a few field goals and extra points, and to go over the schedule for game night. This particular Thursday was picture day, and the players had suited up in their clean, all-black uniforms and posed in the bleachers as a group, affecting the high seriousness that only teenagers can bring to having their photographs taken. Afterward, they'd gone back to the locker room to change and returned to Bernie Cox Field in just helmets, shirts, shorts, and cleats for the usual day-before-a-game run-through.

From the beginning of the week, the team had been off-kilter. A 7–0 win over last-place North Little Rock the previous Friday had not sat well with the coaches, and Rankin had been demoted, leaving untested sopho-more Adam Meeks to take snaps with the first team. Rankin's father, also named Randy and a regular at practice, was morose over the change. "Looks like they've got a new QB. . . . I hope [Randy] gets to play some," he said and paused. "Senior Night," he explained. On Tuesday, rain had washed out a day of practice, and the team had watched film of the previous game. During that period of confinement in the dank locker room, where rain always leached into puddles through the old stadium's cracks and fissures, Cox had told them, "There's no urgency at all about this group. . . . There's a lack of a lot of things in this group.

"Your dislike for me is okay," he continued, perhaps seeking to unify them at the very least in their opposition to him. "Not that you need my permission to feel any way. Because I have a clear conscience. Because I'm not expecting more from you than from any other guys I've worked with. . . . You can hate me. [But] you're going to hate a guy who loves you if you hate me."

By Thursday, the latent hostility Cox had identified, the disappointing performance of the week before, and the quarterback change turned a nor-mally rote session into a cauldron of mistakes and emotional outbursts. The proper players often were not on the field for their specific teams, and the ones who were there were missing assignments or jumping offside.

The offense was as chaotic as if they'd never seen each other before. Kaelon Kelleybrew, the fiercest competitor on the team, threw a ball at freshman kicker Walker Hawkins after a perceived slight. Other players were laughing and cutting up. Cox sent all of them to the bleachers. Instead of making them run straight up and down, he had them loop through one section of the stands—up the steps, across the top row, down and across the bottom, and back up. From the field, the motion of the players resembled some football-themed Pac-Man game stuck in a perpetual cycle around the screen. After fifteen minutes, Cox called a stop to it and sat them in the bleachers in a cruel parody of the team photo taken just minutes before. They were exhausted—nauseated, coughing, chests heaving.

"Take your hats off," Cox said. "We're going to be here just a minute. If you guys want to leave and not come back, then go ahead. We'd been at practice for fifteen minutes when all the bitching started. Offense started bitching, I heard the defense start bitching, I heard cussing each other over here, so we spent the last fifteen minutes of practice walking the bleachers. I'm not going to listen to that crap out here."

As Cox often did, he downshifted his tone to cover simple logistics in exacting detail and then accelerated again to an emotional pitch.

"Guys, we'll have a sandwich for you tomorrow, as soon as you get out of school and get down here. If you guys want to come out here tomorrow and you guys want to play, you be down here and you be dressed by 4:45. We'll start our team meetings at 4:45. Because it's Senior Night, we've got to be off the field by 6:30. So we're moving everything up. If you guys want to come down here tomorrow night and you want to piss me off because you'll be in there and playing grab butt and laughing and talking, you come on. I'll meet you in the dressing room and I'll send your butt back up those stairs. We might get our butt kicked tomorrow night, which we probably will, and I'll tell you what, I gave you an excuse today to justify it. You can blame it on me. Why? 'Cause I put you in the bleachers. So you can tell everybody in your family, all your girlfriends, everybody that you want to tell, that it's my fault, because I've deadened your legs today by putting you in the bleachers. So you blame it on me when you play like crap tomorrow.

That's the way we worked today, like crap. That satisfies most of you, that's the sad thing. You guys can't even get along together on the football field. Every frigging snap, somebody was criticizing somebody on one side or the other. You haven't played a complete football game all year. You won't admit it, but you know that."

He read off the names of his most egregious offenders—Kelleybrew among them, for his blowup at the kicker—and told them to remain to run extra bleachers. "If you want to ask why, then don't stay. I'm inviting you to stay if you want to dress out tomorrow night. If you don't want to dress out, you go to the house. Any questions? You be dressed tomorrow at 4:45. If you don't want a sandwich, you see me. I don't want to pay six bucks for it tomorrow if you don't want it. Questions? Get out of here."

IIIIIIIIIIIIIIIIIIIIIIIIIIIIIIIIIII

Now, as the players looked at the ninety-nine yards of Bernie Cox Field ahead of them to traverse in under eight minutes, with the Catholic defense standing in their way, no one would have blamed Cox or anyone else for feeling less than optimistic about the team's chances. Still, even though Central was behind 20–7 at halftime, Cox had told his players, "It strikes me that if you wanted to, you could take this ball game over. You can still do it." Given his tirade of the day before, his confidence seemed downright insane. His matter-of-fact statement in a tone of detachment—which sounded more like a speech from a political pundit or an investment advisor ("It strikes me . . . ") than the fiery stem-winder he was known for—seemed to be just what they needed to hear. And even in spite of allowing a Catholic touchdown with forty-eight seconds left in the first half, they had returned to the field with an air of confidence, or at least some hope, that they might pull out a win.

Cox held sincere beliefs about transferring what you learn on the football field to life and molding character and being committed to a task, but he didn't dismiss the importance of winning. "You've got to win *some* of the time," he said, otherwise you lose reinforcement that the other things you're trying to say are worth listening to. "You want to take advantage of their interest and talent. If you have the size and talent, you need to win on the scoreboard."

The scoreboard at the other end said they were six points behind. Central needed to win—yes, to have a shot at the playoffs, but also to justify Cox's tirade and punishment, to make his players see those harsh words as necessary lessons, not empty anger.

So Cox put Kaelon Kelleybrew in at tailback, where he hadn't played a down all year.

CHAPTER 2

BUILDING CENTRAL HIGH

ON THE LAST DAY OF OCTOBER IN 1927, Mary Lewis returned to her hometown of Little Rock for the second time since she'd made her unlikely Metropolitan Opera debut as Mimi in Puccini's *La Bohème* the previous year. The New York newspaper critics had been generally kind and sometimes rapturous about her performance. Samuel Chotzinoff of the *World* wrote that her "upper register is brilliant and, when Miss Lewis chooses to make it so, it is sensuous." More important, she seemed to have a diva's necessary ability to connect with her audience, which, as Chotzinoff stated, "was visibly touched."

On her first trip home, some six weeks after her debut, she'd performed in the packed, 1,100-seat auditorium at the high school where she'd been a student more than a dozen years before. Sparing no hyperbole, the *Arkansas Democrat* proclaimed that she "was the recipient of the greatest demonstration of welcome ever accorded any individual in the history of the state." The governor sponsored a reception for her at the capitol, and the mayor presented her with the key to the city.

By the time she returned to Little Rock a year and a half later, she had sung ten more times with the Met's company, as well as at Carnegie Hall, and undertaken a nationwide concert tour. In the spring of 1927, she'd fallen in love with German bass-baritone Michael Bohnen, and their match was such a high-profile society event that New York mayor Jimmy Walker had been enlisted to marry them.

Even more than her singing ability, Lewis's Dickensian life story had captured the public's imagination. Her early history included stints in an orphanage and foster homes in Texas, before the Reverend William Fitch and his wife, Anna, took her in and insisted on a Christian musical education, undergirded by the occasional spanking and prohibitions against godless jazz. When the Fitches moved to Arkansas, Mary's singing in Little Rock churches earned her local praise and attention, but she chafed under the strictness of her home life and the limitations of choir music. After a brief marriage to a high school boyfriend, she traveled to the West Coast, where she sang, swimsuit clad, in a vaudeville show and earned a part in a silent film (obviously more for her figure than for her voice). After moving to New York in 1920, she found a series of chorus jobs that led to a contract with the Ziegfeld Follies, which gave her enough financial independence to undertake serious studies with the famed vocal coach William Thorner. His imprimatur gained her opera engagements in Paris and Vienna, where the positive notices led her back to New York and a successful audition at the Met. In the summer before her second appearance in Little Rock, *Ladies' Home Journal* had published, in three installments, her autobiography to date.

This time, the city had a performance venue worthy of her star power. Twenty-two blocks from the old high school building, in what had been a park on the western edge of the city, had risen a new high school and at its center an auditorium with two thousand seats, just eight hundred less than Carnegie Hall. The school had opened for students in September, but the Lewis concert would be the first public event held there. (Two weeks later, the official dedication of the building would take place.)

The citizens of Little Rock had been anticipating this event since it was announced in September, and on the night of the show, a parade of Hupmobiles and Model Ts, Plymouths and Cadillacs debouched their passengers on Park Street. Swells in tuxedos and their gowned gals hopped from the No. 3 streetcar that made the journey along Fifteenth Street from the Victorian homes downtown or from the one that wound down Prospect Boulevard for the thirty-four-minute trip from the new mansions in the Edgehill and Prospect Heights neighborhoods. The floodlit façade of the school in front of them, whose construction they had followed for a year, filled them with pride.

A central tower, topped with decorative arches fit for a Venetian palazzo, adorned the center section, which was fronted by four pilasters indicating the main entrance. From that anchor extended a pair of three-story wings, each stretching nearly a city block north and south. The crowd converged on the entrance along the walkways lacing the front lawn, their progress detoured by the circumference of an oval reflecting pool. The elegant portico in front of it was a false one, backed by a wall, so the wave of music lovers turned right and left to ascend the stairways on either side that zigzagged them to the foot of a final set of stairs. This winding path allowed the drama of the enormous building to sink in, and from this landing, if they were not rushing to make curtain time, they no doubt stopped to gaze at the magnificent entry marking the grand aspirations for Little Rock's youth. Set off in white limestone against the buff brick background of the rest of the building, the broad pilasters, linked by arches over three wooden double doors, supported human-scale female figures, tipped forward from their twenty-foot-high perches, representing Ambition, Personality, Opportunity, and Preparation. The excitement of the evening was such that Ambition, though her head was modestly bowed and her body cloaked, seemed ready at any moment to throw aside her wrap and perform an aria herself.

Once through the doors, the citizens found the foyer illuminated by six iron art deco light fixtures, each an open globe ringed by a band containing the astrological symbols. Only those Little Rockians who had attended the opera or symphony concerts in New York City or Chicago had seen anything to rival the auditorium in front of them. In the orchestra, more than twenty rows of gray and green seats ("For the benefit of prospective concert goers," reported the *Arkansas Gazette*, "it may be added that they do not squeak") followed a gentle slope down to the stage, said to be the third largest in the country. (Hidden behind drop curtains at either end and along the rear wall were basketball goals, since the stage also functioned as the gymnasium.) Ticket holders searched the seats for the brass plates that matched their numbers and, once settled, took in the finery around them:

the windows and main curtain of deep blue velour, four streamers bearing the letters L. R. H. S. draped from a valance embroidered with a gold tiger's head, and a constellation of ten-bulb iron chandeliers.

Lewis didn't rise from chorus girl to opera diva without a flair for the dramatic, and she knew that to compete with the sensational building, she'd need to make a formidable entrance. Former governor Charles Brough appeared first, and when he asserted that Lewis had declared the building "the finest she had seen at home or abroad," the audience thundered its approval with applause. Lewis emerged from the wings to gasps. "Gorgeously gowned in a striking period creation, Spanish in effect," as the *Arkansas Democrat* described it, she launched into her program, opening with Paisiello's jaunty two-minute "Chi vuol la zingarella" before moving on to fourteen other crowd-pleasing selections from Mozart, Chopin, Strauss, and Massenet. As she finished the final song, "there was continuous applause and the audience sat demanding more."

The range of her selections had showcased her musical fluency in French, German, and Italian, but for her first encore, she reverted to the familiar accent of her upbringing, with a rendition of "Dixie." It was the first time "Dixie" was sung in the high school's auditorium, and thirty years later, in 1957, it would be sung again, with results both comic and sinister.

At the end of the performance, the crowd streamed into the warm Halloween night. Perhaps some of them headed downtown to Rainbow Garden, the city's premier venue for national touring bands and located atop 555 Tire and Service Company ("World's Largest Service Station"), for the costume dance that was scheduled to go until 1:00 a.m. And some no doubt were caught in the thronged traffic on Main Street, where a "large husky youth attired in a mother hubbard gown and other feminine accoutrements" provided a slapstick counterpoint to the high-culture evening they'd witnessed. The night seemed to produce more merrymakers than troublemakers, as the *Gazette* reported, describing the holiday high jinks as possessing "a carnival spirit that has been exceeded by few New Year's outbursts.

"All available police were on duty," the paper continued, "but generally they had an easy time," even though many partyers were thumbing their noses at Prohibition by drinking. On that one night it must have seemed that Little Rock had everything to offer—the raucous, good-natured debauchery of New Orleans and the sophisticated entertainments of Manhattan. And in the light of day, when the fog of alcohol had lifted and the glittering notes of opera had faded, what remained for Little Rock's citizens—or, at least, for its white citizens—was a grand, beautiful building devoted to the enrichment of the city's students. As the *Gazette* opined, the school "is an architectural monument to our sense of beauty and to our civic pride."

Throughout the following week, excitement at the school and in town was building to a crescendo for another event of even greater importance, if the full-page ads taken out in the city's two major newspapers were any indication. "Throw 'em back, TIGERS!" read one, under a panoramic picture of the new structure, which a thirty-six-point headline touted as "The New Home of the Little Rock High School T-I-G-E-R-S." The other ad, in the *Arkansas Gazette*, billed the game between Little Rock and Pine Bluff as "The Premier Football Game of Arkansas." The sponsors of the ads were some of the most prominent businesses in the city, including a few that eighty years later were still operating (if rebranded or merged): Arkansas Power and Light Company (now Entergy), 555 Tire, Terry Dairy (now Yarnell's Ice Cream), and Missouri Pacific Railroad Company (now Union Pacific Railroad). One ad implored readers: "Every student and citizen of Little Rock should give to Coach Quigley and the Tigers the best co-operation, and perhaps the easiest and most effective way is to *attend the game tomorrow* [italics in the original]."

Long before the completion of the new school, coach Earl Quigley had brought a palpable pride to the city with a string of championship football teams. He had become head coach at Little Rock High in 1916, after assisting for two years, and by 1923, he'd won five state titles. Unless a Jack Dempsey fight was approaching, the Tigers and Quigley were always given prime real estate on the local papers' sports pages, which even went so far as to track the coach's annual journey back from his summer home in Oshkosh, Wisconsin, as the team prepared to reassemble in August for the coming season.

The triumphs of Coach Quigley and Little Rock High were not limited to the city or state. His teams were regional powers, regularly defeating the best high schools in Tennessee, Oklahoma, and Missouri. In 1921, for instance, Quigley's Tigers topped Muskogee Central High, which had lost to only one other high school team in three years, and Louisiana state champion Warren Easton High of New Orleans, which had not allowed a point all season until Little Rock beat them 21–3. That undefeated season for the Tigers led to offers of postseason games from high schools across the country. A snowstorm stopped a scheduled game with Peabody, Massachusetts, and as Little Rock High's 1922 yearbook reported, "A game might have been played with Waite High, at Toledo, Ohio, had they not insisted on using a negro in the line-up. Little Rock objected to this and negotiations were broken off." The absence of a closing victory didn't prevent Quigley from earning the yearbook dedication from the students, who "love the spirit of the Tiger Team. It stands for loyalty, perseverance and square dealing."

The celebration of the team and its coach didn't end at the walls of the school. The local Chamber of Commerce presented the state champions with a shield engraved with the team members' names, and, as part of a list of reasons for the team's success, the yearbook staff included: "THE SUPPORT OF THE TOWN. The business men of Little Rock showed an unusual amount of interest in our football games this year."

The regional success of the Tigers fit nicely into the community's and the state's desire to write over the image of Arkansas as a backward-looking backwater full of hillbillies, an idea popularized by the best-selling 1903 joke book On a Slow Train through Arkansaw. (A typical excerpt depicts a frustrated passenger querying the conductor about why the train has stopped and being told there are cattle on the track. When the train next stops and the passenger asks why this time, the conductor replies, "We have caught up with those cattle again.") In the 1920s, though it ranked just outside the top one hundred cities in the country in population (and still hovers there), Little Rock was often tarred with the same brush that swept across the rest of the truly rural state, from the mountain hamlets of the Ozarks to the flat farmland of the Mississippi Delta.

An attack on Arkansas by the country's most notorious journalistic debunker gave state boosterism an added urgency at that time. In a 1921 essay titled "The South Begins to Mutter," H. L. Mencken unleashed his satiric wit on the region in general—"a walking sarcophagus of dead ideas"— and Arkansas in particular. He referred to the state's "trackless, unexplored" lands and "miasmatic jungles," and civic leaders in the capital took exception, responding with a raft of editorials and articles, one of which seemed to prove Mencken's very charges with a xenophobic call for the United States Congress to investigate Mencken's citizenship.

Mencken's magazine, the *American Mercury*, continued to jab at the state over the years. At about the time that ground was being broken for Little Rock's new high school, Mencken published in the *Mercury* a broadly damning essay on Arkansas written by a native son and onetime socialist candidate for governor, Clay Fulks. Full of sweeping generalizations, the article, titled simply "Arkansas," declared: "To be different is still dangerous, and those who have sense enough to be different understand the virtues of discretion." Arkansans, he claimed, "move in herds."

Even before Mencken's piece, Governor Brough, whose term ended in 1921, had proven himself a tireless promoter of the state's resources, lecturing on the Chautauqua circuit about the state's eighth-place ranking in production of "cow peanuts" and touting the fact that Arkansas homes had become "virtually tick-free." After leaving office, he worked for the newly formed Arkansas Advancement Association, which counted among its duties to "influence popular song writers to occasionally insert the word Arkansas in their effusions." (Longtime Arkansas journalist Bob Lancaster has asserted that in spite of Brough's political and academic accomplishments, he "may be remembered as something of a boosterism buffoon.") Mencken had always found this sort of local crowing repellent, and he later pointed out that if Arkansas was going to boast of its high rankings, it should include lynchings.

Little Rock, however, as opposed to the plantation system that dominated the southern and Mississippi Delta parts of the state, was a boomtown for black strivers in the first quarter of the twentieth century. The commercial strip downtown on West Ninth Street was a thriving site of African

American social life. Besides a number of barbershops and clothing stores, the street contained medical and law offices, churches, and, at the main intersection of Broadway and Ninth, the greatest symbol of black prosperity in the city, the building housing the Mosaic Templars of America. This fraternal organization served the black community primarily as an insurance broker and at its peak claimed more than one hundred thousand members. Booker T. Washington was one of them and spoke before a crowd of 2,100 at the dedication ceremony for the building in 1913. For an African American Arkansan with designs on improving his fortunes, Little Rock provided seeming proof that it could be done.

A man like Scipio A. Jones was a perfect model. Born to a slave in Tulip, Arkansas, Jones, whose father is generally believed to have been his mother's owner, moved to Little Rock as a teenager and eventually earned a degree from what is now Shorter College. Studying law on his own while teaching high school, he passed the bar in 1889 and opened a practice in town, forging relationships with many of Little Rock's most prominent white citizens, including the progressive governor George Donaghey. Jones could often be seen being ferried around town in a chauffeur-driven Cadillac. Though he received some criticism from the black community for his coziness with whites and his nonconfrontational nature, he was no elitist; in his most prominent case, he defended, throughout years of appeals, twelve black sharecroppers from the Delta who'd been summarily convicted of murder and sentenced to death for their alleged roles in an episode of racial violence in 1919. Working with the fledgling NAACP and white attorney George Murphy, Jones helped shepherd the case all the way to the US Supreme Court, which eventually decided for the sharecroppers in 1923. They were subsequently all set free by 1925. Jones also became a leader in the state Republican Party, which he prodded to include African Americans, and in 1928, he served as a delegate from Arkansas to the Republican National Convention.

He'd been preceded in the community's esteem by Philadelphia-born Mifflin Gibbs, who had moved to Little Rock in 1871 after attending a convention where he heard its virtues praised—"the comparative infancy of its development, its golden prospects, and fraternal amenities," as he described it in his autobiography. His prose style typically ornate, Gibbs gained a favorable initial impression upon disembarking from a Sunday-morning ferry ride in May across the Arkansas River: "the carol of the canary and mocking bird [sic] from treetop and cage was all that entered a peaceful, restful quiet that bespoke a well-governed city. The chiming church bells that soon after summoned worshipers seemed to bid me welcome." Thirty years later, when his autobiography was published—after a career in law, politics, and business that saw him serve as municipal judge, Republican Party leader, and real estate investor (as well as US consul to Madagascar under President William McKinley)—he still found the town hospitable enough to declare that his "first impressions have not been lessened by lapse of time; generous nature has enabled human appliance to make Little Rock an ideal city."

Jones, Gibbs, and other local black leaders chose to follow the lead of Booker T. Washington, who wrote the introduction to Gibbs's autobiography. Though Washington has been often criticized for adopting what some saw as an Uncle Tom level of accommodation to white prejudice, his pragmatism dictated a temporary acceptance of the status quo and cultivation of sympathetic whites in order to achieve for African Americans the freedom to pursue education and economic advancement. In his memoir, Gibbs quotes from Washington's remarks to a meeting of the National Negro Business League (of which Washington was president) in 1901: "The object-lesson of one honest Negro succeeding magnificently in each community in some business or industry is worth a hundred abstract speeches in securing opportunity for the race. In the South, as in most parts of the world, the Negro who does something and possesses something is respected by both races. Usefulness in the community where we live will constitute our most lasting and potent protection." The consequences of taking a more militant stand, especially in the South, were often fatal, as Robert J. Norrell points out in his recent biography of Washington. "Having conditions forced on him," Norrell writes, "with the threat of destruction clearly the cost of resistance, does not constitute a fair definition of accommodation. It is coercion."

Little Rock, however, true to the belief of Gibbs, did seem to offer a more tolerant atmosphere, or what historian Grif Stockley calls a "less stratified existence available to blacks," than did many other southern locales. Besides providing commercial and political options, the Little Rock area in the early twentieth century was the site of three black colleges and a notable black high school. In more practical matters of social interaction, Little Rock seemed relatively untroubled by race mixing; white and black families often lived next door to each other in certain neighborhoods. And in a 1930 essay for the *American Mercury* called "Traveling Jim Crow," Harlem Renaissance writer George S. Schuyler noted, "In Memphis it is necessary for a Negro to obtain a Negro taxicab. In Little Rock, one may take any cab, whether operated by white or black, and either will call at one's hotel or rooming place at any hour of the day or night."

At a deeper level, advancement was less likely. The black business strip of West Ninth Street gave an owner with means a place to hang his shingle, but, as historian Gene Vinzant has documented, overall, the economy in Little Rock in the 1920s was segregated to a degree even greater than it had been in the previous century when Gibbs had found avenues for his ambition. In this, Little Rock followed the rest of the South, described by C. Vann Woodward in *The Strange Career of Jim Crow:* "There was no apparent tendency toward abatement or relaxation of the Jim Crow code of discrimination and segregation in the 1920's." And as Vinzant asserts, "The tantalizing vision of black prosperity in Little Rock in the 1920s was a mirage that vanished upon close inspection."

Then, in the spring of 1927, as whites in Little Rock were marveling at the construction of their majestic new school, blacks in the city would undergo a vivid and horrifying test of the thin wall of "usefulness" in the community in providing protection, one that would change the makeup of the city and poison the air of opportunity for decades.

IIIIIIIIIIIIIIIIIIIIIIIIIIIIIIIIIIIIII

Rain had already been pummeling Little Rock and most of the South for a month when Floella McDonald, eleven, went missing on Tuesday, April 12,

1927. Her case joined the seemingly unrelated disappearance the previous day of another child, thirteen-year-old Lonnie White, who was later found to have drowned.

Along with more rain on Wednesday, strong winds had struck, demolishing chimneys that hailed their bricks on downtown streets and, in the industrial eastern part of the city, toppling a cotton mill's smokestack and unroofing its plant, and skewering a shed with a twenty-foot plank. In addition, three houses in a nearby African American neighborhood were destroyed and their occupants injured. The flooding forecast for the rest of the week—Easter week—was dire. The Little Rock–Memphis highway was already impassable, and the Arkansas River was expected to overflow its lower bank on the North Little Rock side by Sunday, covering the railroad tracks. Despite the dangerous weather past and future, the main headline in the evening-published *Arkansas Democrat* on Thursday, April 14, was the missing children.

Floella had last been seen at the public library on Wednesday at 6:00 p.m., when she checked out *Mrs. Wiggs of the Cabbage Patch*. Within twenty-four hours, various search parties were ranging over the area, including one made up of seventy-five Boy Scouts at a wetlands south of the city, an area "which has been the scene of several searches for slayers of women who had been brutally murdered," as the *Democrat* reported on its front page. Citing two previous attacks on girls reported to the police in the "past six or eight months," the paper speculated that the perpetrator may have been "a negro moron" who in both instances had been frightened by the screams of the girls and fled, and so was still at large. The police chief and his deputy were marshaling all forces in the search, even as the specter of a flood threatened the city.

On Good Friday, the fierce storm created its greatest havoc, reaching a degree forecasters hadn't predicted. Ten inches of rain fell on the city. Tornadoes touched down in four counties and injured a dozen people. Levees were breached in every part of the state, creating a mass of refugees. The Arkansas River was carrying a third again as much water as it ever had, and the force of the current would become so strong that on the following Tuesday the Baring Cross Bridge, upstream from the "little rock" and holding

Missouri Pacific tracks, was closed because it had been knocked out of line. In the hope of stabilizing it against the pressure of the current and the copious debris—including timber and entire houses—it carried, engineers parked more than twenty cars filled with coal on the bridge. Train traffic into and out of the city had come to a near standstill anyway because tracks in all directions were covered with water and impassable. One train from Memphis that did get through traveled more than eight miles on tracks submerged in water up to the coach steps.

The missing children, however, still merited attention, and the *Democrat* reported that the girl was rumored to have been abducted and held in a "negro shanty." By Easter Sunday, under a composite picture of the houses and families of Lonnie and Floella, flood-related theories were being explored, with police chief Burl C. Rotenberry and his head detective, Major James A. Pitcock, inspecting a stream's ditch near Floella's home that was full of rushing water from the rains. But the paper still held out the possibility that "she was kidnaped [*sic*] by a negro fiend and held prisoner by him."

Still the storms did not cease and the waters rose. The Wednesday after Easter, another seven inches of rain fell in eighteen hours, and the river, whose flood stage at Little Rock was twenty-three feet, covered the highest mark on the Main Street Bridge gauge at thirty-one and a half feet, necessitating an improvised painted mark on the side of the Little Rock Athletic Club boathouse nearby. When the water rose to thirty-three feet, ten feet above flood stage, Little Rock got an operatic demonstration of the river's destructive power. On Thursday morning, April 21, at 4:00 a.m., watchmen at the bridge heard a crash loud enough to sound over the roar of the river; something enormous that had been swept into the churning water—a house, a barn, another bridge—had struck the stanchions. The bridge started to sway and squeal, creating an eerie melody heard above the thundering water. Suddenly, in the darkness of that predawn, flames burst from the parked coal cars, their cargo ignited by friction caused by the shaking structure. The scene briefly illuminated, the watchmen on the bank saw the river tear the Baring Cross Bridge from its mooring and dump two iron spans and fourteen cars packed with fiery coal hissing into the water, leaving on the shore the snapped tendons of cables and telephone wires. One of the watchmen said the iron rails were ripped "as though they were small pieces of ribbons."

For all its destruction, the flood of 1927 left Little Rock isolated but largely unscathed. North Little Rock, low-lying with less natural protection, saw waters rise to the eaves of houses. The devastation in the eastern part of the state—at one point, five million acres were flooded—would have touched especially the African American community in Little Rock, since many of them had sought advancement in the city but left relatives behind in the cotton fields. And tense race relations on the plantations only worsened under the desperate conditions of the flood. John M. Barry, in his book *Rising Tide*, documents that armed whites conscripted black laborers to work on the levees, that many whites overseeing refugee camps "kept the good Red Cross food for themselves," and that the dirty job of cleaning up and the manual labor, like unloading supplies, were derided as "nigger work."

After some ten days of the deluge, the humor and lightness of spirit that have always characterized Little Rock's residents were beginning to return to the town as the water subsided. "The next flood we want is a flood of orders for Franke's Lemon Cake," read an ad for Franke's Bakery. And the *Arkansas Gazette* published over several days a column called "Eddies of the Flood," reporting short, mostly humorous human-interest stories about how ordinary citizens were dealing with the extraordinary circumstances. Then the news turned grim once again.

On Saturday afternoon, April 30, barely in time for the evening edition of the *Democrat*, Floella McDonald was discovered. "Lost Girl's Body Found in Church Attic," read the front-page banner above a brief story. The Sunday edition contained an extended account.

Frank Dixon, the black janitor at the First Presbyterian Church at Eighth and Scott Streets—designed and built only three years before by one of the city's leading architects, John Parks Almand, the primary architect of the massive new high school then under construction—called police on Saturday and told them that in investigating a foul smell, he had found a decomposing body in the belfry of the church. Two patrolmen arrived and scaled the stairway and fifty-foot ladder that led to the bell tower. From the description given of her clothing on the day she had disappeared, they recognized that the body was likely the girl's. The coroner was called, and, to prevent further deterioration, he ordered that the body be wrapped in a sheet and lowered outside the church from the tower rather than removed via the ladder inside. That spectacle aroused the murmuring crowd that had already gathered outside the church.

Police were swift to round up some dozen black suspects, including Frank Dixon and his sixteen-year-old son, Lonnie, who had a record of petty crimes. Another girl showed up at the police station with her father and claimed a man had attempted to lure her, with the promise of a toy, into the church earlier on the day that Floella had disappeared; she identified Lonnie Dixon as the man in a lineup. By 4:30 Sunday, after hours of intense interrogation, he confessed to the crime, at the same time exonerating his father of any knowledge of it, and directed the police to a garage where the dead girl's hat and the library book were found under a floorboard.

At Floella's funeral that same afternoon, a pastor, J. O. Johnson, tried to discourage any resort to violence or mob justice, but by the evening a crowd estimated at two to three thousand had assembled outside the jail at City Hall, demanding to search the building for Lonnie, who certainly would have been lynched if found. Another mob gathered outside the state prison south of downtown, demanding the same. Anticipating such a reaction, Chief Rotenberry had ordered that Lonnie and his father be transported out of the city separately earlier in the day.

As darkness closed over Little Rock, the mobs grew more unruly. At City Hall, police guarded the entrances with loaded shotguns. The mayor, a local minister, and a Supreme Court justice all spoke to the crowd, but it was not placated. To quell the group's anger, Rotenberry finally agreed to let a party of leaders inside. When they emerged to report that Lonnie was not there, the crowd began shouting, "Tell us where he is!" Rotenberry ordered all available police to City Hall, and twenty to thirty National Guardsmen, supplied with tear gas, were called out to assist in controlling the mob. By 11:00 p.m. the crowd had not dissipated and another party was allowed to search the jail. When they returned with the information that the men were nowhere to be found, the mob turned on Rotenberry, who had to be rescued by his men and secretly removed from the area. Eventually, eighteen people were arrested, and the throng dispersed.

Meanwhile, a similar conflagration was erupting at the state prison. Warden S. L. Todhunter requested that police be deployed to the Walls, as the facility was known, but they had their hands full at City Hall. When the group outside the prison was refused admittance, some of the crowd began firing guns at Todhunter's office. As at City Hall, the warden negotiated with the group to allow some inside to search the grounds and buildings, but before they emerged with their report, those remaining outside broke down the main gate and stormed the prison, including the warden's house. Satisfied that Lonnie was not there but fired by a rumor that he had been taken to Benton, in neighboring Saline County, members of the mob left in a "wild scramble for automobiles" bound for that town.

All through the night, armed bands scoured the state, rolling up to small-town jails in Benton, Searcy, and Malvern, unsuccessfully seeking the alleged murderer. The beginning of the workweek Monday morning brought some relief from the massed gatherings, but small groups seemed to renew their anger by visiting the church as rumors flew that the prisoners were back in the city. By the evening, City Hall and the prison were once again the sites of threatening mobs, and splinter groups gathered at other locations in the town. One posse of about thirty-five people showed up at Chief Rotenberry's home and forced its way in, but he had already removed his family to another location for their safety.

Finally, at 1:00 a.m. Tuesday morning, Major Pitcock, a fearless disciplinarian who had once been superintendent at the penitentiary and was rarely seen without a cigar, had had enough. He appeared on the steps of City Hall and called out, "I'll give you ten minutes to get away from here, every one of you—and three of the ten minutes are already gone." Soon, the sidewalk was empty.

Little Rock seemed to have weathered a major storm of social unrest, and when on Tuesday morning the grand jury quickly returned a murder indictment against Lonnie Dixon and at the same time issued a warning that "indictments will promptly be found against anyone disturbing the peace and dignity of this community," the general feeling was that the crisis had ended. After all, Little Rock had not suffered a lynching in thirty-six years, and despite the perception of the state as backward and uncivilized, the city's leaders valued Little Rock's reputation as moderate and progressive and trusted its citizens to heed their call for order.

The governor left town that day to attend a strawberry festival in Van Buren, in the northwestern part of the state. The mayor and the police chief, shaken by the mobs and exhausted, also left town. On Tuesday, the *Arkansas Gazette* ran an editorial proclaiming that "Little Rock escaped the disgrace of a lynching," which "would have been especially deplorable at this time when Arkansas is in the eyes of the nation by reason of the flood." Before that paper was a day old, the disgrace the editorialist thought the city had avoided would come to pass.

||||||||||||||||||||||||||||||||||||

The most congested intersection in Little Rock today is the conjunction of Shackleford Road and Interstates 630 and 430. Traveling from downtown along 630, or the Wilbur D. Mills Freeway, named for the powerful Arkansas congressman of the 1960s and 1970s who brought the road into the federal interstate system, cars have to either exit onto 430 or, continuing straight, slow for the stoplight at Shackleford. There, as the result of a bizarre engineering decision, the interstate that splits Little Rock in two for seven and a half miles from downtown to the western part of the city slows evening commuters from speeds of seventy miles per hour to a dead stop. At any time of day, but especially during the afternoon rush hour, traffic will be backed up for a mile or two. Cars, trucks, and SUVs inch forward through several cycles of the stoplight. Going straight will funnel you onto Financial Centre Parkway, the Anglo spelling spiffing up the aggressively nonlyrical name, where undistinguished office buildings eventually give way to the big-box shopping district of Petco, Wal-Mart, and Best Buy. Turn left, south on Shackleford, and you'll ascend a hill to an office housing Allied Tube and Conduit, TIAA-CREF, and other companies. The next intersection is Kanis Road, an extension of what starts downtown as Twelfth Street.

In 1927, this spot was five miles outside the city limits, unpaved and surrounded by heavily wooded land, but it still took its name—the Twelfth Street pike—from its distant origin downtown. Shackleford didn't even have a name yet, but it was sometimes called simply the "second cutoff road" from the Twelfth Street pike to the Little Rock–Hot Springs Highway. The first cutoff, now John Barrow Road, was a mile closer to town and somewhat more populated. Running straight north and south, this road was beginning to be platted and settled—telephone lines were already in place—but the piney woods around it were still quite heavy. Recent political developments had already ensured that the pace of road construction would soon pick up; in February, governor John Martineau had pushed through the legislature the Martineau Road Law, in which the state issued some $52,000,000 in bonds for improvement and paving.

On Saturday, April 30, a convict named John Carter escaped his work detail from the Pulaski County penal farm, where he was serving a one-year sentence for a misdemeanor assault on a Little Rock woman, and plunged into the thickets of rural Pulaski County. By Wednesday, May 4, unaware of the mob activity that had been occurring over the past few days in Little Rock as he foraged in the woods between the first and second cutoffs, he was likely growing hungry and desperate.

That morning, Carter was near the intersection of the Twelfth Street pike and the second cutoff when a horse-drawn wagon driven by Mrs. B. E. Stewart and carrying her seventeen-year-old daughter, Glennie, passed, on its way to Little Rock. He ran and caught up with the wagon, jumped in, and demanded whiskey, according to later reports. When the terrified women told him they had no whiskey, he declared he would kill them and threatened to strike them with an iron bar he was carrying. Both women jumped from the moving wagon and Carter pursued, first throwing rocks at them and then brandishing a large stick. He caught Mrs. Stewart and struck her a blow to the head that knocked her unconscious. As Carter struggled with

Glennie, an approaching car frightened him, and he disappeared back into the woods. The driver helped the Stewarts into her vehicle and took them into Little Rock to the hospital.

Because the pike was a well-traveled road, the news that a Negro had attacked two white women spread quickly, and by 9:40 a.m. Pulaski County sheriff Mike Haynie was on the scene. He put out a call for all available officers and stationed men along the Twelfth Street pike and the Hot Springs road to keep Carter within the area; he informed those who lived on the cutoff roads that a fugitive was at large. Two pilots, deputized a few months before—an exotic law enforcement tactic in those early days of aviation— circled above the hundred men who had joined the police in the search. For several hours, Carter evaded police and posse, crossing the cutoff roads and diving back into the woods.

Downtown, leaders of the black community, already on edge over the Lonnie Dixon affair, immediately intuited the anger that could be reignited by word of an assault on a white woman by a black man. By noon they had mobilized to meet with Haynie. Attorney Scipio Jones and eight other lawyers, businessmen, and educators offered to assist the sheriff in any way they could and issued a statement that "it was the sense of the law-abiding negroes of Little Rock that the alleged negro assailant should be given full punishment for the crime." This dramatic pronouncement, one that, despite the word "alleged," seemed to foreclose the idea of innocence before proof of guilt, must have been especially painful for Jones to sign on to; for much of the decade, he had successfully defended the rights of habeas corpus for the twelve black men railroaded to convictions in the Delta in 1919 and had seen them all freed by 1925, just two years before. He must have assumed that assuring the white powers of black support for Carter's conviction might save the city from greater racial violence and prevent a lynching, but perhaps none of the black elite of Little Rock could have imagined the horror that would shortly arrive at their doorstep.

Late in the afternoon, the police and volunteer searchers were closing in on Carter. A woman who lived on the upper Hot Springs pike reported that she'd seen a Negro crouching near the road not far from her house, and officers rushed to the site. Sometime before 5:00 p.m., he was spotted again near the road and two officers fired and wounded him. Carter fled again into the woods for a mile before climbing a tree, where he was spotted by two men from the citizen posse, R. L. Snow and E. L. McElvain. Snow raised his gun to shoot the tree-bound man, but McElvain stopped him. Carter climbed down and begged them to spare his life.

The men exited the woods with their captive on the first cutoff road, less than a mile from the upper Hot Springs pike, where soon more than one hundred men would gather. He was placed in a car with a deputy sheriff and two other men, and someone sent for Glennie Stewart to identify him. While waiting for her to arrive, the crowd rumbled for revenge, not only for this attack but for that on Floella McDonald by Lonnie Dixon, whose whereabouts were known only to Chief Rotenberry and the policemen hiding him. Of Carter, one in the lynching party said they were "never letting that negro get to Little Rock so the police can protect him," as the *Arkansas Gazette* reported. The officers present argued to let the law take its course, but the crowd was in no mood for any justice other than its own.

Carter asked for a sip of water and someone gave him "a tin cup from the well close by," adding that it was likely the last he would ever taste. He asked for a cigarette and one was produced with the same comment.

At about 5:25, Glennie appeared, and as soon as she said, "That's the man! That's the man!" two of the crowd seized Carter and called for a rope. Someone produced a part rope, part chain that had been used to secure a calf at a nearby property. They led Carter about thirty yards down the road to the nearest telephone pole and threw the rope over the crossbar.

The ad hoc hangmen played their part by asking Carter if he had any last words, and he requested that he be allowed to pray. They assented, and he started to kneel but was instructed to pray standing up.

"God, here I come on this fourth day of May, 1927. Take me God and have mercy on my soul—"

Before he could speak any more, the lynchers looped the rope around his neck and helped him ascend the back of a Ford roadster. A man holding the other end took up the slack and lay down in the ditch in preparation for the load he would support. Others instructed the crowd to back away from the makeshift gallows and proceeded to place about fifty armed men in a line twenty-five feet away from the pole.

The leaders of the group wanted Carter hoisted to the top of the pole, so that shots from the firing squad would not injure anyone else, but this "plan was defeated by the chain, which could not be passed over the cross bar," according to the *Gazette.* After some minutes of arguing over this difficulty, it was decided that the car would simply be driven out from under him. A complaint that they had "wasted enough time" was followed by the roar of the roadster's engine as the car took off and Carter's body dangled, his shoes about four feet off the ground. He was left there twisting on the rope for a couple minutes before a first shot, followed by a "fusillade" of at least two hundred more from the line of men, struck his body. Despite the force of the ammunition that riddled him, his hat remained on his head.

Word of the execution spread quickly, and another three hundred people showed up. Someone suggested that the body be burned, but another warned that no one should touch it until the coroner arrived. Fifteen minutes later, Sheriff Haynie and other officers appeared and tried to disperse the crowd until the coroner could make his official inquest. When Dr. Samuel Boyce drove up, he questioned several of those still present and, unsurprisingly, could find no one who would admit to having witnessed or participated in the killing. He finally determined that Carter had died from multiple gunshot wounds, trotting out the common term for assigning responsibility to nameless perpetrators in lynchings, "at the hands of parties unknown."

The mob's fury was just beginning.

Haynie later claimed in a statement that the crowd was "perfectly orderly," and he left the body under the coroner's care while he walked a quarter mile back to his car. Boyce later asserted that he was worried about the ambulance from Dubisson's funeral home, the black undertaker, being delayed, so he started toward the city to try to meet him. In any case, the men with the greatest official authority deserted the gathering. While they were absent, the mob reassembled, and B. E. Stewart, the husband and father of the assaulted women, later admitted to a reporter that he had been at the scene and said to the crowd, "Everybody that wants to drag the nigger down Ninth Street [the center of the black business district] and burn him, gimme your right hand," and that every hand, including those of the remaining policemen, had gone up.

In short order, Carter's body was strapped like luggage to the bumper of a Star roadster, which led a procession of dozens of cars toward the city. At about 7:00 p.m., at the intersection of Fourteenth and Ringo Streets, a block from the black Philander Smith College and eleven blocks from the construction towers hovering over the new Little Rock High, the gruesome parade stopped. Members of the mob removed the body from its makeshift bier and secured it head first to the back of another car.

As the sun began to set, the macabre parade began. Hooting and shouting "as if at a football game," blowing whistles and shooting guns, with the body of John Carter bouncing behind the lead car, the caravan moved down Ninth Street, a message to the black-owned barbershops, furniture stores, and nightclubs there, before turning north on Main Street toward the river, the procession by one account being twenty-six blocks long. A left on Markham took them brazenly in front of City Hall, which contained the police department and the mayor's office, both missing their senior officials, who'd assumed the worst was over. Weaving through the streets for more than an hour, causing traffic jams everywhere as people congregated to see the spectacle, the line of cars eventually made its way back to Ninth Street and Broadway, where the body was dumped in the middle of the intersection, on the trolley tracks. Someone drenched what was left of John Carter in gasoline and ignited his corpse.

As thousands converged on the site, they saw the body ablaze. And for three hours, when the fire would die down, "boxes, limbs, furniture, gasoline, oil, kerosene and whatever else that could be procured by the mob were thrown upon the charred body of John Carter, while men and women, many with babies in their arms, danced in a circle and howled and jeered." Some fed the fire with wooden pews taken from the historic, black Bethel AME church on the corner. As the *Arkansas Gazette* concisely summarized, "There was no semblance of order." One account had a man directing traffic with the charred arm of the victim.

As the bonfire raged, rumors spread that blacks were organizing countermobs, so splinter groups left the main conflagration and roamed the black neighborhoods, which were seemingly vacant and eerily silent. "All negro business houses and residences in the vicinity appeared deserted throughout the night," reported the *Gazette*. "That no violence did ensue is chiefly due to the good sense and restraint of the Negroes of Little Rock," wrote Marcet Haldeman-Julius, a Kansas journalist who happened to be in Little Rock during the events and chronicled them in *The Story of a Lynching*, the most comprehensive account, published later that year.

One unlucky black boy wandered into the area of the mob and, once it was discovered that he was carrying a pistol in his pocket, was beaten unconscious. He would have been thrown alive onto the fire, but one leader, standing on the top step of the Bethel church entrance, called for attention. "Listen, men," he said, "don't be fools. We've already righted one wrong and if we ever get our hands on Frank and Lonnie Dixon, we'll right another. But you've done enough for one night. This nigger has done nothing except carry a pistol in a place where he could not possibly use a pistol. . . . Send him down to police headquarters since there seems to be no policemen handy"—this the crowd greeted with laughter and jeers—"and charge him with carrying a concealed weapon." In fact, one source had the police playing cards in the basement of City Hall during the disturbance, waiting for orders from their missing superiors.

In the absence of the top brass, the city council met and decided to petition the governor to call out the National Guard. They reached him in Van Buren and he approved the deployment at 10:00 p.m., also securing a special train to return him to the city. Captain Harry Smith assembled Company H, 206th Coast Artillery, of the Arkansas National Guard at the Little Rock armory a few blocks away and marched them down Ninth Street, approaching from the east, then splitting the detail to enclose the intersection from four directions. They carried sidearms, rifles with fixed bayonets, and tear gas canisters.

The crowd had already thinned from five thousand to two thousand when Smith ascended the steps of the church and announced, "Fellows, there's been a lot of excitement tonight. A man has been killed and burned. That's all over with. . . . We think you've done enough for tonight and believe you ought to go home and go to bed and think over the matter until tomorrow. What do you think about it?" Those remaining responded with calls of "He's right" and "Let's go home," and within a half hour the street was almost clear, with any tarriers being hustled away by the troops.

A fire truck approached the intersection and extinguished the lingering flames of the fire, and a Dubisson and Company ambulance pulled up to take away what was left of John Carter, ashes and bones.

||||||||||||||||||||||||||||||||||||||

The following day, the *Arkansas Gazette* published a front-page editorial decrying the lynching and the mob that had perpetrated it under the headline "Law and Order Betrayed." It began: "The city of Little Rock suffered last night the shame of being delivered over to anarchy." It laid the blame on the "city and county peace officers," who "let a riddled corpse be brought to town for a Saturnalia of savagery," but seemed chiefly concerned that "in millions of homes throughout America, when families gather for the morning meal today, the name of Little Rock will be read with expressions of horror."

The mayor's statement in defense of his and Chief Rotenberry's absences drew ridicule. "I have no apologies to offer," he said. The chief "had only five hours rest since Saturday night and was worn to a frazzle both mentally and physically. I was not in much better condition myself." Even though he said he didn't hear about the lynching until 10:40, when he had been in bed for two hours in Memphis, and didn't arrive in Little Rock until two hours after that, he felt free to surmise that some 250 police officers and citizens would have lost their lives had the mob been confronted. Meanwhile, Sheriff Haynie attested that the lynching of Carter was "orderly." In the face of these assertions, the *Arkansas Democrat* called their statements "childish" and "so weak that they were pitiful."

Over subsequent days, Little Rock's leaders, including members of the Chamber of Commerce, the Red Cross, and the Ministers Alliance, convened in various groups and called upon the grand jury to take action against the public servants who had let them down. The Little Rock Bar Association offered to the authorities and the courts "the services of every member of the association in upholding the peace and dignity of the state, in enforcing the laws," and "in punishing the guilty." A meeting of one hundred or so members of the Chamber of Commerce passed a resolution "deploring and condemning" the execution of John Carter and urging that an indictment be returned against "every officer shown by the facts to have been guilty of dereliction of duty" and against those who had participated in the lynching and the "leaders of the mob that dragged the body through the streets and burned it." More substantively, they offered "to furnish the constituted authorities any amount of money that may be necessary to aid them in bringing all of the guilty parties to justice."

The effect on the black community was profound. C. L. Thompson, the white chairman of the citizens' flood-relief committee, said, "When our workers go out in the county, the negroes flee, thinking they are either mob members or others with no good purpose in mind."

Sentiment in the city was running high to hold someone accountable for the breakdown in civic order. But soon, the grand jury found itself at an impasse. After a week, the foreman, Gordon Peay, and six others wrote to the judge asking that the jury be dismissed, since they were convinced that the nine other jurors were trying to make a few minor figures the scapegoats and "that the whole affair was to be white washed." H. A. Cook, one of the nine in the opposing group, also wrote to the judge, asserting that "[Mr. Peay] seems to have thought that a foreman of a grand jury was expected to dictate the indictments. . . . [He] has insisted publicly and privately that the mayor, the chief of police and the sheriff should be indicted. I wanted to proceed with this question of fixing the responsibility for the mob leadership."

When Judge Abner McGehee agreed to "disorder" the grand jury, it was widely assumed that he would convene another special grand jury to pursue the matter, but for reasons he did not make public, he chose to let the next regularly convened grand jury take it up if it so chose, four months later. Lacking a legal body to make indictments, the community found its resolve for an inquiry waning. And once again, a storm interceded. On May 9 a series of tornadoes struck the state, missing Little Rock but hitting five counties around it, killing seventy-one people and diverting headlines and attention from the legal machinations surrounding the lynching. For three days, the newspapers featured little other than storm devastation.

Ten days later, when the Lonnie Dixon murder case was due for the court docket, the white community seemed eager to dispense with all racial strife as quickly as possible. Notwithstanding the bar association's proclamations that it would do all it could—even financially—to seek justice in the John Carter case, it left the selection of counsel for Dixon to lot: Names were literally drawn out of a hat, two days before the trial. On May 19, in a proceeding that lasted five hours, in a courtroom forbidding spectators and surrounded by police backed up by the National Guard on alert, Lonnie Dixon stuck to a story that his cousin had committed the murder of Floella McDonald. The jury found him guilty in seven minutes. Hours before his execution on June 24, he recanted his trial testimony and admitted his guilt.

||||||||||||||||||||||||||||||||||||||||

During that late spring and summer, there was much felicitous news to distract Little Rock's citizens from the grimness of the trial and execution. The day after the conviction, Charles Lindbergh took off for his solo flight across the Atlantic, and when he landed thirty-three and a half hours later, the already aviation-besotted country became even more obsessed. For four straight days, the *New York Times* spread triple-deck Lindbergh headlines across the front page, and the *Arkansas Gazette* seemed similarly caught up in Lindy fever. When the flier announced that Little Rock would be one of the cities he would visit on his cross-country tour in September, the city once again became enamored with itself.

There was also the new high school building to celebrate. Even before Mary Lewis sang in the first public performance in the auditorium in

October, the school's anticipated opening thrilled the city. Ten days before students filed in that September, a headline in the *Arkansas Democrat* touted the new building as "Arkansas' Supreme Achievement in Field of Public Education." With the size of its auditorium, it claimed, "Little Rock is now in position for the first time in its history to accommodate great assemblies such as national conventions—which has been the ambition of the 'booster' element for many years."

That element was responsible for dubbing the school "the most beautiful high school building in America," a phrase that appeared in the program for the official dedication on November 17. An earlier schedule for the annual meeting of the Arkansas Education Association, held at the new school in the week before the dedication, described the accolade as "the slogan which has been adopted by the city." This subjective but not entirely baseless bit of self-promotion has enjoyed a rich life of its own in the eighty years since it was first coined. In an evolution that would delight any public relations man, the phrase has been variously credited in countless articles over the decades to the *New York Times*, the National Association of Architects (a nonexistent organization), and, most commonly, the American Institute of Architects, which has no record of awarding the building this distinction. Even now, in the official documentation from the National Park Service and in the US House of Representatives bill from 2004 proclaiming the high school a national historic site, the latter body gets credit for anointing it with this title.

In that same month, the city received an unexpected endorsement from afar when the New York *Sun* declared that "Arkansas Travelers Cut a Wide Swath in Commercial New York." The story went on to identify some two hundred men, among them many "brisk boys from Little Rock," who had made an "amazing contribution" to New York City's business and financial worlds. Back home, the *Gazette* editorialized that "here is impressive refutation of misrepresentations and misconceptions of long standing." New York's embrace of Little Rock didn't end there: That fall, the Yankees signed a can't-miss twenty-year-old catcher who spent his teens in the neighborhood around the minor-league Little Rock Travelers' Kavanaugh Field and later played there for the team; after a long career in the majors, Bill Dickey would indeed earn a place in the National Baseball Hall of Fame. How bad could Little Rock be if its native sons—its white ones, anyway—were conquering the Big Apple?

In the black community, the lynching was not so easily swept away by the tide of public relations coups. In its wake, Little Rock quickly degenerated from a relatively tolerant place for African Americans to one that terrified them. Just two weeks before Floella's body was discovered, the *Little Rock Daily News*, a smaller and arguably less edified newspaper than either the *Democrat* or the *Gazette*—it often reported speech by blacks in a broad dialect—editorialized on a fund-raising effort by "colored" citizens to build their own YMCA without white funds: "The negroes of Little Rock are lifting themselves up. We people of the South are too prone to think of the negro in terms of the latest lynching. We often measure him by the man who mows our yards or the women who perform the menial tasks of the home. It is quite possible we are not cognizant of the amazing strides the race itself is taking right here in our midst for its own advancement." Such dawning if still patronizing enlightenment, contradicted by the subsequent violence, wasn't enough to convince blacks to remain in town.

By the winter, the NAACP reported that "many Negroes have moved away from Little Rock as a result of this lynching." The *Chicago Defender*, the leading black newspaper in the country, stated that on the day after the mob action, the Missouri Pacific Railroad sold $2,000 worth of tickets to black "migrants." Census figures may have shown that Little Rock's black population from 1920 to 1930 grew by 12.8 percent, from 17,485 to 19,725, but a deeper examination seems to bear out the anecdotal evidence of an exodus. When one assumes that there were thousands of black refugees from the 1927 floods in Arkansas who were driven from their rural fields and might have been expected to move to Little Rock, the increase seems slight, even more so when compared to the booming growth of the African American population in surrounding cities. During the same period, Houston's black citizenry grew by 128 percent, Memphis's by 58 percent, Shreveport's by 56 percent, and St. Louis's by 32 percent. And Little Rock's white population showed a 30 percent gain. At least part of the lag in growth for blacks in Little Rock must be attributable to the lynching and its deterrent effect on potential relocation there.

Among those who remained, race relations in Little Rock in the aftermath of the lynching clearly worsened. Nearly a year later, a representative from the NAACP traveled to Little Rock to do an investigation and evaluated Judge McGehee's reticence in calling another grand jury; the judge, in an interview, "plainly showed his antagonism to Mr. Peay," the report states, and McGehee further said that he saw "*no reason why the subject of the burning and lynching should come before this Jury or, in fact, ever be brought up again* [italics in the original]."

Neither the participants in the mob nor those officials who allowed it to run out of control ever faced legal consequences, and this denial of justice sent a chill through the air that permitted other atrocities. In the year after the lynching, Boyd Cypert, the district attorney described in the report as "a fairminded man with a decent and reasonable attitude," despaired of bringing cases against whites who killed blacks. He told the NAACP investigator of a case the following winter in which a jury delivered a "not guilty" verdict for "two white boys who went out one night with the definite and expressed intention of killing a Negro, for a lark." Cypert believed that such verdicts were "worse in themselves than the lynching of last summer and showed the hopelessness of bringing any kind of justice where the race issue is involved."

Even Scipio Jones, his legal triumph in freeing the twelve sharecroppers not far behind him, had grown so pessimistic that he advised the investigator against speaking to any black resident of the city lest it make that person a target. The report concluded, "Those with whom I talked felt that the outlook was depressing."

Over the years, the story of the lynching faded in the memory of Little Rock's white citizens. In the African American community, it remained alive, and as it was passed down, it differed in the probable facts in one key element that speaks volumes about the black perception of their status in the city. The black version first surfaces in print in the early 1950s, just twenty-five years after the event, in the memoirs of Edward Demby, a prominent black Episcopalian bishop who was active in the state in 1927. He recounted the story as one in which a white woman had been tossed from the wagon she was driving when her horses spooked. They were caught and calmed by a black man, but a mob of white men suddenly emerged from the woods accusing the man of rape and demanding that he be lynched, despite the woman's pleas to spare his life. Later, James Forman, a black journalist and activist who would become executive director of the Student Nonviolent Coordinating Committee in the 1960s, recalled in his memoir hearing a similar version during a visit to Little Rock in 1958, when he was on assignment for the *Chicago Defender*. In a conversation with three men, one said, "They drug him down this street. They took the benches out of the Methodist church, my church, and they burned the man on Ninth and Broadway. . . . They say he was chasing the buggy and the white men said he was trying to rape the woman." Another added, "I heard the white woman tried to tell them that the man was trying to help her. . . . But, son, sometimes these white people here don't listen to nobody."

More recently, in 1992, Beth Roy interviewed Jerome Muldrew, a social studies teacher at Central, for her book *Bitters in the Honey*. He was born in 1926, and he recalled hearing the story of the lynching as a child. "I was introduced to it orally," he told her, "it was just a thing everyone in Little Rock [knew]," though he identified the lynched man as Lonnie Dixon. When Roy told him that she'd heard the lynched man was innocent, he replied, "That's right." In the context of her other interviews with blacks, she concluded that the story demonstrated how "a common understanding of danger came to be shared by everyone in the black community." That version has endured even into the current century. In a memoir self-published in 2000, Little Rock resident Edith W. McClinton, who was a classmate of one of Lonnie Dixon's siblings, repeats the story of the runaway horses, one that appears in no contemporary accounts, even by those whose sympathies are with John Carter. In other particulars, McClinton's memory is amazingly accurate.

McClinton correctly identifies the lynched man as John Carter, but the conflation of Carter and Dixon still crops up in the narrative of the event in the African American community. In video interviews with black residents on display at the Mosaic Templars Cultural Center in Little Rock, a museum that opened in 2008, several elderly African Americans remembered the victim of the mob as Lonnie Dixon; elsewhere in the museum an exhibit correctly tells the story of John Carter's death and immolation, which occurred at the intersection where the museum stands. To some degree, it's understandable that Dixon's rushed conviction and summary execution could be perceived by Little Rock's black residents as little different from the injustice of Carter's fate, especially since Carter's murderers were never tried.

City leaders' failure to follow through on their promise to punish racial murder and mob action drew a clear line between the black and white communities. Thirty years after the lynching, the breach of that line by nine students would prove that the embers of the bonfire that burned John Carter still smoldered.

CHAPTER 3

SPEECHES AND JUDGMENTS

BERNIE COX HAS A VOICE THAT'S ODDLY SOFT for a coach. Background noise of any kind—an air conditioner, an idling bus, a lawn mower, Central's marching band at practice, even a cell phone's ringtone—might eclipse it.

As he started addressing the parents at a preseason meeting in Central's auditorium, the same one Mary Lewis had christened with her arias eighty years before, the listeners scattered across the orchestra seats leaned forward to hear. His voice may have been soft, but he was delivering his own aria, one that differed in tone from year to year but in some ways was as unchanging as any by Verdi. He hit the same notes in 2007 that he'd been hitting since 1975, his first year as head coach.

Standing in front of the stage rather than on it, he was sure some of the parents wouldn't like what they heard from him, but then, some never did.

The parents he didn't care for were the ones who either didn't participate in their sons' football lives at all or participated too much. The former group saddened him. His opening words to the parents were ones of appreciation for their being there. "It means a lot to us, the coaching staff," he said, "but it means a lot to those kids. . . . You wouldn't believe the number of kids I've coached who finish their career without their parents having ever watched their son play a football game. I don't know why. You wouldn't believe the number of kids at the end of the season who come to me with tears in their eyes—big, strong kids—crying and saying, 'I wish my mother had come to watch me play once.'"

In the latter group were the Central parents who had outsize expectations for their football-playing sons. Perhaps they'd been seduced by the success of Central players from the past, including the one who was in the local newspapers daily as coach of the Arkansas Razorbacks, Houston Nutt. He'd been a transcendent high school quarterback on perhaps Central's best team ever. You'd get some argument that the 1957 team was the greatest, but Nutt's 1975 Tigers had gone undefeated too, and sent a number of players on to college careers. Many, many Central players had gone on to play Division I college football, or D-1 in recruiting shorthand, and many more parents thought their sons should be playing top-level college football. One Tiger dad, whose son was strong but regularly last in sprints and in general put forth little effort, spoke of him as if he were simply biding his time before he started for Auburn.

Cox tried in this initial meeting to head off any parent criticism—and there was always some—by emphasizing the experience of the staff. "We have nine coaches, two of which are here tonight. We have over two hundred years of coaching experience. . . . Over 120 years of it has been right here at Central High School. So your son is getting coached by experienced coaches. I know you've probably talked to parents who have moved their sons from Central High because of me. They didn't agree with my beliefs, my philosophy, whatever. I'm a dinosaur. I'm the surest definition of it. I'm old-fashioned. I believe there's a right and there's a wrong, there's not a lot of gray area there. The things that we do in our program, we have a purpose for doing. I've made the statement many times to many parents: My No. 1 goal out there coaching is to teach young men, to be a very positive example—I know sometimes I'm not—to be better not football players, that's a part of it, but to be a better person, to be a better son, to be a better student, to be a better father. Everything we teach your son on the football field, make no mistake, they can transfer it to any area of their life, at any point in time in the future.

"My prayer is that ten years from now, fifteen years from now, twenty years from now, when your son comes back to Central High School, he'll say that the greatest thing he did was play football at Central High School. We take a lot of pride in that."

Players came back. They came back all the time, for every game. They came down to the decrepit locker room, with its peeling paint and rusty lockers and rainwater pools, and they heard the same voice they'd heard ten, fifteen, twenty years ago, the voice of Bernie Cox.

They were players like John Steed, one of Cox's all-time favorites, who showed up on the practice field the day before the first game of 2007 against West Memphis. An undersize lineman, he hadn't weighed 180 pounds when he came out for football at Central as a sophomore. He went on to become a two-time all-state player at defensive tackle and played nose guard at the US Air Force Academy, where he was the most valuable defensive player in 1988. "He didn't miss a game" at Central, Cox told the 2007 Tigers, "and he played both ways his last two years." Now he was Lieutenant Colonel John Steed, 126th Mission Support Group commander for the Illinois Air National Guard.

Steed looked like he could still run fifteen sets of bleachers in fifteen minutes, and a lot of the players who returned were in great shape, just a couple of years into college ball at the University of Arkansas, the University of Tulsa, or the University of Arkansas at Pine Bluff. Some came back from farther afield, still playing football at places like Grinnell in Iowa and Washington and Lee in Lexington, Virginia. Central has sent lots of students to strong academic colleges. It has always been cited as one of the top public high schools in the country; in 2007, *Newsweek*'s ranking put it twenty-fourth. And there were a lot of players who were at Central knowing they could both play top-tier Arkansas high school football and get an education that would get them into top-tier colleges. While Cox was making players of them, the school's teachers were making scholars of them.

Other returning players, older, grayer, paunchier, came back from careers that had taken them to Los Angeles, Dallas, or Washington, DC. They might be in Little Rock in August to visit family and stroll onto the practice field behind Quigley Stadium, the sweat of an Arkansas summer soaking their shirts, and they'd find Coach Cox saying the same things he'd told them years before. But he had regretfully made some adjustments over the years.

"The main criticism I get," he told the parents in the auditorium, "as a person and as a football coach from former football players who come back to Central . . . is: 'Coach, you're too easy on them. . . . Why did you make us do this in 1980, and these guys are wussies!' I'll give you an example. You parents know this. What did we tell them they would need to come back and do the first day when they reported back on July 23rd, run what?"

The parents knew and they shouted, "Ten in ten!"

"Ten in ten!" Cox echoed. "What did we do in 1980? Fifteen in fifteen. That's a criticism I get. You know what *those* kids tell me? I got a letter from a guy in Iraq, a major in Iraq who played football here. 'The things you guys taught me'—and Coach Callaway, he was here then—'the things you guys taught me have kept me alive for sixteen months. Because you told me, you drove it into me, you said, "You can do this, you will do this." ' He's Special Forces. He said, 'It's made a difference in my life.' The purpose of his note, seemingly, was: 'Don't change, don't change.' But I have. I hate to tell that kid. He was one of the group that ran fifteen in fifteen. Now we've got ten in ten. Why? I've softened up. . . . I'm going to be as blunt as I can. Your sons are not the type of athletes that we had here twenty years ago. If we tried to get fifteen in fifteen out of most of these kids, we wouldn't have a football team."

Of course, other players from the past have made mistakes. One of the best athletes who ever played for Cox was Emanuel Tolbert, a senior during Cox's first season as head coach. After three years of catching passes and taking handoffs from Houston Nutt, Tolbert went on to Southern Methodist University during the Mustangs' glory days in the old Southwest Conference and is still the school's all-time leader in career receiving yards. He later had an eleven-year career in the Canadian Football League, making the all-league team in 1988. He moved back to Little Rock after his pro career was over and began substitute teaching. In 2001, he was convicted of rape and violation of a minor in the first degree and was sentenced to sixteen years in prison at the Ouachita River Unit in Malvern. He has written to Cox, and he's not the only former Tiger serving time in prison who has written to him, and Cox told the ninth-grade football players at their first meeting in the bleachers of Quigley Stadium that when you get a letter from prison, the return address doesn't have a name on it, but only a number. When you go to prison, you lose your name.

Cox told the freshmen that when they went to the locker room that day, there would be a table and on the table would be a notebook and they were to print their names in the notebook, along with their student numbers—so if there were a dozen John Smiths in the school, there would be no mistaking which one it was—and the names of their parents or guardians. He never said "parent" without also saying "guardian" because he had learned over the years that many of his players didn't grow up like he did, with a mother and father and siblings in the same home. Often the grandmother or grandfather would be the one in charge, or an uncle or aunt, especially when the mother or father was fifteen or sixteen when the player was born.

He told the freshmen that he had notebooks just like the one they were going to print their names in that went all the way back to his first year, when Houston Nutt was his quarterback. Yes, the same coach who was now making millions of dollars coaching at the University of Arkansas once had been a kid just like them who had printed his name in the notebook where Cox kept all the grades and tardies and records from the building up the hill, i.e., the school. And he also told them that recently the parole board had contacted him about a former player of his from long ago who was now in prison, and the board was inquiring about what kind of citizen he had been when he'd played for Cox in high school. Cox went to his notebook and told the board what it said, and it wasn't good. Your actions, even your actions now, as a ninth grader, he implied, had consequences. Cox shook his head and you could tell he was sorry about it, but his notebook didn't lie.

In the auditorium with the parents, Cox held up a piece of paper. "This is something an old man named Cox came up with several years ago when I had so many parents fussing about a number of things we do," he said. "It's called a Code of Conduct form. I'm not very smart, but I decided to come up with a form, and on that form we'll address a lot of the issues that I thought were important if your son wanted to play football in our program. I put things like 'Respect yourself,' 'Respect your teammates,' 'Respect the faculty, administration, security guards,' 'Respect the civil authorities.' You have it, you have signed it, and I have it filed. And the ironic thing is, on several occasions, over the past few years, I've had parents challenge me on things, and when I put that down in front of them, with their signature on it, they really get embarrassed. We expect them to follow the Code of Conduct form: no tardies in classes, no disrespect to teachers, be a good teammate, give 100 percent, don't be selfish. Probably for me over the years, the No. 1 thing I see in young athletes today is, they're selfish. I think they get that from the professional athletes who are so selfish. It's all about money. We like our athletes not to be selfish."

The one former player and student who perhaps best embodied everything Coach Cox included on his Code of Conduct form was Roosevelt Thompson. A two-year letterman as a five-foot-seven-inch offensive lineman, Thompson worked even harder in the classroom than he did on the football field. By the time he graduated in 1980, he had already accumulated a list of honors unequaled in the school's history. In addition to being a starting guard on the 9-1-1 team that season, he acted in student theater, worked as assistant editor of the student newspaper, was elected the senior class president, and became valedictorian, the school's first African American to earn that distinction. He scored the highest mark ever recorded by an Arkansan to that point on the National Merit Scholarship exam.

His father was a minister and his mother a teacher, and the family—he had three siblings—lived in a modest house just across the railroad tracks that ran behind Quigley Stadium. You could see the stadium lights from their yard. Moreover, his academic and extracurricular accomplishments were yoked to an unusually humble and selfless personality. Behind the big, square glasses and goofy, toothy grin, behind the face and the grades of a nerd, was a leader who seemed to bestride the school like a colossus, who was able to unite the factions of race and class.

During his senior year, a racial conflict erupted over a student drama production of *You Can't Take It with You*, in which Thompson had a role as the wacky Mr. De Pinna, the iceman. The 1936 Kaufman-Hart warhorse comedy of the eccentric Vanderhof family was a classic—and a Pulitzer winner—but some black faculty members objected to the stereotypical portrayal of the black servants in the script, as well as some of the casting. The superintendent of schools sent an administrator to investigate, and she recommended that the play be canceled. He refused to do so. Thompson stepped forward and defused the controversy by writing a letter to the editor of the

Arkansas Gazette saying that the conflict was justified "only if citizens insist upon finding racism where none exists." The *Gazette* later editorialized that Thompson was "the only hero in the dispute."

That he arose out of the school that had earned a place as one of the country's most important historical symbols of racial strife was a healing irony. In 1979, he was one of two candidates for governor of Arkansas Boys State (the American Legion–sponsored mock state government), a position won previously by future governor Mike Huckabee. Expressing a desire to eventually enter public service and politics, he was already being spoken of by teachers, fellow students, and politicians like then-governor Bill Clinton and senator David Pryor as an eventual candidate for real political office— governor, senator, and even president. (He was born seven months after Barack Obama.)

After matriculating at Yale, he continued to play football, even though his size relegated him to the JV squad; he proudly displayed his height by taking the number 57. Yale captain Tom Giella, now a health care executive in Chicago, remembered Thompson as "dedicated. Never missed a practice in four years. Always positive. I never saw him down or depressed. He had a contagiously positive attitude."

The honors continued to pile up at Yale: He was elected to Phi Beta Kappa as a junior and won the Hart Lyman Prize, awarded to a junior "for character and achievement." At the national level, he was awarded a Truman Scholarship and, in December of his senior year, found out that he had won a Rhodes Scholarship, just like the man he'd worked for back in Little Rock during the summer of 1983, Governor Clinton.

He found time among his academic and athletic commitments to tutor at a grammar school and worked at New Haven City Hall eight hours a week. He was elected president of the Calhoun College Student Council at Yale and as a senior volunteered to be a freshman counselor, where he showed off his impressions of Eddie Murphy and Michael Jackson.

During spring break in March 1984, Thompson was in Little Rock, working on a research project and soaking up the atmosphere created by the Democratic caucuses held there that week, in which frontrunner Walter

Mondale was facing challenges from Jesse Jackson and Gary Hart. The city's black population was divided about whether to throw its support behind the prohibitive favorite Mondale or experience the heady, if largely symbolic, pleasure of voting for an African American for president. On the Thursday after the Saturday caucuses, Thompson was making the long drive back to New Haven. At 5:25 a.m., about one mile north of Newark, New Jersey, on the western spur of the New Jersey Turnpike, the driver of a truck traveling south swerved to avoid a tire in the road, lost control, and crossed the median, crashing into Thompson's northbound vehicle. He was pronounced dead at 6:35 a.m. at College Hospital in Newark.

Dr. Davie Napier, master of Calhoun College and professor of theology at Yale, called Thompson "one of the outstanding students ever to enroll at Yale in modern times." The memorial service a week later at Central High's auditorium drew fifteen hundred mourners, and a grief-stricken Bill Clinton told the crowd, "Roosevelt made all of us who knew him bigger and better and stronger. So today I pray that we think not of what he might have done, but what he did." After the service, his coffin was borne by classmates past tearful faces down the winding front stairs, where white students had set up a gauntlet of insults twenty-seven years earlier for those of his race. At the urging of his classmates, who perhaps best knew what was lost, the school board voted to name the auditorium the Roosevelt Levander Thompson Auditorium.

His death warranted a full page in *Newsweek* and a segment on CBS's *Sunday Morning* show, on which he'd appeared two years before. For that earlier interview, he'd affirmed, "I plan to return to Arkansas, and in Arkansas I'd like to practice law, and probably take part in a lot of politics." Despite Bill Clinton's eloquent tribute to remember him for what he did rather than what he could have done, from the time of Thompson's death in that election year of 1984, when Jesse Jackson was both mobilizing black voters and dividing the Democratic Party, until the fall of 2007, when Barack Obama and Hillary Clinton were dueling for the Democratic nomination, it was impossible not to sometimes think of the role Roosevelt Thompson might have played in the life of the city, the state, and the nation. A Rhodes student a year ahead of him from Little Rock's Catholic High, Bill Halter, was elected lieutenant governor of Arkansas in 2006 and became a candidate for the US Senate in 2010. In Thompson's same Rhodes class was George Stephanopoulos, political operative for Bill Clinton turned network journalist. Hillary Clinton herself, in an as-yet-unreleased documentary about Thompson, *Looking for Rosey,* produced by one of his classmates at Yale, said, "He was truly one of the most remarkable human beings I've ever, ever known. He had a combination of humanity and brilliance that you rarely find." Current Arkansas senator Mark Pryor said in the same documentary, "He was the best our generation had to offer . . . Roosevelt was going to be the first black governor of Arkansas."

Cox loved Roosevelt Thompson, but he loves all his players—or at least the ones who attack the bleachers, the ones who make the greatest use of the gifts they have. Most of Cox's players are not going into politics or law or medicine, though plenty do. Most will not stride onto the national stage, though some have. Most will go on to ordinary jobs in Little Rock as car salesmen and policemen and bank tellers and auto-body shop workers. And because they can play football, some will get to go to college to eventually earn a white collar instead of a blue one when they have no other means for going to college. Cox maybe loves these players even more than he loves the ones whose options are limitless.

Back in Roosevelt Levander Thompson Auditorium, Bernie Cox was talking to the parents about more forms. "We have you sign an equipment issue form," he said. "You and your son agree that you're responsible for any and all equipment that you check out. If I told you what my budget was for football, I think you'd be amazed, not because it's so high, but because it's so low. I'll say this—and I'll say it in front of the superintendent of schools and I'll say it in front of all seven board members—it's pitiful. It's embarrassing. There's no emphasis on helping the athletes in this district. . . . People don't understand. There's a lot of emphasis on AP, and there should be. You go back and look at thirty-five years, and you total up the number of those kids who've gone to college on football scholarships and compare that to some of the other scholarships and what they're worth and the value of those scholarships, yet we don't get any budget at all for football. . . . And that's another reason I appreciate so many of you so much. That's the way we survive—moms, dads, alumni, they've done a lot. . . . There was a time here at Central where I bought every player—we had a hundred kids—a game shoe and a practice shoe. Because we got all the gate receipts. We played Pine Bluff and we'd get six or seven thousand dollars. But we get forty-five hundred dollars. For the year."

Advanced Placement, or AP, courses were on everyone's mind that year. In February, the student body president for 2006–2007, an African American senior named Brandon Love, wrote a college-admission essay called "A Tale of Two Centrals" about the lack of interaction between black and white students and the disparity in the racial makeup of Advanced Placement classes. Without his knowledge, it was distributed anonymously in the late spring of 2007 to every Little Rock School District e-mail address, setting off a public debate about how successful Central had actually been in effecting equality. This debate was not new. When *Life* magazine visited Central ten years after the 1957 crisis, it found students willing to stand in a cafeteria line together and attend the same prom together, but doing little more. "We don't associate with them," said David Baer, a white student and the editor of the school newspaper. "We don't invite them to our parties. We just both go to the same school, that's all." Thirty-five years later, in 2002, in a case before the federal district court, a black Central alum described "the two institutions that existed simultaneously within the walls of Central High: 'Central College' where mostly white students take challenging courses, and 'Central High' where mostly African American students take distinctly less rigorous courses." Love's essay, another five years down the road, essentially reprised that testimony, but its emergence during the year that Central was in the spotlight because of its fiftieth-anniversary commemoration was an embarrassment.

Down in Bernie Cox's Quigley Stadium locker room, there were no two Centrals for the Tigers. "There's some things for which I've been criticized and even praised to some extent, which I don't get much around here," Cox continued in his speech to the parents. "I expect them to flush the commode, because their mama doesn't work here. I'm not going to go around and flush. Pick the trash up off the floor. We've got three huge, fifty-gallon receptacles down there. We ask them to lay their game pants down in one pile, what I call right side out, the outside out. [After a game], they just want to jerk those pants off, and throw them over there, because they're mad, they're upset. And we want them to take their jersey off and lay it with the number on the outside. It works pretty good. . . . I think the little things are important. If your son comes home and hasn't heard one of the coaches out there say, 'Little things make a big difference, do the little things,' he didn't come to practice that day. We tell them that every day. Can that not carry into every area of your son's life?"

|||||||||||||||||||||||||||||||||||||||||||

John Walker must have forgotten about Roosevelt Thompson.

In February of 2007, US District Court judge Bill Wilson handed down a ruling that the Little Rock School District was "completely unitary in all aspects of its operations"—and so no longer subject to federal desegregation monitoring. Five months later, John Walker, the state's preeminent civil rights litigator, addressed the school board in objection to the order. He asserted, with his usual blunt forcefulness, that no racial progress had been made in the district in decades; as evidence, he claimed that Little Rock Central High had never had an African American valedictorian.

Walker was known for not sweating the small stuff. He was a big-picture guy. If he got a fact or two wrong in the service of a larger point, that didn't bother him. "John basically does his discovery in court," Philip Lyon, a frequent opponent in the desegregation cases, told the *Arkansas Times* in 1993, but the courtroom was also where he thrived. Chris Heller, the attorney for the Little Rock School District who has often faced Walker before the bench, said, "He's very good at cross-examination whether or not he had a lot of information going in about the person or the issue."

To many in the city, Walker was one of the reasons the community remained divided. A Little Rock businessman once said that every time Walker "opens his mouth, it sets race relations in this town back ten years." To others, mostly the city's African American citizens, he was the righteous burr in the side of the white power structure of Little Rock, merely seeking redress for decades of wrongs perpetrated on the city's black population. For much of his forty-five-year career in the law, he had viewed the Little Rock school system and its board as the most egregious bulwark the white establishment had erected against black progress in the city, and so he kept challenging it in court. "Kids really matter to him," said Max Brantley, who has covered Walker for years as editor of the *Arkansas Times*. "He's got an ego . . . and John matters to John, but this really for him is about equal opportunity and equal growth."

Approaching his seventieth birthday, he seemed as ignited with principled rage as ever. After Wilson's order in February, the attorney told the *New York Times*, "In 2007, we have people in neckties living in big houses celebrating the return to 1957, a return to the concept of white supremacy." To some, this kind of rhetoric had an antique sound in light of the color of the school superintendent he opposed, an African American named Roy Brooks, who had brought a slash-and-burn mentality to the district's bureaucracy and was happy to see the supervision order removed. "I think that this is a clear indication that 1957 is not 2007," he told the Associated Press at the time. Brooks and Walker, and their separate supporters on the school board and elsewhere, had parried throughout the year. At a time when the community was revisiting its shameful past of resistance against superior educational opportunities for African Americans, the theater of two highly educated, accomplished, and powerful black men sparring over control of an institution as important as the school board might be viewed as progress.

Brooks was not from Little Rock or Arkansas—he'd spent much of his career in Orlando—and his outsider status left him seemingly clueless about the deep and tangled roots of racial struggle in the city. Walker, however, had sprung from the same fertile south Arkansas soil that had nurtured the state's most prominent citizen, former president Bill Clinton; its latest presidential candidate, Mike Huckabee; and, verified by the *Guinness World Records* book at one point, the planet's largest watermelon. All four were from the tiny town of Hope.

While Bill Clinton's writings about his boyhood in Hope in the late 1940s acknowledge the racial separation in the town of 7,500 people, his memories are mostly sepia-toned and nostalgic, like those of his Pawpaw's grocery store with its "jar of Jackson's cookies on the counter, which I raided with gusto." But in the first two decades of the twentieth century, when cotton was king and Jim Crow the unwritten law, Hope was the site of enough incidents of racial murder that it was sometimes called the lynching capital of the South. In her autobiography *Truth*, African American writer Ellen Douglas remembered her mother's story of driving into Hope when the family moved there in 1922 and seeing a lynched black man hanging from the struts of the water tower atop the three-story hotel, "a warning to uppity niggers." Nevertheless, Douglas wrote, it was in Hope that her family "would live happily for some years."

Born only sixteen years later, in 1938, John Walker was both acutely aware of the sting of the South's segregated society and, like the former president and Douglas, nurtured by a family that provided a contented upbringing in that small Southern town. His grandparents, educators who had both earned college degrees in Texas, taught him to read and enrolled him in school at age five. A slight, unathletic boy who acquired the nickname Too Thin Johnny, Walker once said that "if there were 18 of us choosing up sides for a baseball game, I would be the 18th picked." He may have been small, but even at age twelve, he could be confrontational. Once when a white boy in the local drugstore called his grandfather by his first name, the young Walker bristled and insisted the boy address the older man as "Mister."

He found his natural intelligence fired by an excellent black school system, historically developed by Henry Clay Yerger, for whom the high school was named by the time Walker enrolled there in 1950. Despite the lack of facilities—one day a week, Colored Day, was reserved for students to use a nearby University of Arkansas site—the school, which also served in the summer as one of three teacher training sites for blacks in the state, provided a competitive and rigorous education. Linda Chesterfield, a former Arkansas state representative and a 1965 graduate of Yerger High, once said of her education, "The teachers had very high expectations of us. We knew gerunds and participles; we knew Antony's oration at Caesar's funeral." In a short study of Hope's "black elites" published in 1980, John Walker's Sunday school teacher recalled, "John could read five times faster than he could speak, and he could speak three times faster than most of his classmates could listen."

Such lessons of language and rhetoric, and skill in them, served Walker well in Houston, where his parents moved after his sophomore year, and he became a star debater and the student body president at Jack Yates High. After graduating, he joined a group of black students seeking to be the first of their race to be admitted to the University of Texas in the fall of 1954. After accepting the applicants, the school withdrew its offer, reportedly because it was waiting for the disposition of the second *Brown* case. Walker heard, however, that underlying the rejection was the fact that one of the black students wanted to play football and neither the university nor the Southwest Conference (SWC), in which Texas played, was ready for that. (It wouldn't be until 1965 that the SWC signed its first black football player, Jerry LeVias of Southern Methodist, and until 1968 that Texas offered a football scholarship to its first black player, Leon O'Neal.)

If football indirectly denied him his place at Texas, it also prompted the student to file his first civil rights lawsuit—he sued the school over the denial of his admission. A district judge ruled that Texas's plan to send the students to a black college for two years prior to having them matriculate at Austin was acceptable under the law, but it didn't work for Walker. Disappointed—and, because of his legal expenses, broke—he decided to enroll at Arkansas Agricultural, Mechanical, and Normal College in Pine Bluff, where he could stay with an uncle. A sociology major, he became involved in some civil rights protests there, including one where he was sent to challenge the segregation of a public swimming pool even though, as he admitted in a speech in Little Rock in 2010, he could neither swim nor pay the admission price.

After his graduation in 1958, he moved to Little Rock and signed on with the Arkansas Council on Human Relations, an interracial activist organization. As Ernest Green prepared to become the first black graduate of Central High, the city remained the site of racial ferment and pinballing legal maneuvers. At the end of the summer that year, the US Supreme Court took the rare step of convening a special August session to deal with *Cooper v. Aaron*, the first desegregation case it elected to hear after *Brown* and one arising out of Little Rock's struggles. Its origins lay in a case brought against the Little Rock School Board, prior to the crisis at Central, on behalf of thirty-three black students from the city who had tried to register at white schools in January 1956 and been rebuffed. By the time it reached the Supreme Court, just before the new school year opened in 1958, its crux was whether the school district would be allowed a two-and-a-half-year delay in implementing integration because of the potential for violence. The decision by the highest court, reversing a federal district court ruling, was unequivocal, stating that the "constitutional rights of respondents [black students] are not to be sacrificed or yielded to the violence and disorder" in the community. To bring added weight to the assertion that *Brown* must be followed regardless of the external circumstances, all nine justices signed the opinion.

On the same day the Court ruled, September 12, 1958, a defiant Governor Orval Faubus ordered the Little Rock senior high schools closed. Both white and black students scattered to private, out-of-state, or nearby nondistrict schools, took correspondence courses, or didn't go to school at all. While legal wrangling ensued, the high schools remained closed for the entire 1958–1959 year. Strangely, Little Rock teachers still had to report to their empty classrooms to get paid, and the students were allowed to participate in extracurricular activities. To deny them that right, Faubus said, would be "a cruel and unnecessary blow to the children," so despite losing so many players to transfer, the Tigers fielded a football team that ended up No. 2 in the final state rankings, losing only one game to an in-state opponent.

In the spring of 1959, a crucial school board election pitted segregationists against moderates, and a coalition of businessmen, who acted more for economic expediency than on principle, and black voters mobilized to defeat the segregationist candidates by narrow margins. It was a victory for moderation, but not necessarily for swift desegregation.

On the legal front, after *Cooper v. Aaron*, integration in Little Rock was "driven by cases decided elsewhere," said Dr. Jay Barth, a professor of politics at Hendrix College in Conway, Arkansas. As the schools were set to reopen in August 1959, the state legislature passed the Pupil Placement Act, a law designed to ensure minimal integration. Almost identical to one passed in Alabama, it gave school boards the power to deny a student admission to a particular school for a range of reasons, notably excluding race. Using this wide discretion, the board denied the applications to attend Central of two of the original nine—Thelma Mothershed, whose heart problem was deemed a hindrance to her ability to negotiate Central's stairs and scope, and Melba Pattillo, who "seemed to attract trouble." By the end of July, only six black students had made it through the administrative gauntlet and were assigned to previously white schools. So, after two years, Little Rock had a third fewer black students in white schools than before.

For years to come, this system of "tokenism" was merely a quieter substitute for "massive resistance"; as Elizabeth Jacoway has stated in *Turn Away Thy Son*, her meticulously researched examination of the crisis at Central High, "Members of the Little Rock School Board expended tremendous amounts of energy in succeeding years, screening and limiting black applicants who wanted to transfer into the formerly all-white schools. Most of them never bought into the moral imperative that was at the heart of the *Brown* decision."

For a young graduate and nascent civil rights crusader like John Walker, this period provided a heady education in activism, realpolitik, and the law. One white leader described Walker during that time as "disarmingly modest but as sharp as a briar." Walker foresaw that the important civil rights battles in the years to come would be fought in the courtroom, where he would take aim primarily at the school system's inequalities. Walker left Arkansas for graduate studies, first at New York University and then at Yale Law School.

Skilled courtroom orator that he proved to be, he was determined not just to talk the talk. When he returned to Little Rock in 1965 with his wife and his four young children, he bought a house in an all-white neighborhood, Broadmoor, across from then Little Rock University, now the University of Arkansas at Little Rock. On principle, he did it to provoke residential integration, and his family suffered for it. "It was not a pleasant experience," he said in a 2000 interview with the *Arkansas Democrat-Gazette*. "Our fence was burned and we had to have night vigils. We lived there four years and no neighbor ever visited our house." While there, he would join the first of the desegregation lawsuits that have defined his career.

In 1966, with the *Clark* litigation, a series of suits that challenged the stonewalling pupil assignment laws employed by the district, Walker began his run as the most significant voice for black plaintiffs seeking equal treatment in Little Rock's schools. The nation's highest court helped him with various decisions. *Green v. County School Board of New Kent County* (1968) ruled against "freedom of choice," which had replaced outlawed pupil placement plans across the South. In *Green*, the court charged districts with an "affirmative duty" to institute a "unitary system in which racial discrimination would be eliminated root and branch." John Walker would argue the meaning of "unitary" in federal court for years to come.

In 1971, *Swann v. Charlotte-Mecklenburg Board of Education* gave a green light to busing, and other means that might be "administratively awkward, inconvenient, and even bizarre," as a remedy for racial imbalance. School districts in urban areas that decreed attendance by proximity, it said, were doing little to promote integration since the neighborhoods themselves were often segregated. Little Rock fit that profile, but the prospect of busing, fully implemented in the city by 1973, began to drive whites out of the school system to private and suburban schools. The percentage of black students in the district was soaring (from 48 percent in 1973–1974 to 65 percent in 1981–1982), and the Little Rock School District sued the two majority-white school districts in the county, the North Little Rock and Pulaski County Special districts, contending that they, as well as the state, were contributing to segregation.

Walker was allowed to join the case in 1984 as counsel for the "Joshua intervenors," a class of plaintiffs representing "all past, present and future African-American or black public school age children of Pulaski County, Arkansas, and their parents or guardians." In a decision that would have a profound effect on Little Rock's schools and demographic makeup, federal judge Henry Woods of the Eastern District of Arkansas ordered the three school districts to consolidate in the spring of 1984, less than two weeks after the memorial service for Rosey Thompson.

When the case was appealed to the Eighth Circuit in St. Louis, it landed on the desk of Judge Richard S. Arnold, like Thompson and Walker a product of Arkansas and the Ivy League. He had entered Harvard Law School in the fall of 1957, just as the Central High crisis was exploding, and later admitted he was "humiliated" to have to tell his new classmates that he was from Arkansas. From the time he was appointed to the Court of Appeals for the Eighth Circuit in 1980 until his death from lymphoma in 2004, a career covered in Polly Price's recent biography, *Judge Richard J. Arnold: A Legacy of Justice on the Federal Bench*, he heard some twenty-eight appeals of cases involving Little Rock and school desegregation. The last of these was adjudicated just months before he died, and his decisions would literally shape the district and the composition of the schools.

The Eighth Circuit had no objection to the findings of fact in the lower court, but still denied that consolidation was the most appropriate remedy. It would, as Arnold wrote, cause "the destruction of three popularly governed units of a local government, and substitution in their stead of one judicially created and judicially supervised school district," a violation, he said, of the "deeply rooted" tradition of local control of schools. As a compromise, the court extended the school district's lines to be largely consistent with the city limits, but denied it full consolidation.

The Eighth Circuit also ruled that the parties to the case—primarily the state and the county school districts—should reach a settlement by 1989. The settlement included a payment from the state to the three school districts of $109 million to fund desegregation programs and $3 million in attorneys' fees, an amount that would be brought up again and again in criticisms of Walker. Woods, whose decisions Arnold kept overturning despite their close friendship, finally recused himself from any further desegregation cases, but not before issuing a stinging rebuke: "Thus we are now in the throes of another of the many appeals perfected in this case, some of which have accomplished nothing but enrichment of the participating attorneys. On this subject the time has come to speak frankly. Lawyer fees paid by the three districts in this litigation have been grossly exorbitant." Arnold did not agree, deciding that "the efforts of counsel in this case are worthy of substantial recognition," including work dating back to *Cooper v. Aaron* in 1956. Though Walker had displayed copies of million-dollar checks in his office before, both Heller and

Brantley dismissed the idea that Walker had become wealthy from the deseg-regation cases. "He probably hasn't been paid in a decade or more" for work on those cases, said Heller, and Brantley stated that "he's provided more free legal advice to people in the community over the years" than anybody.

The settlement was an extensive document calling not only for better racial balance in the numbers of black and white students in the schools, but also for a reduction of the achievement gap, use of interdistrict and magnet schools, court approval of the opening of new schools, and the establishment of an Office of Desegregation Monitoring by the district court. In the face of such complexity, the parade of legal challenges marched on. Walker, as repre-sentative of the Joshua intervenors, continued to prod and harangue until the scales were further righted. And he always knew that should he be defeated in a lower court, the Eighth Circuit was a very friendly place for him to argue.

While his rhetoric has often been explosive, his triumphs in the courts over his career have been less like detonations at the foundations of the status quo than like a slow, continuous drip that gradually wears away the rock beneath it. Brantley counts Walker's numerous victories in economic terms for the black community; they have provided, he said, "a pathway to the mid-dle class for an uncountable number of black people in Little Rock," and those families, in rising, "have prospered in other ways" and become leaders and won elections. By 1996, three of the seven school board members were black.

Walker fought on, and if he was showing no sign of weariness with the desegregation battle, others were. By 2001, in a motion contested by the Joshua intervenors, the Little Rock School District was granted "partial" unitary status in the district court, a decision affirmed by Arnold in the Eighth Circuit. He handed down his decision in March of 2004, when his lymphoma was already progressing, a condition that kept a regretful Bill Clinton from appointing him to the Supreme Court. Arnold would be dead six months later. "This litigation began in 1982 and has been in and out of this Court and the District Court several times," he wrote in his last deci-sion on the topic, "it is complex to say the least." Arnold was a believer that judges should have "passion" for the cases before them, and he had lived with his home state's and adopted hometown's shame of 1957 through numerous attempted and abandoned remedies. In his last decision, as he knew he was nearing his own end, it's not inconceivable that he also passionately wished Little Rock's troubles to come to a close. In upholding the district court's ruling, it must have seemed the end was in sight.

As close as he may have felt to the city's history of racial strife, he remained at an intellectual remove from the brick-and-mortar reality of Central High, as Price recounts in an anecdote. When Justice Sandra Day O'Connor was visiting Little Rock for an event and Arnold was scheduled to take her back to the airport, he asked her if there was anything else she'd like to see before she left. She answered that she wanted to see Central High, and Arnold, though he'd lived for years in the city and had spent so much of his career weighing the legal ramifications of desegregation inaugurated by events there, had to call his secretary for directions to the building.

One of the Joshua intervenors' objections in the case before Arnold was that racial disparity existed in extracurricular activities. If Arnold and O'Connor had stopped by Central's football practice, especially in the late summer of 2004, they would have seen at least one refutation of that in the defending state champions. The Tigers began 2004, the school's one-hundredth year of playing football, with four straight shutouts and ended the regular season 9-1 entering the playoffs. From there, they rolled over their opponents, most memorably in the semifinal game before more than ten thousand fans at Quigley Stadium against undefeated Springdale of northwest Arkansas, which was ranked No. 18 in the nation and averaging nearly forty points per game. As a team under Bernie Cox, Central's players had unified to overcome the residential boundaries that long separated Little Rock's races, the barriers that John Walker had himself once breached and ones he said in 1993 were "the result of one race maintaining for itself polit-ical and economic control over the other."

One feel-good team, however, or one courtroom victory, did not make a community whole. It merely showed what might be possible, just as Rosey Thompson had shown what might be possible. And the triumph could disap-pear as quickly as the last seconds of a game or a life in a car crash.

It could be forgotten as soon as it was gone.

CHAPTER 4

"WE GOT NO LEADERS"

"ONLY GOD CAN JUDGE ME."

Tim Dunn was translating his arm for the coaches. A series of Chinese characters was tattooed on his left forearm, and when he stopped by the coaches' office before practice, one of them asked him what they meant.

Dunn was a senior tailback who'd transferred from North Little Rock High in the spring and participated in workouts then. Though a reputation for fumbling followed him to Central, he'd impressed with his speed and strength. Throughout the summer, he'd worked out with Lee Thompson, a burly former Central running back, the team's PA announcer, and Rosey Thompson's younger brother. Most mornings, while Brian Cox, Bernie Cox's son and the team's trainer, was supervising his own summer conditioning and weight-lifting program at Quigley Stadium, Lee Thompson would pull his air-conditioning service van through the gate and for the next hour give Dunn some individual instruction. Thompson was only blocks away; he now lived in the same house where he and Rosey had grown up.

||||||||||||||||||||||||||||||||||||||||

Though Dunn was faster and stronger than any other back, in the early days of preseason practice he was splitting time with Bo Dillon, a hardworking senior who always finished every play ten yards farther down the field than anyone else. Dunn had the potential to be a breakaway back, but Dillon was a workhorse. Dillon's father, Tony, a regular at practice and as voluble as Bo was silent, claimed that Bo was going to be the first white tailback to start at Central in twenty-five years, but white or black, there was no question that the position was not going to be as strong as in recent years. The previous season, Charles Clay, at six foot three and 215 pounds, had borne the load, and in the back-to-back state championship seasons of 2003 and 2004, Mickey Dean had provided a slashing toughness that seemed lacking from the current Tiger backfield. Sometimes, at practice or in the office, the coaches simply looked into the distance and said his name with longing: "Mickey Dean."

In the Bernie Cox era, Central had excelled on defense and would continue to do so in 2007. The anchors were Jared Green, a quick defensive tackle almost as broad as he was tall; Reed Caradine at defensive end; diminutive but fierce nose guard Quinton Brown; and two senior defensive backs in their first year with the Tigers football team, basketball star Kaelon Kelleybrew and a transfer student from Stuttgart, Arkansas, A. J. Williams. It had become clear in preseason practice that Williams was an impact player. He had trouble running the bleachers, but on the field, he owned perhaps the best football instincts of anyone on the team. He was an elusive return man, a ball hawk on defense, and, having played some quarterback at Stuttgart, a potential threat to run or pass from the offensive backfield, where Cox was also considering using him.

||||||||||||||||||||||||||||||||||||||||||

Cox's emphasis on defense was a source of frustrated amusement for his friend and longtime colleague Norman Callaway, the assistant head coach who worked primarily with the offensive line. During the first week of practice, Cox had told the coaches that he wanted to stress basic defensive skills: "We're gonna attack and read. We're gonna go low to high." He ended his instructions to them with a sigh and said, "If we shut people out, we've got a chance." Later, Callaway observed wryly about the previous season's team and Cox's defensive mind-set: "We average twenty-six points per game and it's the defense that won."

Even after the first few days of practice, the coaches had pinpointed the team's primary weakness, and it had nothing to do with offense or defense. "It will depend on chemistry, if it develops," said Callaway. "The 2003 and

2004 teams, they had it. They were all friends." On the field, Clarence Finley announced his opinion of the team to the offense at high volume. "Everybody's just going through the motions," he said. "Not a leader on the team. Better take off those Tiger shirts. If we don't get a leader out here, we're going to be in trouble. You're not fuzzy! You've got no hair on your balls! Randy, this is your team. You need to be a leader right now!"

After the Wednesday practice of the first week, the coaches descended to the office, their hats sweat stained from the effects of the relentless summer heat. Finley clicked on the ancient window-unit air conditioner, which was wedged into a wall crevice since there were no windows to the outside. One coach opened the full-size refrigerator against the far wall and took drink orders for the others. He tossed gum and cheese crackers around the room from containers on top of the fridge.

IIIIIIIIIIIIIIIIIIIIIIIIIIIIIIIIIIIIIIII

When Cox began to speak, Finley automatically reached over to turn off the air conditioner, which shuddered to a stop.

"What grade would you give us for the first three days?" Cox said.

"B," said Larry Siegel.

"B minus," said Darrell Seward.

"If I'm just judging by the offense," said Finley, "then I'd have to say a D. That's just being honest. I'm sorry. Randy Rankin is not a leader."

"He's not," agreed Callaway.

"That's why I'm going to have to be on him," said Finley, "to make him into a leader. He wasn't here today. He said he had two ear infections, but he just wasn't here. We shouldn't have to be teaching him, he should be teaching."

Adding to the anxiety in the room was a series of injuries. Besides Rankin's ear problems, Tim Dunn had fractured his collarbone and was going to be lost for several weeks, and the most accomplished lineman, De'Arius Hudson, had broken his ankle.

Cox returned to the paperwork on his desk, including that for the players who would need to take the bus home after practice. The addresses ranged all over the city, from the Granite Mountain neighborhood in east

Little Rock to John Barrow Road in the southwest. On the wall beside Larry Siegel's desk was a map of the attendance zones for the Little Rock School District. The one for Central followed the southern bank of the Arkansas River from east of the airport all the way to the Pinnacle neighborhood fifteen miles to the west, along with a patch of the recent Chenal development west of Interstate 430. This included some of the poorest neighborhoods in the city and some of the most expensive, including those surrounding the old-money Country Club of Little Rock and the nouveau riche Chenal area.

But the truth was that there was a lot of porousness in these boundaries and easy ways around the zoning restrictions. Central, for example, was an international studies magnet school, so if a superior football player (or basketball player or drama or chemistry student) wanted to attend Central instead of, say, J. A. Fair High School, he would declare an interest in international studies and agree to take the required courses. This option opened the door to charges of recruiting among schools. Recruiting for athletics was specifically forbidden by the Arkansas Activities Association, the governing body of high school sports in Arkansas, and penalties could be assessed for those deemed to do it, but it was rarely proven. Even beyond the boundaries of the school district there were easy ways to transfer, and coaches raised eyebrows and sometimes official protests over some of the more blatant moves.

In the office, there was all kinds of banter about suspicious player acquisitions. One coach mentioned that Central Arkansas Christian had accused Central of recruiting, which drew some mirthful looks since the private schools, with fewer restrictions, had always been the first to draw such criticism. Another noted that North Little Rock's new head coach had brought his quarterback in from Mayflower, in neighboring Faulkner County, where he'd coached the season before. "How'd he do that?" someone else asked. The player's family moved, was the answer. In an age when free-agent pros hop around to different teams for the biggest paycheck, the students and their parents were savvy enough to know how to get into the schools that might be the best fit athletically, often absent any recruiting by coaches. A parent might give the student's home address as the address of a relative in the zone. A student with divorced parents who lived in different zones could choose the home address for the school he desired. Wealthy parents, it was rumored, sometimes bought dilapidated houses in the "'hood," letting them sit empty but listing them as their main residences. And the district's "M to M" transfer rules—that is, "majority to minority"—allowed liberal movement; students of the majority race at a school in one district could transfer to a school where they would be in the minority, as part of a plan to provide greater racial balance. Thus former record-setting University of Arkansas football star and current pro Darren McFadden, though he had lived in Central's district, two blocks from the school, had been able to choose to attend Oak Grove High in the Pulaski County Special School District.

Will Rollins, who transferred to Central before his junior year from tiny Arkansas Baptist High School, wanted the challenge of playing for a school in the largest classification, 7A. From a family of devout Christians, he was home-schooled until seventh grade. His father had been a football star in West Memphis, a brother had gone to Catholic High and played football there, and by the time Rollins was a sophomore, he was growing into too strong a player for the small Christian school. (He'd enrolled at Catholic High for two weeks in ninth grade, but hadn't liked it.) The coaches at Arkansas Baptist often kept him out of contact for fear he might hurt some of his own teammates, thus potentially depleting a team that had barely enough suited up for a full offense and defense. "I never had more than thirty players on a team," Rollins said.

Before he even set foot in a classroom, Rollins had some idea of the change he was about to experience. "I'd never seen anything that big before," he said of the school building when he visited a practice in the spring. But, as a potential fullback, he liked what he saw and heard there. "The first thing he asked me," Cox remembered, "was 'Do you hit in practice?'"

For a superior student like Rollins, there was no academic sacrifice in attending Central, where he could get all the AP classes he wanted. "What he was concerned about," Rollins recalled of his spring conversation with Cox, "was me getting a good education. He told me all the things I'd better watch out for. He said there's good people up there, you've just got to find them." Rollins decided to make the leap to Central after praying about it for two years. "I felt like God was calling me to do something different with my life," he said.

By Friday of the first week of practice, Rollins was feeling more comfortable, but he and the rest of the team would have done well to heed the advice Rollins's father had given him. "If they yell at you," Mr. Rollins had said, "let them yell at you. Just go 100 percent." Cox had blown up during Thursday's session of bleachers, when a few players hadn't followed bleacher protocol, and made them run extra. "Start with two feet on the bottom, and when you get to the top, you put two feet on the top!" he'd shouted over the heaving gasps of seventy boys. "You're going to do it my way, or you're not going to play!"

Practices on Thursday and Friday of that first week had lasted nearly four hours each in 93°F heat. Asked what he had learned during his first five days as a Tiger, Rollins replied, "I learned about bleachers." Damien Lee, the big junior tight end, had distinguished himself with both his pass-catching ability and his mouth, dubbing himself Hands "R" Us after one catch. As the players gathered around Cox on that Friday, he told them, "It's been a pretty good first week, but some of you have not given us everything you could." But then he switched topics, leading with a seemingly puzzling question: "How many sets of brothers do we have here? The Greens. Bo and Chase Dillon." He paused. "Over the weekend, I want you all to go up to your mother and give her a hug and what are you going to tell her?"

The players who'd spent previous seasons with Cox knew the answer and shouted it in unison: "I love you!"

In the coaches' office afterward, Finley lifted the foil from a catering-size aluminum pan of barbecued sausage and chicken wings he'd cooked at his house. His father had been a chef at Sims, one of the best barbecue joints in Little Rock, and Finley himself had spent a year in the catering business. His advice: "Don't ever go into business with your brother. I tried it one year, got right back into coaching."

Like the week of practice, the food wasn't quite right, in his opinion. "The wings went a little too long, about four and a half hours," he said. "Should have been on four. They got a little dry. They're good, but if you'd had them at four, they would have been just falling off the bone." No one else was talking. Their mouths were full.

||||||||||||||||||||||||||||||||||||||||

On Thursday, September 27, 2007, the Little Rock School Board held its first meeting after the Tuesday ceremony to commemorate the fiftieth anniversary of the integration of Central High School by the Little Rock Nine, and pork was on the agenda. The Partners in Education program, a Chamber of Commerce initiative to bring business support to schools, presented to the board for review and approval a new partnership between Corky's Ribs and BBQ restaurant and Central High School. Melanie Fox, from Zone 3, which included the Heights (where the Country Club of Little Rock was located), moved to accept the new partnership, and Dianne Curry, from Zone 7, which covered mostly minority southwest Little Rock, seconded the motion. It carried unanimously. That the board agreed unanimously even on something as innocuous as what barbecue might be served at football games must have come as a surprise to those in the community who had followed the past nine months and more of acrimony, recriminations, turf battles, charges of racial discrimination, electoral gamesmanship, and shrill hectoring.

The Little Rock School Board had long been a battleground for the opposing factions in Little Rock, the organization that had most often embodied the rift between black and white, progressive and segregative. Indeed, throughout the first half of the twentieth century, in Little Rock and elsewhere across the South, the white power structure usually controlled school boards and paternalistically oversaw the administration of the Negro schools.

Two years after the opening of the new Little Rock High School, the board oversaw the completion of a new building for Little Rock's Negro students. Contributing funding for the construction of the school, which was to have an industrial arts emphasis in the manner of Booker T. Washington's Tuskegee, was the Julius Rosenwald Fund, named for and supported by the president of Sears, Roebuck and Company. Over the course of the decade and a half between 1917 and 1932, the organization funded the building of nearly five thousand schools for black students across the country. Some of the same architects who had worked on Little Rock High designed the school, located nine blocks east of Little Rock High, and at the dedication ceremony in 1930, it was called "the dream of the colored people of Little Rock come true . . . far beyond in beauty, and modernity, and size what the boldest had ever hoped for." The cost for the building was $425,000, of which $67,000 came from the Rosenwald Fund, and in 1931, it became the first black high school in Arkansas to be accredited by the North Central Association. Students from all over the state moved to Little Rock to stay with relatives so they could matriculate. Still, others objected to the vocational focus of the curriculum (dictated by the Rosenwald Fund) and sought to ennoble its liberal arts offerings by naming it for the prominent poet, novelist, and playwright Paul Laurence Dunbar.

Nevertheless, it was significantly less opulent than the new high school for white students (and more than $1 million less expensive), with thirty-four classrooms and limited space for recreation. It had no gymnasium or athletic fields at all. One football player remembered walking to and from Crump Park, fifteen blocks away, for practice, "making for a very long day." The schools were separate but hardly equal.

Throughout the 1940s and 1950s, per-pupil expenditures for black students in Little Rock began to inch closer to those for white students, reaching 67 percent in 1943 and 93 percent in 1952, but no move toward greater equality came without a fight. In 1942, a Dunbar teacher filed suit over the disparity in salaries between black and white teachers in the district, a case taken up by Thurgood Marshall and the NAACP. Various rulings and appeals took the case into 1945, when the Eighth Circuit overturned a lower court's judgment for the school board. The degree of the district's reluctance to budge on equal salaries can be gleaned from Marshall's notes, in which he asserted that "the other side really means business" and had employed "top-flight lawyers."

Even in the best of times, school board service is largely a thankless job, normally unpaid and rife with bureaucracy, budgetary wrangling, and factionalism. If the original *Brown* decision resulted in, as Richard Kluger writes in his history of the case, *Simple Justice*, "a reconsecration of American ideals," when the Supreme Court handed down *Brown* II, emphasizing "varied local school problems," it essentially decreed that implementing integration was in the hands of local authorities. The overt response in Little Rock after *Brown* I was that the district would obey the law of the land, but superintendent Virgil Blossom's plan—starting with the high schools and working for full integration over the next seven years—was by any definition a strategy of "gradualism" if not outright delay.

Further complicating matters, by 1957, two more new high schools were to open in the city, Hall High in the city's mostly white western section and Horace Mann High in mostly black east Little Rock. The former shielded parents residing in wealthier white neighborhoods from having to send their children to a school scheduled for desegregation—"gerrymandered" is the word Elizabeth Jacoway uses in her book to describe the attendance zone excluding blacks—and the new black high school potentially blunted objections by the black community that their school was woefully out-of-date or that white citizens were getting preferential treatment. In the end, Central stood alone at the center of the integration fight.

The six-member school board at the time of the integration crisis was stocked with officials who were either part of the major business interests in the city or proxies for them. Two avowed segregationists were defeated in the March 1957 elections by candidates supported, both financially and logistically, by the "civic elite," who hoped to avoid controversy so as not to stanch growth and industry, and by voters of the largely black fifth ward. Despite these nods toward progress, an Eisenhower civil rights investigator found the integration plan one of "evasion, not sincere compliance." All six school board members—as well as Blossom, the architect of the integration plan—lived in the Heights, an area then included in Hall High's zone, thus exempting them from any direct experience with integration.

Jacoway describes the performance of the school board during the 1957 crisis as having a "characteristic lack of force," allowing segregationists to outmaneuver them in controlling public sentiment and Governor Orval Faubus to overpower them with the mechanisms of politics. Five school board members resigned in November of 1958, during the year when the schools were closed, and in the following elections, a split slate of three avowed segregationists and three more-progressive candidates representing the city's businessmen was elected. Turmoil ruled as the integration battle moved through the courts. When segregationist school board members threatened to fire forty-four teachers and administrators whom they had identified as favoring integration, a citizens' group organized a recall election in May of 1959 and succeeded in removing the board members, news that landed on the front page of the *New York Times*.

As the schools opened again in 1959, Little Rock was "tired of trouble," the *Times* reported. The city resolved to obey the minimum of the law, as many other Southern states had also decided, and the plans it put in place for decades to come received continual federal oversight. A report prepared by the University of Arkansas at Little Rock in 1997 described the "constant presence of instability over the last 40 years. . . . Since the crisis at Central High, a new or revised pupil assignment plan has been introduced approximately every five years. Each has grown out of litigation and then has become the subject of litigation."

As for the school board, African Americans did not begin to assert some electoral power until 1966 with the successful campaign of T. E. Patterson, the first African American member and a well-known local educator. Whites, however—and in particular white business interests—continued to dominate the board for years. In an essay in the *Arkansas Historical Quarterly* published in the summer of 2007 to provide a fiftieth-anniversary retrospective of the school crisis, Ben F. Johnson III traces the way the white elite first united with the black community to defeat ardent segregationists after the 1957 crisis, then proceeded to use their power to manipulate housing patterns and school construction to perpetuate de facto segregation. Johnson details how William Rector, a prominent real estate investor who developed the west Little Rock neighborhood of Pleasant Valley in the 1960s (where Bernie Cox now lived), engineered a "purge" of liberal forces from the school board. Shortly after, Rector changed the landscape of education in the city by building in his neighborhood a private school that was soon to be called Pulaski Academy, one of the wave of "seg academies" constructed across the South to avoid the busing given court sanction in the *Swann* decision. He declared that his school would be open to all, but let his true intentions be known by saying: "I even hope we'll be allowed to play 'Dixie' if we want to without having a riot about it." It was the start of a still-growing trend in Little Rock toward private school construction. Johnson notes that by 2000, Little Rock ranked in the top ten among metropolitan areas in the percentage of white students attending private schools, while also remarking that as recently as 2003, Pulaski Academy awarded only one black student a diploma in a class of 102 seniors. He concludes: "Notwithstanding the importance of the original school crisis in the nation's civil rights history, the conservative takeover of the school board by 1970 . . . more decisively shaped the development of education in Little Rock over the following decades." Rather than the "massive resistance" of overt segregation, this period marks what Johnson calls a time of "affluent resistance" in which white parents blamed court decisions for causing the decline of educational quality and forcing them to pursue other educational opportunities for their children.

And so they did in Little Rock. Over the next thirty years, the demographics of education in the city changed dramatically. Besides the skyrocketing rate of private school attendance, whites in Little Rock were also abandoning the city for the surrounding areas and their predominantly white schools. In 1977, a US Commission on Civil Rights report stated, "Many Little Rock citizens fear that a widening gap exists between the schools and the larger community because of the continuing white middle-class flight to the suburbs." That trend marched ahead unabated. The 2000 census numbered the white population of suburban Little Rock and North Little Rock at 88.7 percent. And a Brookings Institution study in 2006 ranked the Little Rock area second in the country in the percentage of exurban residents, with almost a quarter living in neighboring-county communities like Bryant and Cabot, whose populations are overwhelmingly white.

As a result, the percentage of African American enrollment in the public schools ballooned, so that in the 2006–2007 school year, the number of white students in Little Rock public schools stood at 24 percent. Compared to Dallas and Birmingham, Alabama, for example, whose white enrollments for the same period were a staggering 5 and 1 percent respectively, Little Rock's number didn't look so bad, but the city had received millions of dollars over the years to right its integration wrongs, and black students were still trailing their white counterparts in performance.

Part of this exodus no doubt correlated with a rise in gang activity in the 1990s. The city reached its all-time high murder total of seventy-six in 1993, which placed it sixteenth in the country and spawned an infamous HBO documentary, *Gang War: Bangin' in Little Rock*. An investigation by the *Arkansas Democrat-Gazette* estimated that one of every eight teenagers in the public schools was a gang member, and the neighborhoods around Central were ground zero for the turf wars. The 1993 season also gave Bernie Cox his worst record as a coach at 1-9. Whether or not gang violence was to blame for keeping players off the team—losing them to the streets or to their parents' fears of what might happen if they weren't at home—the team photograph for that season shows only forty players in uniform.

If any school was stemming the tide of white flight, it was Central. The trophy cases that lined the halls were as packed as the halls themselves in vivid testimony to a history of athletic and academic excellence. In the decade before the fortieth anniversary of its integration in 1997, 10 percent of the state's National Merit semifinalists came from Central, and nearly half of the black semifinalists from Arkansas had been Central High students. Governors, lawyers, doctors, and prominent businessmen alike sent their children to Central, and students throughout its history have regularly won admission to the most competitive colleges in the country. In a 1993 survey of college-admissions directors—the same year gangs were patrolling the neighborhoods surrounding the school, it is worth noting—Central was one of the twenty-six public high schools in the country most frequently named as best preparing its students for college admission. If Central's record of academic and athletic accomplishment had not been so impressive for so long, it's probable that Little Rock's percentage of white public school students would have dropped to Dallas's range.

But in the lead-up to the fiftieth anniversary, it was the school board that drew all the attention, and not for the right reasons. If Little Rock had hoped to smooth over the racial rifts that had always cleaved it, the noisy school board offered a case study in how not to get along.*

In a runoff election for Zone 7, in southwest Little Rock, in October of 2006, Dianne Curry defeated Tom Brock, giving the board a black majority for the first time in its history. The news went out widely over the wires, the flip side of reports from forty-nine years earlier: Now the African Americans were in control of the schools. With less than a quarter of the students in the schools being white, John Walker told the press, "why shouldn't it be a black majority School Board." Skip Rutherford, a former school board president and Clinton insider who had become dean of the University of Arkansas's Clinton School of Public Service, struck a hopeful and even-handed note: "Most people when they get on the school board tend to view issues not by color but by what's best for the students."

The most pressing issue facing the board in the fall of 2006 concerned the polarizing Roy G. Brooks. He had been hired in 2004 after a successful run as superintendent in Orlando. His hiring was not without controversy, with the five white board members at the time voting to sign him and the two black board members, Katherine Mitchell and Micheal Daugherty, supporting interim superintendent and former Central principal Morris Holmes. Both men are African American, but when the board defeated along racial lines a motion to give the job to Holmes and then in the same meeting voted to hire Brooks, some voices in the audience rumbled that the votes were "racist."

Brooks, who had been praised for reorganizing the bureaucracy of the Orange County, Florida, schools and improving performance, vowed to do the same for the Little Rock School District and make it the "highest achieving district in the nation." Two years into his term, the number of schools in the LRSD deemed "failing" under No Child Left Behind had dropped slightly from twenty-seven to twenty-four, but some of his initiatives had angered union teachers and African American activists. He'd courted private money, including some that came from the publisher of the local daily newspaper, the

*Keith A. Nitta of the University of Washington, Bothell, and Joseph Y. Howard of the University of Central Arkansas have deftly summarized the school board's fractures during this time in "The Little Rock School District: A Community and School Board Divided," published in 2008, by *Electronic Hallway*, Evans School of Public Affairs, University of Washington.

Arkansas Democrat-Gazette, which heaped praise on his policies in its editorials. He'd closed schools in black and Hispanic neighborhoods and promised to build a new facility in a largely white, wealthy one. His reorganization plan eliminated 101 central office jobs, which some claimed disproportionately affected African Americans. John Walker weighed in with the assertion that "the only thing he stands for is putting black people down."

When three seats on the board were up for election in September 2006, the two African American candidates supported by the union each won a seat, thus changing the board to majority black for the first time in its history; the newspaper had endorsed their white opponents, as well as the winning candidate not supported by the union in the third race, between two white women. In February 2007, Judge Bill Wilson's order declaring the district "unitary" was handed down, but the board itself became even more fractured. In a closed meeting in March, board president Mitchell began proceedings to fire Brooks for cause, charging that he had "made disparaging comments" about board members, including Mitchell herself; "threatened and harassed" employees; and ignored concerns of African American parents.

A board vote in April to suspend Brooks fell again along racial lines, with the four African American members in favor of the disciplinary action. *Democrat-Gazette* editorials began calling the board majority the Gang of Four, a reference to the group of Mao Tse-tung supporters during the Chinese Cultural Revolution of the '60s and '70s. Brooks fired back at the board, suing its members for violating his contract, and more legal wrangling began.

As the beginning of the school year—and the integration commemoration—approached, it became clear that the election in September for Micheal Daugherty's seat would be a crucial event in the future of the district.

|||||||||||||||||||||||||||||||||||||||||

The August heat pounded down upon the players. They ascended and descended the bleachers, their cleats rattling the aluminum like hail on a tin roof. Lee Thompson, Rosey's brother, was watching the annual ritual and smiling. He said to nobody in particular, "You're supposed to be hollering 'I love these bleachers.'" The forecast had called for four 101°F days in a row.

A. J. Williams, the transfer from Stuttgart, was having trouble. He was one of the best athletes on the team, but his stamina was suspect. He hadn't spent four years running up and down Quigley Stadium's slope, so it might as well have been Everest. Kaelon Kelleybrew, who was playing football for the first time in three years, had just joined the team after spending the early part of the summer with an Amateur Athletic Union basketball team. According to Coach Cox's calculations, he had ninety-two bleachers to make up because of all the practices he had missed. He was rangy and fast, but his inexperience in negotiating the stands cost him and he slipped and fell, opening a gash on his leg. He saw Brian Cox to have the cut wrapped and taped.

Players had been missing practice, for reasons legitimate and not. One had heat exhaustion. One had told Coach Callaway he had to work for the next two days. "He was just smiling," Callaway said. Earlier, when the phone in the office rang, before anyone could pick it up, Callaway said, in a high, teasing voice, "Coach, I can't come to practice today."

Cox was more tolerant of the absences. He named a player who had missed practice the day before and said, "He called my house last night and said, 'Coach, my cousin committed suicide and we had to go out of town.'

"I used to just send them to the bleachers when they missed, but now I listen to them. I was probably too harsh about that earlier. . . . I had a player from 1976 who came back and told me, 'Remember when you'd stand at the foot of the stairs [to the locker room] and say, "Where are your books?" A lot of [players] don't get support at home, the parents saying, 'What did you do today? Where are your books?'"

That day the offense was showing its weaknesses, the most frustrating being a simple lack of determination. Callaway bellowed at one lineman: "Every year, every day: zero effort. I'm tired of it." During a water break, as the players shuffled toward a hose perched across two sawhorses and punctured with holes so the water arced out to allow for multiple drinking stations, Finley shouted mockingly, "Walk over there, walk over there, don't run like Southside," invoking the memory of the team from Fort Smith that had beaten an undefeated Central in the first round of the playoffs the previous fall.

The players continued to wilt. When the offensive huddle was lethargically composed, one of the players himself complained to quarterback Randy Rankin, "C'mon Randy, that's your huddle," prompting Finley to add, "We got no leaders. I'm not gonna be the captain. I haven't been a captain on a football team since 1977."

After practice that day, the last without pads, the team was gathered in its semicircle around Cox. Callaway threw an inhaler he'd been given for safekeeping to one of the linemen who suffered from asthma.

"Here's the challenge for tomorrow," said Cox. "We'll be in full pads. I hope it's hotter. I want it to be hotter. That's your challenge: How will you respond?

"Here's what happens: You'll leave here and where will you go? Some of you will go to work. Some of you will be partying, lying out at the pool, in the *sun*! You'll be wasting energy you could be giving us. It's 1:12 now. Think about what you're going to be doing at 3:12, 4:12, 5:12.

"About the seventh whistle [out of ten for the bleachers], I'm looking up and seeing you dragging up to the top. I want to see who's going to meet the challenge.

"The bleachers are beating you. We're going to let those bleachers that can't fight back defeat us. Like Southside last year. They turned us every which way but loose. They found a way to win.

"Who did what they had to do?"

"Southside," the players answered.

"We can't even meet the challenge of hot weather and bleachers. There's a lot of preparation that goes into meeting goals. Success is not a dream.

"I picked up two cups [in the locker room]. This is your warning. Some of you seniors, get that trash. Your mouthpiece will be attached to your face mask. That's the way we do things at Central High School. I'm trying to put a little structure in your life, a little discipline in your life. You run away from the *d* word faster than you run out here. But you need discipline in life to be a success in life. There's no limit to what you can do."

The practice had been four hours and five minutes long. As always, when Cox finished, one of the players, usually senior defensive end William

Bennett, called out, "Lord's Prayer on three, Lord's Prayer on three. One . . . two . . . three . . . ," and the players recited the prayer in unison before breaking up and plodding back to the locker room.

Cox descended to the office to attend to the infinite paperwork. A big binder sat on his desk, labeled "FOOTBALL 07-08 ELIGIBILITY," with academic information about everyone on the team. If a player didn't maintain a C average, to remain on the team he had to attend a study hall, called the Supplemental Instruction Program (SIP), twice a week, either in the morning or the afternoon. Because of football practice, the only one that a football player could attend was in the morning, before classes. If the player missed or was even tardy to one, he was ineligible. In 2001, Central forfeited a state championship in basketball because a player had missed a study hall. "Every nine weeks," said Cox as he tapped the binder, "I send a roster around with their student numbers . . . to see if there's any problems. I have my wife read off the name and number from the roster, and I check the paperwork. I double-check it and I still worry about it."

When the other coaches filed in and took their chairs, the talk turned again to the lack of offensive cohesiveness. "I'm not a Randy Rankin fan, as you know," said Cox, "but we wouldn't have won Conway in 2005 if he hadn't come in and run the option. And he took us to ten wins last year. Randy's gonna be Randy, but you've got to give him some credit."

Darrell Seward, who resembles former Pittsburgh Steelers coach Bill Cowher with his thinning hair and brushy mustache, was the last to enter the office, carrying a construction-grade measuring tape. He had been redrawing the practice-field lines, and his hands were dusted with lime.

"Coach," said Callaway to him, "I think that right hash mark was about two inches off," and the other coaches laughed good-naturedly at their colleague's fastidiousness.

"I know," Seward fired back. "That's why I was out there. Sometimes I wish I was less anal-retentive, but that's just the way I am."

The next day, the clatter of plastic echoed in the locker room as, for the first time this season, the players slipped shoulder pads over their heads and tested the fit by having a teammate hammer them with his fists. In the coaches' office, Bernie Cox told the staff that he didn't want any real tackling today, that the defense should just "wrap them up."

A player entered and waited for Cox to notice him before saying, "Coach Cox, I got somebody to watch me do my five bleachers, is that cool?" The comment drew laughter, primarily at the improbability of Cox replying, "Yeah, that's cool," words that would never cross his lips.

From his desk near the whirring air conditioner, Finley looked up from his portable DVD player, which was playing an instructional video from the St. Louis Rams about special teams, and said, "We got some good kids, we do."

Stan Williams added about one of the players, "His mother told me, 'He's not like me. I done weed, crack cocaine, never been caught.' Just shows we got to look out for these kids."

Finley repeated, "We *got* some good kids."

On the field, as the players adjusted to the weight of the equipment and faced each other in two lines for half-speed form-tackling drills, Seward instructed his defensive backs in proper technique. "I don't want to see anyone using the top part of the helmet on a hit," he said. "Eyes up, ground up, chest up, garbage up. Some of you got those tight hips. I don't see that in the hall with those gals. Eyes, ground, head, lunge!"

During one drill, Damien Lee was sent off the field for fighting. After practice, he came into the coaches' office and asked to speak to the group. He was wearing a torn, dirty T-shirt bearing the likeness of William Shakespeare. The year before, he had played Romeo in a scene from the play at a Shakespeare festival hosted by a local college. He apologized and said, "I wasn't being a leader."

Seward said, "You know what happens if that happens in a game."

"Two weeks."

"We need you."

It was the Friday of the first week in August, a little more than two weeks before the first scrimmage of the season, against Benton, a much smaller school in neighboring Saline County. Before practice in the office, the coaches were contemplating the weekend and talking about the systems they had for watering their lawns.

"I have seven stations," said Callaway.

"I have four stations," said Siegel, "fifteen minutes each."

"I have weeds," said Finley. "My yard looks like my face—messed up."

At the end of practice, Cox was in a more sanguine mood than he had previously been. "You picked it up on the last three days," he told the team. "We're a lot closer to where we want to be. We're not there yet . . . but I have seen signs of leadership. I have personally witnessed some of you talking to your teammates."

Later in the office, he was reviewing the personnel and was impressed with the physical nature of the team, which was composed on both offensive and defensive fronts of just the kind of players he liked. Offensive tackle Taylor James-Lightner, a superior student who had won admission to the competitive Governor's School summer session and was also a standout in the choir, was only five foot ten, but according to Cox he had great feet and tremendous arm and lower-body strength. De'Arius Hudson, whom Finley described as weighing "350 and biscuit with butter on it," had a broken ankle, but when he returned, he would be a formidable left tackle, since, as Cox said, "You grab his arm, it's like grabbing that wall." Most of the defensive front five was rock solid. Reed Caradine, a stand-up end who took a number of AP classes, had already drawn major-college interest. Jared Green was an immovable but cat-quick tackle ("Nobody's going to stop Jared Green," Cox said), and Quinton Brown, whose five-foot-seven, 250-pound size was a benefit at his nose guard position because he could get under anybody, drew high praise from Callaway, the offensive line coach: "He just manhandles whoever we put in front of him."

||||||||||||||||||||||||||||||||||||||||||

Early in the morning ten days before school started and eleven days before the Benton scrimmage, one by one, the players' cars cruised through the gate in the ten-foot wall surrounding the stadium, turned right up a rise, and pulled into parking spaces behind the southeast stands. Bernie Cox's compact Nissan truck was in its usual spot facing the wall, closest to the rusting light stanchion and nearest the stadium ramp. Larry Siegel drove a red Mazda Miata convertible, the one concession to flashiness for the defensive coordinator with a mop of gray hair who led the team's Fellowship of Christian Athletes group. Rickey Hicks, a lineman who was one of the school's best-dressed students, drove a black Chrysler 300 with tinted windows and a vanity front license plate that read "BLACK PEARL." Dallas Odom, the junior lineman who sometimes got up before dawn to hunt before practice, pulled into the lot in his SUV, country music blaring through the rolled-up windows.

In the office, Callaway was digging through the tackle box that held the spare snaps and screws for helmets and pads. He took out a pair of pliers to open a stubborn Gatorade bottle. Seward had two stacks of three videotapes each on his desk, the corners perfectly flush with a group of file folders, their contents identified by typed stickers on the tabs. When Cox scrawled out the practice schedule and number of minutes devoted to each session on the dry-erase board ("St/Cals 20, Bleachers 20, Passing 20 . . . "), Seward took out a lined sheet of his own devising and filled in the premade grid with Cox's list. As always, Stan Williams copied down the schedule twice and handed one list to Clyde Horton, the retired Central coach who in recent years had been helping out as a volunteer.

Cox reported on a player he had suspended—a senior who had missed practice—and was reinstating. "He was very . . . apologetic," he said. "He had tears in his eyes, told me how much he wanted to play. Early in my career, I didn't give enough latitude. I saw things in black and white because that's the way I was raised. I ran a couple of kids off that I shouldn't have, and I really regret that. If there's one thing I would tell a young coach coming up today, it's that—try to understand the circumstances."

In addition, Cox had received some information about how the fiftieth-anniversary commemoration was going to affect the team. On Saturday, September 22, they would be allowed into the stadium to watch film of the Pine Bluff game from the night before, as they always did on Saturday mornings. Because of the security arrangements for former president Bill Clinton's appearance, no one would be permitted to enter the stadium on Sunday. School would be out of session the following Monday and Tuesday, when the main ceremony would be held.

Then it was back to practice preparation.

"Ends need to work on hook blocks," said Cox.

"We've got to have some pass rush," added Horton.

During the period designated for the two-minute offense, the players were slow to line up because some of them chose the water hose that was farther away. Cox sent them to the bleachers. They did their ten to the top of the thirty-nine benches and returned to the practice field for read drills—which develop players' ability to "read" the action happening around them—while Cox told them, "You wasted a ten-minute period with farting around. What you do right now is extremely important. All you're thinking of is, 'I'm tired and broken down.' This is what wins and loses ball games right here. And you're not going to play for your teammates because you're tired and broken down."

The next day, he told the coaches before practice that if they let up on the players, "we're doing them an injustice. I want them to know that we haven't gotten what we expect of them. We had seven seniors on defense yesterday and not one of them was doing anything to pick anybody up."

"You've got to stay on this bunch all the time," added Finley. "We've got to be the cheerleader, coaches, everything."

"If they fart around in the first three minutes," Cox said, "we're going to spend the next seventeen minutes in the bleachers. We're their conscience. They don't have one."

On the way out to the practice field, Callaway said, "It's going to be one of those days. I've been here too long."

Soon there was some confusion about which personnel should be on special teams, and Cox sent them again to the bleachers. From the top step of the east stands, you could see over the wall of Quigley Stadium to the house at the northeast corner of Daisy Gatson Bates Drive and Jones Street. The gables of the house were visible in the background of team pictures from the 1930s and 1940s, but it had suffered fire damage and was vacant—like many others in the neighborhood—the windows covered with plywood, as if a hurricane were about to bear down. But today, workers were painting the whole thing white, plywood and all, for the crowds and cameras that would be arriving for the anniversary a month away.

On the Thursday before school started, the parents hosted a team dinner, without the coaches, at the Whole Hog Café, a Little Rock barbecue spot. Some of the seniors were wearing the official T-shirt from the fiftieth-anniversary commemoration. Like teenage boys everywhere, they piled on the food in enormous portions and there was a constant low rumble of noise and laughter and the occasional shout and shove. One parent told the players that all the adults were going to leave the room and suggested that each senior say something. Good-natured but a little confused that they'd been left on their own, they fumbled around until Quinton Brown, the undersize nose guard, stood at his place. Just before he began to speak, James Giese, another lineman, said, "Stand up," drawing a burst of laughter from the group and a high five from a teammate.

As senior after senior spoke, there was both confidence and fear: "If we come to play together as a team, I don't think there's anybody who can beat us except ourselves," and, remembering how the last season had ended, with a blocked punt against Fort Smith Southside, "I don't want to lose like that this year."

After the meal, the players streamed into the parking lot and drove to quarterback Randy Rankin's house in the Hillcrest section of the city. His father had invited them back to watch videos of Central's last championship season in 2004. While Randy was setting up the DVD player, Kyle Temple, a big tackle with a mordant wit, said, "We're all going to bond by watching *The Devil Wears Prada*."

Set to music ranging from "In Da Club" to the team's unofficial theme, "Eye of the Tiger," the video was a rousing collection of slashing runs, devastating tackles, and crisply executed plays from a team that went 13-1 and shut out seven opponents on the way to a second straight state championship. For the first time all night, the players were rapt and inspired.

At practice the next day, with the video's soundtrack still ringing in the Tigers' ears, Rankin encouraged the seniors to run and hustle everywhere. "It's our last summer practice," he said. As the players darted around the practice field, the coaches seemed energized by their effort, delivering compliments seldom heard, like "Everybody, great job!" At the end of the practice, Cox began his speech by saying, "On three, everybody give yourselves three claps," followed by "Three . . . two . . . one . . . " and three sharp, unified cracks echoing between the stadium wall and the back of the school. "I like the way we moved our feet," said Cox, "the entire practice. Wherever we go, if we move our feet, we're going to get there, right?"

"Yessir!"

On Monday, after the first day of school, the coaches entered the office in ties and slacks and dress shoes for the first time since the spring and began changing into their coaching shorts and shirts. Seward carefully folded his pants, rolled his belt, and then asked Callaway if he could borrow scissors. Callaway dug through his tackle box and produced a pair. Seward took them, snipped a dangling string from the hem of his pants, and handed them back to Callaway.

Talk turned to the school's principal, Nancy Rousseau, and the big inflatable Tiger mascot, which the coaches had nicknamed Champ. Apparently, during a game at Texarkana, she had been impressed with the inflatable mascot there, the enormous red head of a razorback hog (just like the University of Arkansas's), whose mouth, complete with bared tusks, the team had run through at the beginning of the game as the band played a rousing fight song. She had decided to order a tiger for Central. When it was inflated, it wasn't a fierce beast with glistening teeth that might strike fear into their opponents, or even a rampant jungle cat with massive paws and extended claws. Once filled with air, it sat on its hind legs like a kitten about to swat a string, its face gentle, a figure of playful concentration.

"Don't make fun of that tiger," said one coach.

"She loves it."

"It's got its arms spread like it's going to hug you."

"But don't make fun of it. She paid $2,000 for it."

For all the joking, Nancy Rousseau, a native New Yorker who had become principal in 2002 after more than two decades as an English teacher and administrator in both private and public schools in Little Rock, had proven to be both hands-off and highly supportive of the athletic programs. She let the coaches run their own shows, but she also was a visible presence in the stands at every football game, often clad in a tiger-striped jacket. If she sometimes instituted rules that seemed draconian (like a ban on backpacks that weren't made of clear plastic), she had also kept Central near the top of the nation's public high schools and shepherded it through a period when its physical plant needed upgrading. The recognition that Central was "an icon of civil rights," she said, made her leadership approaching the fiftieth anniversary "a big responsibility." Central "sets a tone," she added. "When Central does well, the community smiles."

Cox was focused on the scrimmage the next day. "I don't want Quinton Brown playing thirty snaps. What's he got to prove? What's Jared Green got to prove? We don't have a lot of time. We play next week. The countdown begins."

On the field, Damien Lee used his downtime to talk with the coaches about the first day of school.

"I got three numbers today. I didn't have to do anything except smile and they slipped them to me," he said to Stan Williams.

Williams replied, "I saw you holding hands with a boy in the hall."

Lee immediately shot back, "That was your daughter. She shaved her head." Then he asked Larry Siegel, "What do you teach?"

"World History."

"Regular."

"Yes."

"You should teach AP. The teacher put the class to sleep today."

The next day, the team first dressed out in helmets and shorts for a run-through before putting on game uniforms and boarding the bus for the half-hour trip to Benton.

Finley and the rest of the coaches wondered how the Tigers would respond in true game conditions.

"They don't watch football," he said. "They don't play in the street. They'd rather do this"—he cupped an imaginary Xbox controller and moved his thumbs up and down over it—"than play football. They watch the highlights."

Williams teased him that maybe if he had such strong opinions, he should be the head coach.

"Don't bring out the ghetto in me," Finley warned him. "Shoot, I can't even spell 'head coach.' I tried it one year. Moving that twelve inches"—the distance from his desk to Cox's desk—"is tough."

In Benton, the field was beautiful natural grass; unlike Central's, it looked as if it hadn't been stepped on yet this season. Behind one end zone was a large Baptist church; behind the other was a horse in a yard.

Cox's pregame speech took place on the field—since it was just a scrimmage, they didn't use the locker rooms—and was simple and direct. "You need to take advantage of every snap you get," he told them. "You need to play with some urgency. You need to grow up a little. You need to become a more mature football player. We can be pretty good, guys. How many times have I told you that. Probably too many. Play hard. Be a good sport."

The scrimmage was sloppy, with delay penalties and several off-target centers to the quarterback when the team was in the shotgun formation. Benton moved the ball too easily on the Tiger defense, angering Jared Green, who complained that the right end wasn't containing. Cox told them, "Go to the football, go to the football—you're going to the player." Among the good moments were a Rankin touchdown pass to Lamont Lacefield off a great play fake and another touchdown pass to Kaelon Kelleybrew, who had been at practice for only two weeks. Tim Dunn, the speedy tailback, delivered one hit on a run that knocked a Benton player out of the game.

But back at Quigley after the scrimmage, Cox was not happy and gave the team a grade of C minus.

Up at the school, the annual rituals of a new school year were beginning. The next day, the first block of classes was devoted to the annual "black-white count," as the coaches termed it. A green form was placed in every teacher's mailbox to tally the student "census," with a designation for race, as required by the Arkansas Department of Education. As the coaches prepared for practice in the office, they discussed the process. Some of the students had questions of their own about the count. What should they count themselves as, if their parents were of different races? About supervising the survey, Seward said, "You can be whatever you want to be in my class. The district only recognizes black, white, and other."

When Cox entered the office, he was still boiling about the performance at Benton, and not only about that by the players. He thought the coaches had performed just as sloppily. He asked them why they weren't gathering the team together during time-outs. He asked them why they weren't in the office at 2:20 that day. He threatened to withhold their coaching stipends.

Shortly afterward, Seward told the defense that "there isn't a coach here who didn't get his ass chewed out because of the crap that went on last night." And when Cox addressed the team at the end of the day, his disappointment was palpable. "What are you committed to? Tell me. It's not to this program. . . . You know what's embarrassing to me? We're not going to be able to run our Tiger package [a four-receiver set from the shotgun]. You know why? Because we don't have anyone who can get the ball back to the quarterback. . . . I'm not going to go out there and be embarrassed in a football game—historically the greatest school in America, the second-most wins in high school, *in America*! And we're going to go out there and get in Tiger formation and snap the ball over the quarterback's head. No, we're not. . . . I wish you'd play for your team and your teammates and for yourself. You won't do that. You can change that attitude, guys."

They didn't have much time to change it. The first week of school was done, and the game-week schedule started on Monday. The Tigers' defensive front was strong, anchored by Jared Green at tackle, Quinton Brown at nose guard, and Reed Caradine at defensive end. Linebacker Hunter Sinele was not as athletic as some of the other players, but he had a great football mind and made up for being a step slow by thinking a step ahead. Kaelon Kelleybrew had established himself at safety with his athleticism and his "ornery" attitude, and A. J. Williams was the fleet corner who could stay with any opposing receiver and would be a dangerous kick returner.

The offense was more of a question mark. The line was experienced but had been racked by injuries. Will Rollins was a solid blocking fullback. At tailback, Bo Dillon was a bruising if unspectacular runner, and when he was out, Tim Dunn provided a change of pace with breakaway speed. Rankin could be an elusive scrambler and a decent passer, but was prone to erratic play. What the offense really lacked was a vocal, respected leader, a role filled on defense mainly by Green and Sinele.

The preseason was about to end. But not before Cox had the final word. After the players gathered around him, he announced that SIP would start next Wednesday and he had seven players who were on the list to go. If a player missed one session, he would not be able to play for the season. Cox called it a "state law," though technically it was a policy of the Arkansas Activities Association, the governing body for high school athletics in the state. The purpose was to get a player's grade point average above 2.0. "You dug your hole," Cox told them, "you dig your way out of it."

Next he said that he had received reports from the security guards at the school that some of his football players had been "disrespectful." He said that those players who were involved—"and you know exactly who you are"—should see him and "fess up" before Monday. "Or your option is, Don't play. You're not going to represent me, these other coaches, this football team, this school, yourselves, if you're going to be a jerk and be disrespectful. We're going to stop that. We sent your names out Monday, and we couldn't go five school days without getting in trouble. And that's a shame."

He further singled out Quinton Brown, Aaron Nichols, Jared Green, and all the other starters from the previous year and told them to come see him before Monday and explain to him why they had not been performing up to par. "Everybody on this football team that played last year," he told them, "you have a long talk with yourselves over the weekend—with your parents, with your teammates, with your 'hood, your friends, your gang members, whatever it is, your bangers—you come back Monday and tell me whether or not you want to play on this football team. If you don't come by and tell me that you want to play, and convince me that you want to play, that you're going to come out here every day and give it everything you have, then I will make the decision. You guys who played last year, you should be out front, you should be leading, you should be setting an example. You're not doing that.

"We're no better off today than we were the first day. Five weeks, guys, five weeks. That's not that sour ground you smell, that's us. We stunk it up today. You guys argued with each other, screaming and hollering about different things. . . . One week from tonight, we play. . . . I'm trying to put on the football field a group of kids that have a love for the game, that have a respect for the game, that have respect for their teammates, their coaches, themselves, the school, all the fans that are going to come watch you play, the opponent, but will you get out there and will you play like you have that respect?

"This weekend I will make a list of all the football players I expect to see me before we practice on Monday, twenty-six or twenty-eight kids. I'm forcing you to respond in some way. If you don't, I'll know the answer."

He strode off toward the stadium to supervise the running of bleachers.

The other coaches followed at a distance. "I don't know why he gets so frustrated," Finley said. "He's too good a coach to get so frustrated. He gets frustrated and the kids get frustrated."

IIIIIIIIIIIIIIIIIIIIIIIIIIIIIIIIIIII

The ringtones started singing on Saturday—Common, The Game, Kanye, and Lil Wayne; Timberlake, Kid Rock, Linkin Park, and Toby Keith. Meet at the practice field on Sunday afternoon. After church. They showed up in baggy jeans and T-shirts and flip-flops and hats cocked to the side. Clothes covered with outsize logos: Polo and Gucci and Nike. Or Disney characters or camo. Not many Razorback hogs or Dallas Cowboy stars or Chicago Bulls.

They chose up sides for two-hand touch and immediately took positions they never played, doing all the things they wouldn't be allowed to do in practice. Defensive end Jared Green lined up at split end. Defensive back Aaron Nichols made a reception and weaved his way around the hands reaching out to down him, then ended his run with a touchdown dance. They threw flea flickers and ran triple reverses. They leapt for chest bumps and executed elaborate high fives. They were joyous.

That morning, in the local paper, they had been named the preseason No. 1 team in the state.

CHAPTER 5

MAKING A STAND

"WORST THING THAT CAN HAPPEN TO A BUNCH OF KIDS," said Cox. "Some kids can handle it, but not these kids."

"After that newspaper article," said Finley, "you've got to really stay on them. That's just how this bunch is."

"We've got to keep the bar raised high," said Seward. "And keep on them."

Seward remembered something and looked puzzled. "Rollins texted me that he'd be late for practice yesterday because he'd be in church."

"Yesterday?" said Cox. Sunday?

"And Ke'Won called to ask if the field would be open."

"Practice fields are always open," said Cox, "if they want to come practice. Doubt they will."

Today, on the Monday before Central hosted West Memphis in the season opener, instead of waiting until after practice to gather them around him, Cox called the team together after calisthenics, but kept them in their lines. He demanded first that the senior line leaders, the guys in the front row, hand in lists of everyone in their lines. He then told them what he thought of being voted No. 1 in the state when you haven't played a down. "The people across the state of Arkansas have determined that you're the best football team in the state," he said. "It doesn't mean a thing, but they honored you. I don't like it. All it does is put a target on your back. But if you like being No. 1, you'll commit to being No. 1. The challenge is yours."

In the locker room before practice, the team had sat on aluminum benches watching tape of West Memphis. "Cornerback is crucial this week," said Larry Siegel. "Once you establish the run inside, you can do anything you want to."

Seward, the defensive secondary coach, stood beside the big television. "They're going to try to bull you with the run," he said. "That will take some discipline. Do a great job every snap of reading the release of that guy," and he pointed to the wingback.

Privately, Siegel said, "West Memphis has some good athletes. They will be a huge test for us."

Before practice the next day, the skies were threatening rain. Kyle Temple, the big offensive tackle, looked up at the clouds and said, "Coach Cox has a direct line to Jesus and told him not to let it rain from 4:00 to 6:00. Six-oh-five, it can pour."

The rain held off, as Temple predicted, but there was bad news that seemed to imply no heavenly favors for the Tigers—James Giese, a lineman who had been working at center, had fractured his wrist, depleting the already thin depth chart on the offensive front.

During the block-and-tackle portion of practice, Finley exhorted, "I want the crackback more physical. I want to hear it!" The crackback block can be a devastatingly effective maneuver for springing a running back around the end. It calls for a wideout, sometimes in motion toward the ball before the snap, to target an interior defensive player with a blind-side hit, thus impeding—or ending, if he's knocked off his feet—his pursuit. As long as the block is executed above his waist with the offensive player's head in front of the opposing player, it's legal. Because of the danger of injury to the knees, anything below the waist on the crackback is penalized. The cut block, where below-the-waist contact is allowed by national high school rules, is a legal block, but only within a certain zone close to the ball, which normally restricts the diving move at the ankles and legs to linemen and linebackers. For years, outlawing the cut block had been the subject of debate at all levels of the game. After one of his players was injured on a cut block play, University of Alabama coach Nick Saban commented, "Cut blocking has been a part of the game for a long time. A lot of players get hurt because of cut blocking. I don't think there's any question about that, but I also feel that every player has a responsibility to play the cut blocks." He continued, "I don't know how you [make the block illegal] without making a huge impact" on the game.

Later, when the first offense lined up against the first defense, Finley was happy with the resulting effort. "We don't give y'all enough praise," he called out to the offense. "I'm on your side." Soon, however, one of the players poorly executed a cut block, leaving Johnathan Green, Jared's brother, on the ground holding his right leg. Jared was incensed. "We got a game Friday," he shouted. "Why are you going for somebody's legs?!"

After practice the next day, Cox told the staff that he'd answered a couple of calls from parents complaining that a coach had told one player to hurt another. Finley explained that he'd told one of the linemen to cut block, but not when the defensive player wasn't looking. As soon as it happened, Finley jumped all over the blocker, a fact that Larry Siegel backed up.

Cox addressed the issue with the team in his end-of-practice meeting, telling them that there was some kind of misunderstanding and that if anybody heard a coach telling one player to injure another, then "you should resent it," and he wanted to hear about it.

The controversy pointed up the sometimes-adversarial relationship between the coaches and parents, which seemed to affect the team and the staff. That very day, as Callaway and Williams were supervising the running of the fourth-quarter sprints, Callaway commented about one player, "He's always last. He's lazy."

Williams replied, "Just coach him, don't get personal, because his father's over there writing stuff down."

Callaway looked truly depressed. "I'm getting too old for this crap," he said.

The fact that Norman Callaway was as old as he was, 65, and still coaching on a high school football field for his forty-first straight Arkansas fall was a tribute to modern medicine—and luck. In 2003, he was scheduled to go in for a hip replacement, but when they injected him with dye in preparation for the surgery, the doctor told him that he was going to stay in the hospital not for his hip, but for his heart. He needed an immediate triple bypass. It would be another two years before his hip would be replaced, and the doctor also mentioned that he'd eventually need a knee replacement owing to an old surgery after college, when "they scraped right down to the bone," as Callaway tells it. The result was that he walked slowly and with difficulty, especially up and down the stairs leading to the coaches' office. All of his complaints—about his aches and pains and age or anything else—were always leavened with a good-humored quip, so his unadorned disgust over the parental oversight implied in Williams's warning showed an unusual weariness with what his profession now required of him. Not like the good old days . . .

IIIIIIIIIIIIIIIIIIIIIIIIIIIIIIIIIIIIII

Cox's frustration reached its pitch on Wednesday. He had to send fourteen players back to the locker room because they lacked some piece of their proper practice uniform or equipment that was required. His postpractice speech lasted twenty minutes. For five weeks, along with the other coaches, he had harangued and cajoled, stroked and stoked, but he had still been unable to figure out this group of kids, whom Larry Siegel called "paper-thin in attitude." What could he do to bring out their best? His default stance was to blame it on the generations; this generation didn't rise to challenges. They sought only pleasure and didn't see the meaning of sacrifice—for teammates, for fans, for yourself. They didn't love football because they had so many other loves: their Xboxes, their music, their TV shows, their girls.

They had the talent. There were big kids and fast kids, but only a few of them burned with the fire that would make them run through walls, that would carry them up the last steps of those thirty-nine bleachers so they could be first, that would lead them to study game film on their computers instead of checking their Facebook pages.

"Monday is Labor Day," he said. "There's no school and no buses. We will practice. Right now, practice is scheduled for 4:00. . . . We got through early today—what we did, we came out here early today because we thought it was going to rain. We wanted to get as much as we could out of the way. Well, here it is 5:19 and we're through. Tomorrow, we'll be in our helmets, shirts, and shorts."

He repeated that Monday was Labor Day. "Some of you, right now, the first thing that's in your mind is, 'How am I going to get out of that?' We've been doing it for thirty-six years at this school—I'll put it like this, some of the better teams we've had never had a gripe. You won't gripe to me, but you'll gripe to someone else. You're not dedicated like some of the others, you're not committed. It's obvious every day. I've tried to explain every day. That's why we do it, so you won't forget. You're not dedicated. You're selfish.

"You guys are not nearly the football players you want to be or think you are. You could spend some time getting better on your own, but you won't do that. I've gone so far as to ask some of you to watch football on TV and put yourselves out there on the field and just read, but you won't do that. You've got something more important to do. Just like those fourteen guys out here who weren't dressed properly. I'll give you the same example I gave them: Some of you will pay sixty or eighty dollars a ticket to go to a concert, I don't know who it might be, to watch somebody get up there and make a fool of themselves—that's my opinion and I'm entitled to it!—I bet if you start for that concert, I'll bet you anything that I own and you own, you'll never forget your what? Tickets! But you'll come out here without a shirt, without shorts. Because that's more important.

"All we're asking is that you make this important too. After that playoff game last year, every person who calls me, would you like to guess what's the first question I hear? 'How you gonna do this year? You got a lot of kids coming back, how did that loss in the first round hurt you? How did they respond in the off-season? *You guys should have won that ball game!*' That's what I've heard over and over and over and over and over. You guys never thought about it. . . . Coaches holler at you over and over and over about the same things, and you have a very good excuse for not doing it. Guys, what you can do, you can fill your lives up with excuses. You're going to be full of excuses all your life, and the more excuses you use to justify something, the easier it is to use an excuse to justify something else. 'I'm tired, Coach.

Gosh, I weigh 280 and it's hot out here.' You're paving the way right there, you're paving the way. That's what's wrong with our society today.

"Guys, you can be a lot better. I don't want that to be your epitaph. I don't want us to finish this season 6-4 and play that tenth game and not make the playoffs and stand in front of you and say, 'Guys, you could have been better than you were.'

"You go around once in life. We'll never play West Memphis again after we play them Friday night in 2007. How many of you guys have a conscience? How many of you even know what a conscience is? Ten hours a week, that's all we ask of you. In 1966, I started coaching high school football. I know some of you guys might not understand this, and a coach said— I knew what it meant because I'd grown up on a farm—he made this statement and the kids understood it too because they were from a rural community. He said, 'Guys, the hay is in the barn.' That means, we've got a ball game and we can't do much else. Did we put enough hay in the barn in the last five and a half weeks to be successful? We'll find out."

The next day, the players seemed buoyant in just shorts, T-shirts, and helmets, relieved of the weight of their normal armor. During the warmups, the team chanted a call-and-response that had been passed down for years.

Split end Lamont Lacefield shouted, "What you gonna say about it, Aaron Nichols?!" and Nichols replied, "I say, 'Let's get them Devils, bay-beeeeee!'"

And the rest of the team called in unison, "All right!"

For the first time, when the echo rebounded off the empty stadium stands, the bleachers seemed to be cheering them on rather than taunting them.

Cox seemed to have softened from the day before and concluded the practice by saying, "After all we've said, there's not a coach out here who doesn't want to be here. We love coaching, we love kids, we love you. Sometimes you have to set guidelines for good people."

For game day, the locker room was decorated with a large sign reading "Beat Devils," with a painted tiger paw on it. After they had dressed, the players sprawled on the floor with headphones piping in psych-up music. Seward told the other coaches, "I like the way I saw the majority of the kids handling themselves in the building. . . . The ones I saw were real business-like: 'You ready for tonight, Coach?'"

The last thing Coach Cox told them before they headed to the field was "Enjoy it." And they filed down the hall under the east stands and reached up to touch the horseshoe nailed above the door.

|||||||||||||||||||||||||||||||||||||||||

They were not ready. The first half of the game seemed to prove every doubt Cox had expressed in the previous six weeks. Mistakes are always common in the first game of the season, but nobody looked sharp. Tackle De'Arius Hudson jumped offside, quarterback Randy Rankin fumbled snaps, someone roughed the kicker, other players were out of position or not on the field when they should have been. Clarence Finley commented, "Terrible football game. I'd hate to see the No. 2 team." The only bright spot was a dazzling forty-six-yard punt return by A. J. Williams, "the one athlete we've got out there," according to Cox, but then the offense sputtered after a bad center-to-quarterback exchange.

Fortunately, West Memphis was just as sloppy, drawing delay-of-game penalties and pass-interference calls. "They're trying to give us the damn game," said Finley. "We can't score with a calculator." At the half, the Blue Devils led 3–0, having kicked a thirty-four-yard field goal on the final play of the second quarter.

Back in the locker room at the intermission, Cox brought the team together immediately and told them they were deficient in exactly the ways he had lectured them about the day before. "I hope we're not making a statement in the first half about what this team is all about," he said. "We found a way to screw up everything we tried to do in the first half. Guys, our offense is pathetic, it stinks, it's horrible. We ended up losing yardage two different times we should have scored. If that's the kind of football season you want to have, that's what we'll have. We're not fighting back. That's the saddest thing to me, you're not fighting back. If we don't perk up, offense, three points will beat us. That's it. I'm not fussing at you, I'm trying to wake you up.

"You're not focused, like we talked about yesterday for forty minutes. . . . I know you don't give a crap, but it disappoints me for you. No. 1 team in the state. Sloppy, sloppy, sloppy. We actually have guys out there who are really playing hard, working their butts off. They deserve better than this.

"I'm going to have so many questions this weekend. If we don't win 40–3, I'm going to get, 'What happened?' That's why I hate to be ranked No. 1. Sports people all over the state: 'Mighty Tigers, mighty Tigers, what happened to the mighty Tigers?' I can't tell them what I think, I can't tell them what's in my heart. But I can tell you: You played horrible. You need to get focused. Some of you need to get out. Do something else with your time every day. . . . Get in your meetings." And the defense and offense broke apart to meet with their individual coaches.

Back on the field for the second half, Bo Dillon promptly fumbled the second-half kickoff and fell on the ball, leaving Central backed up on its own 7-yard line.

The defense continued to play "sound," as Cox had told them they had at halftime, but the offense was still reveling in dysfunction. At one point on the sidelines, Rankin turned to fullback Will Rollins and said, "Why don't you fucking block somebody?!" Rollins leapt at him and they had to be separated.

Late in the third quarter, West Memphis had driven to the Tigers' 19-yard line. The Devils tried to throw a quick out pattern to the split end, but A. J. Williams stepped in front of the receiver, picked off the ball, and dashed down the home sideline for an eighty-six-yard touchdown and a 7–3 lead.

As the game wound down, the Central defense remained solid, but West Memphis engineered one last push to the Central 7-yard line with only a couple of minutes remaining. Three successive running plays were stuffed. With twenty-seven seconds left on fourth down, the defense sniffed out a tackle-eligible pass and dropped the receiver for a two-yard loss to secure the narrow win.

The players were jubilant in the locker room. They high-fived and hooted as they slipped off their uniforms and changed directly into street clothes, not bothering to test the locker room's ancient showers. They laid their jerseys and pants in a pile on the locker room floor while Cox supervised the procedure and corrected the new players who left their jerseys or pants inside-out. The pile grew as each of the seventy-four players added another piece of uniform to it.

Satisfaction over the close win soon turned to pensiveness in the coaches' office. Randy Rankin came by and apologized for his part in the offensive debacle, telling Cox, "I didn't have a clue out there."

When he left, the postmortem began.

"I thought they were pretty good," Callaway ventured.

"A.J. played a heck of a ball game tonight," said Seward.

"He's a heck of an athlete," said Siegel.

"We knew that, though," said Finley. "We've got to find some way to get him the ball on offense, too."

"It's going to be a delicate time next week," said Cox. "Tim Dunn is down. Randy's down."

"We can't beat this bunch down," said Finley. "You've got to coach till you drop. We've got to keep working with them."

"We've been over this for six weeks," said Seward, suddenly animated, "and we keep saying the same crap over and over again. It's redundant. We know what we do have and what we don't have. We've got nine ball games left and it's up to us to put something together and let's do it."

A minute of silence and sighs ensued.

"You look at that last series," continued Seward. "We needed to get a first down and we got one. Dunn ran hard and Bo got the first down, on that series. . . . I don't want to lose sight of those good things that did occur tonight. And I think we have—this staff."

"I understand what you're saying," said Finley, "but we've got a big issue offensively. We have to find a way to score to be successful."

"The first thing I want to do is eliminate all the offensive breakdowns—the fumbled snaps, the negative plays," Cox said. "If we think we're coaches, then we've got to coach those kids to do better than that." After a pause, he seemed to question the efficacy of his own methods. "We don't need to browbeat those guys, and I know I do it too much."

When talk turned to a crucial fumble by tailback Tim Dunn, Finley broke the tension and lightened the mood with an indication of his own definition of browbeating: "If it was 1978, I would have slapped his black ass white. He'd be white as snow."

By 11:00 p.m., they had talked enough about the game and moved on to other issues of the new school year: their classes, parental involvement, and the latest school board news.

All week, the lead story in the *Arkansas Democrat-Gazette* was the Arkansas Supreme Court's dismissal of a case challenging the buyout of the contract of ousted superintendent Roy G. Brooks by the Little Rock School District. The decision allowed Brooks to collect $635,000, an astronomical sum for a district where a teacher's salary averages $48,306. A picture of Brooks on the front page of the paper had caught him in a "What, me worry?" pose of shrugging acceptance of his good fortune, palms upraised. Darrell Seward did his best impression of the picture while commenting on the absurdity of a board in a district that was so strapped for funds paying so much money to get somebody to quit.

By 11:30, they were finally ready to leave, realizing wearily that they'd be back in the morning to watch film and analyze the game further. Everyone walked upstairs to the concourse, then up the ramp where the stands opened to the Arkansas summer sky. It was cool for that time of year, and the darkness obscured the detritus of popcorn boxes and drink cups that the maintenance staff would sweep up between the bleachers the next day. The locker room, however, was already tidy. Bernie Cox had cinched tight the bags that lined the fifty-gallon drums where the players had thrown the tape they'd unwound from their wrists and ankles, the boxes that had held their pregame meal from Firehouse Subs, and the remnants of the torn-down "Beat Devils" banner, its exhortation now a mission accomplished, however sloppily. The bags sat in the back of Cox's Nissan truck, and he hauled them away, saving the cleaning staff the job of removing the refuse of his players.

|||||||||||||||||||||||||||||||||||||||||

Bernie Cox had never required his coaches to give up their full weekends, even during the season, to the study of film and preparation for the game to come. Sundays were sacred; all the coaches were devoted churchgoers. The morning after a Friday night game, they met at the stadium for a few hours to watch tape and do more tidying up in the locker room. At 8:00 a.m., Darrell Seward was hosing down the floor, Larry Siegel was picking up shoulder pads left out from the night before, and Cox was removing game pants from the enormous Huebsch commercial dryer and carrying them back to the equipment room off the coaches' office, where they'd be folded and placed into cubbyholes according to size.

That job completed, they marched upstairs to an office off the concourse now used primarily to count the proceeds from admission and concession sales. A booster had donated a bulky, fifty-inch rear-projection TV, to which Seward hooked up a portable camera with remote-control playback. The whole operation was almost laughably makeshift compared to those at some of the private schools or schools in other districts that have near-professional "video coordinators." At Central, one of the parents, a man who taught video production at a local university, had recruited his students to work the game camera from a tripod at the top of the east stands.

While Seward was fiddling with the camera, Callaway said, "Cartoon time."

The tape started, and it became obvious that the student operator had had a little trouble framing and following the play correctly. One of the coaches joked about making "modifications" for the cameraperson. "Modification" was the catchall term used at the school for dealing with students who had learning problems.

When A. J. Williams's punt return flashed by, Stan Williams commented, "Let's keep him. Let's not fire him."

As the first half wound down, Finley, who along with Callaway was in charge of the offense, said, "Defense looks good. They need to fire my ass."

"Me first," said Callaway.

One spark of hope rose at the end of the tape, when Central stopped West Memphis for four straight plays at the end of the game. Cox offered,

"I've never coached a championship team that didn't make a goal-line stand."

||||||||||||||||||||||||||||||||||||||

You'd never hear Bernie Cox say it, but he must have felt it, along with every-one else: The Tigers were fortunate to have McClellan High next on the schedule. Quarterback Randy Rankin said, "It's a good second game to have." Over the previous three seasons, the McClellan Crimson Lions had won just six games.

When McClellan High opened in Pulaski County in the middle of the school year in 1966, Arkansas had one of the most powerful congressional delegations in the country, its influence far outstripping the state's popula-tion or importance in other areas. John L. McClellan was the senior senator, first elected in 1942 (he served until his death in 1977), and his colleague in the upper house was William Fulbright, a Rhodes scholar elected two years later, who had already given his name to the international exchange program that remains his greatest legacy. Along with Wilbur Mills, the chairman of the House Ways and Means Committee, they gave Arkansas an outsize voice in the running of the country.

By 1966, all were nearing the height of their fame and authority. Though a noted conservative Democrat, McClellan first gained prominence for his opposition to Senator Joseph McCarthy's witch hunting for communists in the 1950s. Later, McClellan's stern leadership of the Senate Permanent Sub-committee on Investigations, which looked into labor racketeering by the likes of Jimmy Hoffa, landed him on the cover of *Time* magazine as the "Man behind the Frown." When he appeared at the dedication of the school named after him in May of 1966 (introduced by Mills), his namesake public-works project, the power-generating dams and locks that make up the enor-mous McClellan-Kerr Arkansas River Navigation System, was well under construction.

As staunchly Democratic as the three lions of the legislature were, they spanned a wide ideological spectrum. Nevertheless, in 1956, all had signed the Southern Manifesto, which pledged to overturn *Brown*. The most surprising signatory was the liberal Fulbright, who admitted to favoring a "gradualist" approach to integration and hewed to the line of popular sentiment in the state with his belief in local control of schools. Mills had had an eye cocked toward the electorate and was sure he would be beaten on the issue if he didn't sign. But for McClellan, signing was a matter of bolstering his already strong social-conservative bona fides among his constituents. During the 1957 events and their aftermath, McClellan spoke out "at every opportunity against the Supreme Court and the *Brown* decisions," according to Elizabeth Jacoway's *Turn Away Thy Son*.

The first students entered the new McClellan High School in January of 1966, and the school and its neighborhood matched the man: working class, white, and conservative. McClellan addressed nearly one thousand attendees at the opening ceremony for the school and urged them to be educated "to the limit of their capabilities" to prevent a "Communist aggressor" from gaining superiority over the United States. (The denouncer of communist witch hunts saw no contradiction in denouncing communists from Southeast Asia during the Vietnam War; he knew his audience.)

The month before McClellan spoke, the *Arkansas Gazette* had run a ten-part series called "Race and Residence" that examined the racial composition of Little Rock's neighborhoods, especially as they related to aggressive urban renewal projects. The result, the series concluded, was that "the western reaches of the city steadily are becoming whiter and the old central and eastern sections steadily are becoming blacker." Part eight of the series looked at the experience of "the first Negro family"—a lawyer, his wife, and four preschool-age children—"to break the color barrier in the all-white subdivisions of western Little Rock." The patriarch, a young John W. Walker, two years out of Yale Law School, explained his decision to locate his family in Broadmoor this way: "It irritated me no end that the only houses I could get were houses 15 to 20 years old in the [downtown] area that white people were leaving."

Half a year into their residence there, the Walkers' house had become an occasional target for vandals, and the family members themselves, at best, were pariahs. "The policy in Broadmoor is to ignore the Walkers," an anonymous neighbor told the *Gazette*. The family had little contact with their white neighbors, except, Walker's wife commented, when one came seeking signatures on a petition asking the school board to locate a high school in southwestern Little Rock.

McClellan High, which was just outside the city limits at the time and part of the Pulaski County Special School District, would already have been under construction at the time the petition was being circulated, but the perceived need for yet another, inevitably white, high school in that part of the metropolitan area gives some indication of the alacrity with which whites were leaving the inner city. By 1970, the *New York Times* reported in a story about resegregation in Little Rock, "Whites have fled to the suburbs by the thousands to escape desegregation." Over the previous two years, the United States Commission on Civil Rights sent staff to investigate potentially discriminatory real estate practices in Little Rock and found its housing patterns "a game of musical chairs in which black families moved to areas vacated by whites." Many of those whites, especially ones in the working class who would qualify for Federal Housing Administration loans and who had lived in the racially mixed neighborhoods around Central High, whose enrollment was 35 percent black by 1970, moved to southwest Little Rock and Pulaski County. Code words in real estate ads directed black buyers to all-black or "transitional" neighborhoods: "Anyone May Buy" and "Walk to Central High" were some of the most common. "Cloverdale and McClellan schools" told a different story. While a white builder told the commission staff that he "never had any call from black families asking for Southwest," a black real estate broker attributed the supposed lack of interest to a pragmatic acknowledgment of white control and prejudice: "If I tried to get listings in white subdivisions, the white banks and lending institutions would put me out of business."

The gradualist theory of integration, in wide practice throughout the South, abetted the process of resegregation by allowing whites the time to search for new homes outside the city center, knowing that the snail's pace of integration wouldn't reach the suburbs for years. For the decade and a half after McClellan was built, the area was reliably white. "Southwest was a city unto itself," said Keith Richardson, one of Central's coaches, who worked mainly with the freshmen.

As a fifth grader in the late 1970s, his older brother, Ken Richardson, was bused from Wrightsville, a largely African American community east of Little Rock, to Watson Elementary, a half mile from McClellan, and his YMCA track team practiced at the McClellan track. "The first time I ever heard the *n* word coming from somebody white," he said, "we were walking [to the McClellan track], and a truck with five or six white boys in it [came by], and they were just, 'Nigger! Nigger!' "

As recently as 1981, the seniors on the McClellan football team were all white, with a few blacks sprinkled among the underclassmen. There was one black cheerleader that year. Then things began to change. Judge Henry Woods of the United States District Court issued his decision declaring that the solution to the thwarted desegregation of Little Rock schools should include merging the county's three school districts. His decision caused whites to seek housing outside the county's jurisdiction, or to transfer their children to or establish private schools. Though most of his ruling was over-turned on appeal, the Little Rock School District subsequently expanded its reach to be virtually equal to the city limits, and McClellan became incor-porated into it.

In the familiar cycle, as had happened around Central, desegregating the schools in a neighborhood drove out the whites—in the case of south-west Little Rock, usually to properties in Bryant and Benton, across the county line. Between 1990 and 2000, in the two census blocks surrounding McClellan, the percentage of the black population went up from 44 to 72 percent, and by 2007, the school's enrollment was more than 90 percent black. Crime also rose, some of it attributable to gang activity, and eventu-ally "Southwest" became one of the city's neighborhoods synonymous with drugs and violence. Real estate discussion boards warned families moving to Little Rock to stay out of "09," or the 72209 zip code, which included McClellan. Halfway through 2006, eight of Little Rock's thirty-three mur-ders had taken place in the area.

Ken Richardson, who went on to become a star student and football player at Central in the early 1980s before matriculating to Stanford, now represents southwest Little Rock on the city's board of directors. He was elected in 2006 from Ward 2, which falls south of Interstate 630, the barrier that "separates whites from blacks both physically and psychologically," according to Dr. Jay Barth, professor of politics at Hendrix College. Though what Ken Richardson calls the "segregated" school in Wrightsville is where he "first got that sense of competence," he's wary of any perceived positive effects of McClellan's present racial makeup. "Some view that kind of isolation as a protective factor and others view it as a risk factor. No, it wouldn't be my preference that you'd have any school in the city be 90 percent one color or 90 percent the other color. . . . We're all robbed of some really unique life experiences when we don't have opportunities to interact with people who don't look like us."

For 2002 McClellan graduate Antwan Phillips, however, now a Little Rock lawyer who went from the mean streets of Southwest to the piney woods of Bowdoin College in Brunswick, Maine, his near-single-race high school experience allowed him to ignore race and not battle its preconceptions every day. "I never felt like a minority," he said. "There was never a need to band together." At McClellan, the AP classes were filled with black kids like him, so he wasn't faced daily with the academic division that was evident at Central.

A self-described optimist, he and his friends felt that "going to McClellan was like joining a fraternity," and they "almost embraced the stigma attached to McClellan," feeling that it was "a testament to character or toughness" to get through it. When teachers and fellow students at Bowdoin would find out he was from Little Rock, they would always ask if he went to Central, a question he understood since the school was so well known. But when people in Little Rock asked him the same question, he bristled at the assumption that high-achieving black students come from only Central. "No," he would tell them emphatically. "I went to John L. McClellan High."

Still, McClellan's proficiency scores in literacy and math were the lowest in the district by far, a quarter below Central's. Among black students alone, the gap was narrower, but McClellan still lagged behind Central, 15 percent to 28 percent in literacy and 9 percent to 22 percent in math. Phillips admitted that there were people in the neighborhood who would "take measures so their kids wouldn't have to go to McClellan," or, put more poetically by Keith Richardson, "When you've got this beautiful light shining at our school [Central], it dims everything else out. A lot of the kids that we get probably should be at McClellan."

In basketball over the years, McClellan had won seven conference titles and ended as state runner-up twice before winning the state championship in 2010. The Crimson Lions football team had been less successful. The school enjoyed one glorious season in 1994, going undefeated in the regular season and reaching the state championship game under the direction of coach Ellis "Scooter" Register. He quickly decamped for El Dorado, in south Arkansas, before returning to Little Rock for the job at Catholic High in 2003. Since that run in 1994, the football team had slid into consistent mediocrity, and sometime horrendousness. With virtually no white players on the field, stereotypes about the team had flourished. One veteran coach in Little Rock, when queried about McClellan, responded that they played a "TND." Asked what that stood for, the coach, who was white, whispered, "typical nigger defense," which he explained meant that they lined up in an unpredictable variety of fronts and pursued the ball in an undisciplined manner.

When Central arrived at McClellan by bus for the game, Central coach Stan Williams reminisced about the time a fight had broken out—not on the field, but between a couple in the two-story apartment building past the south end zone. One of them had thrown a TV off the second-floor landing during the game. In 2005, that same street just outside the football field's fence had been the site of a murder. During the trial, the murderer's ex-girlfriend had testified that when she'd asked him if he had committed the crime, he'd said, "Yeah, but don't worry about [it] because . . . they think Southwest did it."

The game was a rout, 49–0. Once again, A. J. Williams and the defense looked spectacular. After a safety by the Tigers, Williams took the Lions' free kick back sixty-nine yards for a touchdown. He also intercepted a pass.

"They're bad," said Clyde Horton, the veteran defensive line coach.

"They're worse than that," said Finley.

The easy win, though it was no test at all, left spirits soaring. Everybody got to play. Late in the game, Cherard Grant, a junior substitute defensive back, returned a punt forty-seven yards but ran about half a mile to do it, weaving back and forth across the field at least three times, eluding all Lion attempts to bring him down and leaving the Tiger sidelines in stitches. Even Kyle Temple and Rickey Hicks, the senior linemen whose fight during practice earlier in the week had left Temple with an injured shoulder, made up.

Back in the coaches' office late that night, the report came in from the scout about the Tigers' next opponent, Arkansas High, in Texarkana, and it was grim: "You'll need all you got this week."

CHAPTER 6

ROAD TO RUIN

TEXARKANA IS A DIVIDED CITY IN A GOOD-HUMORED WAY. It straddles the state line between Arkansas and Texas, and in the 1930s the federal government built a courthouse right on the border, the west door in Texas and the east door in Arkansas, with the foundation made of Texas granite and the walls of Arkansas limestone. Now, in addition to housing US courts, the building functions as a post office for two different zip codes, one in each state. One of the city's leading tourist attractions is a photographer's island in front of the structure where visitors can have their likenesses captured bestriding both states.

In frontier times, the separate jurisdictions were more important, with the border representing a goal line for fleeing felons hoping to escape legal pursuit, often noted in Arkansas warrants with "G.T." for "gone to Texas." The towns cooperate in many public services but operate separate school districts and have two separate high schools, Arkansas High and Texas High, though both are called simply Texarkana by the fans in their respective states.

Arkansas High could not be more Arkansan. The school had used the razorback mascot for its sports teams before the state's university in Fayetteville made it famous, so its identical logo and colors have grandfathered protection from the normally fiercely guarded licensing and marketing rights. The result is that Arkansas High resembles a kind of miniature major-college program, a potentially intimidating fact for central Arkansas kids who grew up as fans of the university's teams.

Wearing the familiar-looking Razorback red uniform for Texarkana was one player who seemed as if he'd come from the university (and would eventually go there), a stocky, speedy running back named Dennis Johnson. One of the most highly sought-after recruits in the state in 2007, Johnson was entering his senior season after rushing for 1,500 yards as a junior and leading Arkansas High to the 6A state championship in 2006. At Quigley Stadium that year, before the Razorbacks ran the table to the title, the Tigers' defense had held Johnson to only nine yards rushing on twelve carries, winning 14–7 as Charles Clay scored the clinching touchdown with thirty-seven seconds left. "He's never been bottled up like that by anybody we've played," Texarkana coach Bill Keopple told the *Arkansas Democrat-Gazette* after the game.

Texarkana returned a strong team, but Darrell Seward didn't see a reason to do anything different from the year before. "He hasn't gotten that much faster," he said of Johnson, "and he had a better line in front of him then." Most of Central's defense was back, but the offense was the real problem. How was Central going to score? When watching film of A. J. Williams's kickoff return for a touchdown in the McClellan game, Finley had said admiringly, "Just like listening to jazz. He's smooth. He's special. You can't coach that, but he makes you look like you can coach." So Williams began getting some reps at tailback, and even worked on a halfback pass. He didn't lack for confidence. He wasn't one of those who were "fragile" in attitude, as the coaches had so often repeated. After connecting on a long pass play during the week of the trip to Texarkana, he turned to the players and coaches arrayed behind the huddle and said, "I got an arm, don't I?"

In the distance, as the ball was being run back in, a security guard from the school could be spotted making his way slowly across the practice field toward Cox.

|||||||||||||||||||||||||||||||||||||||||

That same week, the school board election set for the following Tuesday was heating up. Micheal Daugherty, the incumbent who had been in office for twelve years, was seeking reelection in Zone 2. Covering much of central Little Rock, the zone was shaped like a gun, with Interstate 630, Little Rock's east-west corridor, as the barrel and the bulk of the constituency falling south of that line to Asher Avenue. According to figures compiled from the 2000 census by Metroplan, a regional research and planning group, the population of 24,243 in the zone was 64 percent black. Daugherty, who is black, had become a target of the editorial page of the *Arkansas Democrat-Gazette*, which in its customary tone of folksy sarcasm had styled him a "member in good standing of both Little Rock's school board and its Gang of Four," the latter the paper's name for the black majority who had voted to oust Roy Brooks.

Daugherty hadn't helped himself in the press by failing to show up at community forums, unlike his opponents Mike Nellums, a black administrator in the Pulaski County Special School District; Drew Pritt, a community gadfly who was a member of both the Stonewall Democrats gay activist organization and the National Rifle Association; and his most serious challenger, Anna Swaim, a white mother of two who was communications director for the Arkansas Forestry Association and was receiving substantial support from the business community. But then at this point, Daugherty didn't have to answer to the community as a whole, only to the voters of Zone 2. He already had the endorsement of the Classroom Teachers Association, the district's dominant union, and most of the African American leaders in the city, including a ministers' alliance and John Walker. After the Eighth Circuit court had declared the district unitary in February, Daugherty had sided with the majority, in a vote the press inevitably described as falling "along racial lines," to negotiate a settlement with Walker's clients, the Joshua intervenors, who were contemplating appealing the ruling. Swaim saw no reason to pursue those negotiations in the wake of the decision and asserted that No Child Left Behind requirements would provide sufficient supervision of desegregation.

In one community forum, a representative for Daugherty said the candidate's previously scheduled school board meeting prevented him from attending and then gave an essentially contentless statement merely thanking the League of Women Voters for holding the forum he wasn't attending. Swaim, her three-ring-binder campaign book open in front of her, projected the image of a bright student, presenting herself as someone who could "rise above the board's current personality and personnel conflicts."

The editor of the liberal weekly *Arkansas Times*, Max Brantley, sounded in a column as if he didn't know whom he might support: "I'd be conflicted if I lived in Zone 2. Daugherty is due credit. But his defeat could change a destructive board dynamic. As it stands, the white board members need not bother to show up."

That week, historian Elizabeth Jacoway, whose book about the 1957 integration crisis had just been released, was on a local public affairs show and, in seeming reference to the school board's infighting, said, "There's so much bitterness in Little Rock right now. . . . It's been amazing to me how strong the feelings are about what happened in 1957, and that spills over into our interracial interactions in the present. That is a tragic component of the present situation—that there continues to be so much hostility and suspicion across the color line."

||||||||||||||||||||||||||||||||||||||

At practice, Callaway narrowed the offensive line's splits, since Texarkana played a "gap eight," a scheme in which the defense tried to shoot the gap between the linemen. "They're not going to stay put," he told the offense.

Cox had taken care of the travel arrangements, with the two-and-a-half-hour bus ride being the longest the Tigers would take all season. For this away game and others, the booster club had bought the Tigers new black duffel bags adorned with the school's logo, a large C surrounding an LR. Cox encouraged the players to wear khaki pants and their game jerseys, but he didn't insist on the pants because he knew that some of them didn't have khaki pants and couldn't afford to buy any. "I want you to represent yourselves in a way that does honor to Central High," he told them. "You are going to Football City. I want us going down there looking as sharp as possible." He had called the Western Sizzlin' in Hope to arrange for the pregame meal for fifty-five people, including the coaches and the bus driver, to arrive at about 3:00 p.m. As he always did, he had been trying to make sure everything was in order. The security guard and the player he took away changed all that.

Apparently, on that Wednesday Kaelon Kelleybrew had decided to skip school, but he hadn't wanted to miss practice. By the time his mother and the school administration got things sorted out, he was on the football field, where the guard came to get him. Where he'd gone and what he'd done were between him, his family, and school officials, but his unexcused absence earned him a ten-day suspension and a prohibition against participating in extracurricular activities. More important for his future with the team, he had also violated Cox's Code of Conduct, particularly the rule stating, "Be a positive example in your classes." He obviously would not be making the trip to Texarkana, nor would he be able to practice or play during the suspension. It was up to Cox to decide whether he should be kicked off the team.

Kelleybrew was a high-spirited kid, one who would not hesitate to get in the face of a teammate who was not performing well. Some of the coaches called him "ornery," a not uncomplimentary term, yet he had not been in any fights, unlike, say, the normally laid-back and witty Kyle Temple. On a team of generally phlegmatic characters, orneriness was the closest thing they had to leadership, and the coaches valued it. Known as a superior basketball player, Kelleybrew had come out for football for the first time since the ninth grade and immediately had become one of the top players on the team. He'd run the ninety-two bleachers he'd accrued for missing practice while playing AAU basketball over the summer. In the first two games, he'd been a ball-hawking safety and a sure tackler on defense, he'd returned punts, he'd been the primary receiver in the team's four-wideout "Tiger package." He'd shown up every day and never complained. He'd worked

hard. The recruiting letters from college coaches that Cox placed on the
jerry-rigged table by the coaches' office door were for guys like him, players with D-1 potential. Now he was gone, and Cox had to choose whether
he was gone for good.

Meanwhile there was still a game to play, fifty-four others from Central
High going to Texarkana, thirty-eight of them players wearing the Tiger
black and old gold.

On Friday, when the bus arrived at the Western Sizzlin' off the freeway
in Hope, a giant watermelon was on display near the front, the enduring
symbol of town pride that had predated Bill Clinton's birth there and out-
lived his presidency. No matter what Clinton, the "man from Hope," accomplished, watermelon was still king here.

Clyde Horton, the longtime coach now retired and volunteering with
the team, sat down and said to his dining companion, "Look at the way
the black coaches sit together and the white coaches sit together." Seemingly without thinking, Finley, Williams, and Keith Richardson had
taken one table and Siegel, Seward, and Callaway another. Cox was sitting with his son, Brian. The players also had largely segregated themselves by race at the various tables. What did it mean? Maybe nothing.
But on a more unified team, would Horton have noticed the division? Or
had the school board election, the talk of historic desegregation, the special sections in the papers, and the anniversary interviews on the local
news made everyone more sensitive to the ways the races fail to mix when
left on their own?

Football City was everything Cox had said it was. The 7,703-seat stadium was smaller than Quigley, but it looked larger since its concrete stands
rose from ground as flat as roadkill. That the field was artificial turf surrounded by a full-size track increased the illusion of size (the number of
lanes in Quigley's track had been reduced to make the field big enough for
soccer, and it was no longer used for meets). At one end was a brand-new
fieldhouse, its side painted with a huge "Home of the Razorbacks" and its
decorous entryway staffed by a receptionist.

At 4:00 p.m., when the Central bus pulled in, some fans were already in their seats for the 7:00 kickoff. Closer to game time, the stands began to fill and Texarkana became as red and raucous as Fayetteville: The band struck up the Razorback fight song, the crowd began to "call the hogs" ("Woooo, Pig! Sooie!"), and the team emerged from its end of the fieldhouse through an enormous inflatable hog head, just like the one that disgorged the University of Arkansas players on football Saturdays. It was times like this that mighty Central, the bigger school in the bigger conference, seemed like an underdog.

Still, Callaway remained confident. He reminded his players to close down their splits, and he recalled what a good week of practice they'd had. "Wednesday," he said, "we did not miss a blocking scheme the entire day. Make it fun. It's a challenge. They have not been beat since we beat them last year." Cox concurred: "You are blessed. You are the No. 1 team in 7A playing the No. 1 team in 6A." Seward chimed in, "If you all take care of 6 [Johnson's number] like you did last year, you'll make our jobs a lot easier."

The defense made Seward a prophet. Johnson's first carry went for two yards, and two more went for no gain. For the whole first quarter, every play seemed to end with Jared Green rising from the bottom of the pile and releasing from his grip the legs of Johnson, or the Texarkana quarterback, or anybody else who had had the effrontery to carry the ball. The offense, however, was not helping; it couldn't put three good plays together. Rankin stayed in after every unsuccessful third down to punt and had even boomed a high forty-five yarder over the head of dangerous return man Fred Rose, the state's fastest 100-meter performer at 10.50, to pin the Razorbacks at their own 10.

At the beginning of the second quarter, after another failed third down, Rankin retreated to punt again and struck a short line drive, right to Dennis Johnson, who was deep man this time. Johnson, who had the state's fourth-fastest 100-meter time at 10.77, took the ball at a full run and blew by the first line of tacklers straight up the middle before angling right for an easy fifty-seven-yard touchdown. Cox had warned the Tigers earlier in the week,

"We don't have anyone on our football team who can outrun two of their guys," and he'd told the Texarkana newspaper, "We are struggling on special teams right now and that could cost us Friday night."

The defense proceeded to make up for the special teams lapse. Midway through the second quarter, as a freight train horn sounded on the tracks behind the stadium, William Bennett, the left end, got a clear path to the quarterback and swatted the ball out of his hand before he could pass. Jared Green nimbly scooped up the fumbled ball on the second bounce and dashed seventeen yards to the end zone.

On the sidelines, Rankin was ecstatic and also amazed. "Tomorrow's my birthday and I said, 'Jared, what are you going to give me for my birthday?' and he said, 'A touchdown.' He hadn't scored in four years! How weird is that?"

The half ended with the score tied 7–7. In the locker room at intermission, Callaway told the offense: "You look like you're behind 44–0. We said we were going to have fun. Let's have fun. It's working."

Then it didn't work. Bo Dillon broke free on a run in the third quarter and then inexplicably dropped the ball without anyone touching him and had to fall on it. With two minutes left in the third period, Rankin injured his shoulder on one run and had to come out of the game. After the Tigers failed on third down in that series, Rankin returned to punt from the Razorbacks' 44, hoping to pin them deep in their own territory. He hit a high one that Johnson took at the 12. The coverage was there, but Johnson juked the first man, who flailed at him, then he cut right, splitting two more tacklers and avoiding a pileup at the 25 before breaking toward the Texarkana sideline. The Tigers' Lamont Lacefield took a good angle, but Johnson's combination of muscle and speed allowed him to shrug off the attempt to push him out of bounds. Two blockers smothered the final potential tackler, Rankin, at the Central 25 and Johnson hopped over them and trotted into the end zone. The Texarkana fans were all on their feet, whooping and cheering as Johnson crossed the goal line for his second TD on a punt return.

Back at the other end of the field, three Tiger players were sprawled on the turf: Two of them, Damien Lee and Ke'Won Jones, soon stumbled to their feet and limped off; A. J. Williams remained down.

By the time heads in the stands had turned from Johnson's score to where Williams lay, Brian Cox, the team trainer, was already over him, along with Arkansas High's trainer and Central's team doctor, Brian Hardin. The crowd's din lowered to a murmur as Williams continued to lie supine. As the seriousness of the injury grew more apparent, the huddle of adults around Williams grew. An EMT crew arrived with a stretcher. Coaches Callaway, Richardson, Seward, Stan Williams, Adam Acklin, and Bernie Cox stood by while the medical staff knelt beside the player, securing a splint around his left leg below the knee. His helmet and shoulder pads were removed. Family came out of the stands, the women looking out of place on the field with handbags and heels and stylish jeans. Finally, the medical crew transferred him to the stretcher and cranked it up to waist height, Williams's upper body canted to where he could see the crowd. Bernie Cox seemed to wipe something from his face, and he walked to A.J.'s side and tenderly patted his shoulder. As the stretcher turned to wheel the player away to the ambulance and the hospital in Texarkana, he looked over at his teammates on the sidelines and stoically raised his left hand in a wave. He was still wearing his gloves.

The injury had come on a clip that wasn't called. One of the Tiger linemen was running in a controlled way down the middle of the field, surveying the play ahead of him. When Johnson faked the first man, the Tiger player speeded up, throwing off the timing of the blocker approaching from his left, whom he didn't see. The Razorback propelled himself into the number on the back of the lineman's jersey, sending him flying off his feet. At that very time, Williams was pursuing Johnson across the field as he made for the sideline, and the Tiger player's body, all airborne 230 pounds of him, struck Williams's left leg just as he planted it on the turf, fracturing both bones in his lower leg. When something like that happens, it's a horrible accident, but you wonder why it doesn't happen all the time, how bodies accelerating and hurtling toward each other with such speed don't cause such damage more often. It was nobody's fault.

The game ended 14–7. Cox and the rest of the team were subdued in the locker room. First he addressed the whole game, not just the injury. "They hurt us on every single phase of special teams," he said, not recognizing the literalness of "hurt." "A lot of you gave great effort. I appreciate that. It doesn't matter how much effort you give if you put the ball on the ground. We're not being fair to the defense, guys.

"You guys who believe in prayer, keep A.J. and his family in your prayers. He poured his heart and soul into this program from the day he came on campus."

It was a long ride back up Interstate 30, the longest trip of the year made longer by the losses, of game and teammate. Cox received a call on his cell phone and announced to the bus that A.J. had broken both bones in his lower leg and would be transported by ambulance to Little Rock, where he would go into surgery the next day at Arkansas Children's Hospital in Little Rock.

When the bus neared the city, the driver exited onto Interstate 430, the bypass that runs north and south, connecting I-30 and I-40 so a driver traversing western Arkansas from, say, Razorback Stadium in Texarkana to Razorback Stadium in Fayetteville wouldn't have to go through downtown Little Rock. For this bus, downtown Little Rock was the destination and the driver turned onto Interstate 630, very near where John Carter had accosted the women eighty years before. Everybody in the bus, especially the coaches, was certainly grateful for the speed and convenience of the road, the better to get them to the school sooner and then home sooner and to sleep sooner to forget about the painful night.

||||||||||||||||||||||||||||||||||||

Interstate 630 is also called the Wilbur D. Mills Freeway after the former Arkansas congressman. Because of an affair Mills conducted with a stripper named Fanne Foxe (the Argentine Firecracker) that brought down the chairman of the House Ways and Means Committee at the apex of his career in 1974, the road has also been known colloquially as the Fanne Foxe Freeway. At previous times in its stop-and-start existence, it has been called the East-West Expressway, the Eighth Street Expressway, and, in its one incarnation when only a mile-long section between Pine and Dennison had been completed in 1969, the World's Shortest Highway. "I remember when I was a kid," said Dr. Jay Barth, the Hendrix College professor who has studied the effects of I-630 on the community, "you'd come out of the city and get revved up to go on the interstate for a mile, and then you'd go right back in the city. It was kind of a bizarre traveling experience through Little Rock."

As long ago as 1930, access into and out of the city by car was deemed a problem. An urban plan by John Nolen of Cambridge, Massachusetts, proposed a "Thoroughfare System" that included widening Eighth Street and making it continuous. Over the next twenty-five years, a major corridor that would connect east and west Little Rock seemed always to be on the drawing board, but the idea gained urgency after the 1957 integration crisis. Businessmen in the city worried that attracting companies to Little Rock would be impossible amid the education turmoil and racial strife, and their fears were justified. By most accounts, no new industry chose to locate in Little Rock for four years after the conflict at Central High made international headlines. A major road project might be perceived as a sign that Little Rock was pointing toward the future. Bill Bowen, a local banker and community leader at the time, wrote in his autobiography that "Little Rock was in dire need of positive programs to bring it out of the crisis—both economically and psychologically."

Financing the road was the real problem. The city couldn't get a bond issue approved and the state wouldn't fund it, so by 1969 the orphaned one-mile stretch was all there was of the highway. Federal money was the only option, and city leaders were fortunate to have a powerful friend in Congress in Wilbur Mills. In a 1971 article in *Life* magazine, presidential columnist Hugh Sidey called him "The Republic of Wilbur Mills" and wrote that he was the "literal coequal of the president, as far as money matters are concerned." Mills was able to bring the road into the interstate system with a clever bit of budgetary legerdemain that was his specialty: The mileage allowance for interstate highways had already topped out, but by rounding down the allocations of other states he found enough excess mileage to apply the balance to the 7.4 miles for I-630 in Arkansas. The approval had been in the works for a while and was seen as something of a fait accompli, but he'd been sworn to secrecy until after the elections of 1970, in which he ran unopposed. In a November 12, 1970, speech to the Little Rock Rotary Club, which was meeting in the packed Tiki Room of the Albert Pike Hotel, Mills announced that he'd been able to bring into the federal system the road "between Morning Sun and Evening Shade," two tiny Arkansas towns in his district. The crowd howled with laughter, then applauded when the true announcement was made: I-630 would get its approval as an interstate and the 90 percent funding from the federal government that went along with it.

As happened in so many cities, the planners sited the highway through the parts of town where the land was cheapest, low-income neighborhoods. Since urban renewal practices were already changing the composition of downtown neighborhoods from mixed to largely black, Little Rock's African American population was more significantly affected by the eminent domain seizures required by the route. Rising to challenge the construction was the Arkansas Community Organization for Reform Now (ACORN), later to become the national group known by that acronym. The *Arkansas Democrat* summed up the opposing sides this way: Proponents claimed the highway would provide "easier access to downtown commuters, thereby joining Little Rock's estranged East and West Ends," and detractors proclaimed that it would "widen the gap and become a . . . barrier between neighborhoods." Realizing that an eminent domain fight was futile in the courts because of precedents, ACORN filed suit contending that sufficient environmental-impact studies had not been done, and the group won several delays before the Eighth Circuit overturned the lower court and allowed construction to continue. The ribbon-cutting ceremony for the last section completing the route was held on September 30, 1985, with Wilbur Mills, a decade past his rapid, scandalous fall from power, still sounding a wistful note: "It's been said that the easiest way to grow old gracefully is to look back selectively."

In 2007, twenty-two years after the completion of the freeway, there was strong evidence, both academic and anecdotal, that it had perpetuated or worsened the racial divide in the city. Before the building of I-630, urban renewal programs had started the trend toward racially homogenous neighborhoods. This slum-eliminating initiative became a major priority for local business leaders after 1957. Raymond Rebsamen, whose interests included printing, insurance, automobile dealerships, and real estate, responded to the Central crisis by founding the Urban Progress Association, defined by one former participant as "a new, self-appointed power structure." Claiming that what had happened at Central "was blown up all out of proportion by those who profit from turmoil, confusion, and hate"— though it's not clear who these profiteers were—Rebsamen and his cohort thumped the drum for the comprehensive razing of neighborhoods (even though some of the targeted properties were in good shape), citing what he said was the slogan of the Little Rock Housing Authority: "Urban renewal is good business and good for business."

As a result, many black families from mixed neighborhoods were impelled to relocate into more-segregated areas or into housing projects that were, for all practical purposes, reserved for warehousing African Americans. In an area called West Rock, located not far from the Country Club of Little Rock, eighty black and three white families were moved out. As the *Arkansas Gazette* put it in 1966, "The total clearance of West Rock wiped out the only Negro neighborhood that rubbed shoulders with all-white Pulaski Heights," the city's most exclusive enclave. In studying measures taken by the Little Rock Housing Authority, which didn't have a black board member until 1965, historian John A. Kirk has written that "city planning policy shaped race relations more fundamentally over the long term than the short-term effects of the school crisis."

The construction of what eventually became I-630 changed the composition of more-mixed neighborhoods, but perhaps more important, it became a boundary that was—and remains—both palpable and psychological, a part of the geography as real as a river or ravine and a symbol for conceiving of the city as a place of two separate constituencies.

By 1980, an analysis of census data was showing, according to Jay Barth, "hypersegregation created by this barricade." In a presentation of his research during the summer of 2007, Barth employed an arsenal of graphics to prove a trend toward separation of the races, using pie charts indicating population by race in each census tract. With blue representing white population and red African American, he clicked through a series of maps from 1957 through 2000. In 1980, when the bisecting line of 630 first appeared on the map, the pies jumped significantly to one color or the other, blue north of the freeway and red south of it. "Did the folks who put this road here intend to do this?" he asked. "I think they clearly put it in that space because it was the cheapest place to put the thing. I don't think we can prove an intent to create a divide, but I think the effect of the divide is very, very clear." In analyzing the results of a survey of racial attitudes by the University of Arkansas at Little Rock, Barth also discussed the idea of "social trust," a sociological concept that, he said, basically "equals the spirit of community." Maps charting responses to the survey by geography showed that those residing south of 630 were less trusting across the board, of their co-workers, their neighbors, their fellow church members, and the police. This "trust gap," he continued, is a "huge problem" and "something the leaders of the community have to tackle."

Barth saw some points of hope: The growing Latino population shifted the demographics into a more complex mix that might undercut old attitudes; development along the river, both downtown and to the west where a recreational trail bridge crossed to North Little Rock, introduced spaces without such a freighted history, where the races come together; and the survey revealed that most people believe they can effect change in their communities.

Judged by more-anecdotal evidence, the barrier of 630 serves as a way of thinking and talking about the city that bolsters stereotypes and preconceptions. On Web sites like City-data.com, discussion boards about relocating to Little Rock commonly warn against going anywhere "south of 630." That paints with an awfully broad brush an area that includes the historic Victorian homes of the Quapaw Quarter, the governor's mansion, and the University of Arkansas at Little Rock, not to mention Central High. At one forum on race in the run-up to the anniversary, Walter Kimbrough, the president of Philander Smith College, the 120-year-old historically black institution on Daisy Bates Drive just east of Central High, spoke of needing to unite the constituencies on "either side of 630."

|||||||||||||||||||||||||||||||||||||

The freeway had undoubtedly given most Central coaches an easier way to get to work. Bernie Cox, Larry Siegel, and Adam Acklin all lived in subdivisions west of I-430 and joined I-630 at that interchange. Darrell Seward and Norman Callaway both lived in the community of Maumelle, north of the Arkansas River, and took 430 south to 630. Keith Richardson lived outside of Little Rock in the Saline County town of Bryant and came up I-30 to 430 to 630. Stan Williams lived in Sherwood, Arkansas, north of the river, and joined the freeway at its eastern end. Only Clarence Finley lived in Little Rock and south of 630, in a neighborhood off John Barrow Road created in the 1970s, cut from the woods where John Carter had hidden.

It was almost midnight when the bus bringing the Central players (minus one) back from Texarkana exited 630 at Woodrow and turned right. At Twelfth Street, where the four corners held three places to buy beer and an out-of-business funeral home, the bus turned left and headed east. It turned right on Park Street, and when it crossed Daisy Bates Drive, it slowed down and stopped in front of the school, where the players sang the alma mater, just as they did after every away game:

Hail to the old gold,
Hail to the black.
Hail! Alma mater,
Naught does she lack.
We love no other, so let our motto be . . .
VICTORY
LITTLE ROCK CENTRAL HIGH!

The bus turned right at the next corner, Sixteenth Street, and stopped outside the sliding steel door in the concrete wall around Quigley Stadium, and the players and coaches walked though the gate, no longer No. 1.

CHAPTER 7

FACE TO FACE

FOX IN A BOX IS A FOOTBALL DRILL OF GLADIATORIAL SIMPLICITY.
One offensive player and one defensive player face off against each other in
a narrow corridor formed by teammates standing on each side. On the whistle, the two clash, as a back tries to run through the corridor. Though the
drill had been a staple of Bernie Cox's repertoire for years, the Monday after
the Texarkana game was the first time he'd used it with this team. Fox in a
Box was a way to get back to playing Bernie Cox football, smash-mouth
football, and ultimately, field-position football. The players and the coaches
shouted encouragement, insults, jokes, critiques, and compliments; Central's
marching band (The Stereophonic Storm of the South) was practicing
nearby, and the pounding of the drums lent a martial air to the mini battles
being fought between the rows of players.

"Horrible, horrible!"

"It's hard to hide it out here, Reed, hard to hide it!"

"Somebody run through somebody! Run through him!"

"You never moved your feet!"

"Make a hole, guys, make a hole!"

"Come off the ball, let's go, baby, let's go!"

"That's why you don't play, right there!"

"Keep it up, Bo, keep it up."

"Why wait three downs to do that? You cost us two touchdowns and
you finally decide to do a little bit of something!"

"Pancake him, pancake him! Good job, Giese!"

"You got knocked back two out of four times. Can't play getting knocked back, offense."

"Get your head up, tailback! Way to be tough, but get your head up."

Variations on the drill are common at football practices at all levels, and something like it was run by coach Earl Quigley in 1927, as described by the *Arkansas Democrat:* "Formerly, the men went out individually and fell on the ball, but Thursday, Coach Quigley paired the boys off, sending both of them down at the same time after the pigskin." It was another way in which Bernie Cox was a dinosaur. All those fancy passing teams, like the one right in Bernie's Pleasant Valley neighborhood, Pulaski Academy, which sometimes threw fifty passes a game, pleased the fans, but when an opposing team could really manhandle them, they folded. That's what had happened in 2004, when Central lined up in the state semifinal against the Springdale Bulldogs, with Mitch Mustain, the alleged best high school quarterback in the country, and Gus Malzahn, the alleged offensive genius, at a packed Quigley Stadium. The Tigers knocked them around and broke Mustain's arm and won 30–21, though it wasn't even that close. They kicked West Memphis's butt the next week, 41–7, to win consecutive state titles, bringing Cox's total to seven. Before he won the previous year, he'd gone without a title since 1986, but the 2003 and 2004 seasons had proved that he could still forge a team out of toughness and discipline. And maybe he could do it with this group in 2007.

How tough were they, though? How many times had the coaches said they were fragile? An acknowledgment that this group needed some stroking was written on the dry-erase board in the coaches' office the week Cox instituted Fox in a Box: "Praise is the word of the week!!" And now the team also had serious personnel problems, particularly in the defensive backfield, with the losses of A. J. Williams and Kaelon Kelleybrew. "I'm going to move Aaron [Nichols] to safety," Seward said, "till we get Kaelon back, if and when that's ever going to happen."

The upcoming opponent was the Tigers' long-standing rival Pine Bluff, the only high school in the state that could brag of an equally rich football history.

Like Little Rock, Pine Bluff was an Arkansas River town, about forty-five miles downstream from the capital. It grew with the cotton trade at the end of the nineteenth century, and over the next hundred years became a center for railroads, munitions, and paper products. The founding of Branch Normal College, later to become Arkansas Agricultural, Mechanical, and Normal College and then the University of Arkansas at Pine Bluff, made the city an education destination for African American students, including John Walker. In the segregated days of the first half of the twentieth century, Pine Bluff High School fielded a number of superior football teams with players like the Hutson brothers, future Pro Football Hall of Famer Don and his twin brothers Ray and Robert. The rivalry with Little Rock meant their matchup was always the biggest game of the year. Nicknamed the Zebras, the team was immediately distinguishable on the field by its striped uniforms—on the jersey sleeves or sometimes the socks. After integration, Pine Bluff maintained strong athletic programs, producing professional athletes like baseball star Torii Hunter.

The meeting between Central and Pine Bluff in 2007, the ninety-third in their history, would be the last for a while. Because of declining enrollment, the Zebras were dropping to a lower sports classification and so wouldn't be a conference opponent. But this game was also significant because at halftime, the 1957 Central team, which had gone undefeated and been named the nation's best of that year in at least one poll, was being honored on the fiftieth anniversary of its accomplishments.

The Tigers that season were coached by Wilson Matthews, a no-nonsense former marine and an often profane disciplinarian who would go on the next fall to become the right-hand man for Frank Broyles, the head coach at the University of Arkansas, for a decade. At Central in 1957, as much as he could, Matthews shielded his players from the turmoil that was going on outside the school and in its halls, but that was hard to do when the 101st Airborne had landed its helicopters and parked its jeeps on his practice field. He made them move. When the general in charge of the Central deployment decided to take for his headquarters Matthews's office, the same one the current Central coaches used, Matthews reportedly called in and told a colleague, "Tell the son of a bitch to get out." Matthews lost that battle.

He did, however, keep control of his team. In a preseason team meeting, he told the players, "Don't look out the window and worry about what's going on outside. If I hear of any of you getting involved in any of this, you are finished with football. You will answer to me." A rough man, he nevertheless earned great loyalty and respect from his former players, who still held a reunion every year.

Brian Cox, Bernie's son, spent six years working on a book, *Tiger Pride*, that meticulously documents the century of football at Central High between 1904 and 2004 in 507 oversize pages of game accounts, photographs, and statistics. In the course of his research he'd come to know many of the players from the Wilson Matthews era. He took it upon himself to organize a ceremony honoring the fiftieth anniversary of that great team and set it up for halftime of the Pine Bluff game. He commissioned an impressive national championship trophy, engraved with all the players' names, since they had never received one.

One of the stars from the team was Ralph Brodie, who was the student body president during that tumultuous time. He'd been a thoughtful, measured voice during the crisis, especially in an interview with Mike Wallace, who was then a reporter for the *New York Post* (before gaining fame as a correspondent for the TV show *60 Minutes*).

"If you had your say, speaking personally," asked Wallace, "the Negro students could come to school tomorrow?"

"Sir," Brodie answered, "it's the law. We are going to have to face it sometime."

As the fiftieth anniversary approached, Brodie was one of twenty-six people, including two of the Little Rock Nine—Carlotta Walls LaNier and Minnijean Brown Trickey—who served on the commission charged with planning the ceremony. His self-defined role for a number of years had been to document and represent, primarily through his book *Central in Our Lives*, what he called the "third side" of the story, neither that of the Little Rock Nine nor of the forces of massive resistance, but instead the experience of the 1,900 students who "accomplish[ed] that which they were expected to accomplish when the year started." The football team's undefeated season, Brodie wrote in *Central in Our Lives*, "gave the student body a positive boost and helped keep morale high inside the school." While no one questioned that the voices of those white students deserved to be added to the historical record, Brodie's insistence that the "good folks going on with their lives" in the face of the turmoil were worthy of praise and that "everyone who stepped inside Central High that year exhibited courage every day" rubbed some people the wrong way.

Brodie and some of the other white alumni of the era found an impetus for defending themselves after the 1997 anniversary commemoration. Spearheaded by President Bill Clinton, the event was the first to honor the nine in a big way, with a gathering of 7,500 on the lawn capped by the grand symbolic gesture of Clinton and then-governor Mike Huckabee opening the doors of the school for the students forty years after they had been turned away. But surprisingly, the speech that angered some alumni was not Clinton's, but Huckabee's. Calling on the full repertoire of rhetorical skills he'd practiced as a Baptist preacher, he declared: "There are some times when as we look back on our history we are disturbed, and we ought to be disturbed. The children of Israel wandered for forty years in the wilderness, and in many ways Arkansas and the rest of the nation has wandered for forty years in the wilderness as it relates to race relations.

"Essentially, it's not just a skin problem, it's a sin problem. Because we in Arkansas have wandered around in ambiguity, all kinds of explanations and justifications. And I think today we come to say once and for all that what happened here forty years ago was simply wrong. It was evil, and we renounce it."

He went on to recount a moving story of visiting the Yad Vashem memorial of Holocaust remembrance in Jerusalem with his eleven-year-old daughter and seeing her write in the comments section of the guest book, "Why didn't somebody do something?" This seemed to many to be a direct rebuke to those 1,900 students who had stood by while their nine black classmates were tormented.

Wesley Pruden, a Little Rock native who became editor in chief of the *Washington Times* and was the son of one of the segregationist leaders from 1957, called the event Holier Than Thou Week in an opinion piece in the *Times* and took exception to Huckabee's characterization of the treatment as "evil." Pruden laid it at the feet of "men and women imprisoned in their own time and experience." Echoing that sentiment was James Reed Eison of the class of 1958, who that year had been captured in a photograph stabbing an effigy of a black student. He told the *Democrat-Gazette* after Huckabee's speech: "I'm angry at the judgments. . . . We were products of our time and should not apologize."

In 2007, Brodie was the sometimes deft and always defiant carrier of this flame, and he won the whispered admiration of many white peers in Little Rock for his willingness to defend his classmates "against the negative historical light in which they continue to be cast," as he put it. He had even lobbied for a speaking role at the official commemoration (which was not granted). Terrence Roberts, another of the Little Rock Nine, seemed to be addressing Brodie's efforts directly when he declared in his 2009 book, *Lessons from Little Rock*, that he wrote it "to counter those ever more vocal revisionists who would re-write history to say that things were not as bad as some suggest, that the nine of us were warmly embraced by the majority of white administrators, teachers and students at Central High."

At a forum on education and race on September 20, Brodie appeared on the dais with Minnijean Brown Trickey, who could barely restrain herself from rolling her eyes at his recitation of the positive statistics about his white classmates, like the fact that Central had twenty-two National Merit semifinalists or that the students were more focused on football than on what was happening with integration. Brown Trickey, nevertheless, struck a conciliatory tone at the forum when she declared that it was the decisions and actions of adults that drove events. "White kids were not in charge and we were all pawns," she said to applause.

Attendance at the forum, though, was sparse, and notably lacking in white faces. A member of the audience, Katherine Wright Knight, a former president of the teachers' union, pointed out the thinness of the crowd, which also earned her a round of applause, before saying, "We do have a racial divide within the city, within the school." Perhaps the low turnout could be attributed to commemoration fatigue. Perhaps it was owing to the location: a well-intentioned church in a strip of stores along Colonel Glenn Road/Asher Avenue where the size of the parking lot seemed to indicate a degree of optimistic delusion among the onetime developers. This part of Little Rock, yes, south of 630, had been criticized as long ago as 1930 by urban planner John Nolen as "narrow and unsightly Asher Avenue, which must be paraded to every one traveling to Hot Springs via Little Rock." With its auto-body shops, lumberyard, and after-hours clubs, Asher Avenue remained just as it had been described seventy-seven years before.

|||||||||||||||||||||||||||||||||||||||||

"There's a lot of crap going on and I'm hearing about it," Bernie Cox said to the team on Tuesday of the week before the Pine Bluff game. " 'It's your fault.' 'No, it's your fault.' It's going to stop. The bickering is over.

"I heard a lot of crap about Randy Rankin punting to their returner. I told Randy to do that! If you want to bitch, you come to me.

"We've got problems. You're good kids, I love you to death, but we've got problems. We've got seniors on this football team who won't break down [in a tackling position] on a punt. Seniors!

"You know what the headline said the next day in the Texarkana paper? 'Punt, Central, Punt!' I was embarrassed. And we're still doing some of the same things this week that we were doing last week.

"You did have a great Fox in a Box yesterday. And I saw more aggressiveness in a couple of drills than I've seen all year. You've got to try to commit to doing it all the time."

Tuesday was also election day for the Zone 2 school board position, and there was talk in the coaches' office about the race. In the *Democrat-Gazette*'s story about the election that morning and in an editorial, the paper had repeated ten-year-old charges that Micheal Daugherty, an employee at Arkansas Medical Research Testing, had committed "apparent perjury" (in the words of the city attorney's office at that time) by claiming in a federal deposition to have earned a doctorate. No charges were ever filed, but Daugherty hadn't provided proof of his degrees. One of the coaches said he'd heard that Daugherty had become angry at someone at Central's office because she had called him "Mr. Daugherty" rather than "Dr. Daugherty." Stan Williams closed down the conversation when he announced to his colleagues: "I'm a Daugherty man, and I'm tired of talking about that mess."

Lined up behind Daugherty were the most powerful black and progressive forces in the city. He'd received the endorsements of the Little Rock Classroom Teachers Association, a number of black state legislators and ex-legislators, a flock of influential black ministers, white longtime civil rights activist Brownie Ledbetter, and John Walker, as well as former Razorback basketball star Scotty Thurman. The African American community wasn't always so unified, according to Max Brantley of the *Arkansas Times*. The effort at a united front had begun the year before, when Roy Brooks was creating waves in the bureaucracy and the school board was controlled by a white majority that was supported by the business interests of the city. "For a period there," Brantley said, "there was an effort on the part of the Little Rock business establishment to get behind the school district and they decided that it would probably be better if the city school district didn't implode. No shit, right? . . . And they brought in Roy Brooks, who I thought was an idiot. . . . He sold himself to the first rich white guys who came to see him, and they happened to be people who have been historic enemies of the public school system, beginning with Walter Hussman," the publisher of the *Arkansas Democrat-Gazette*.

Brooks began pushing for a merit-pay initiative, which Hussman and the regularly conservative editorial page of the *Democrat-Gazette* also lobbied for and the teachers' unions objected to. "[Brooks] said, 'Sure, I'll take your money to do this little school test you want to run, this teacher merit pay thing,'" Brantley continued. In the fall of 2006, Tom Brock, the incumbent in Zone 7, which included southwest Little Rock, was up for election after having been appointed earlier in the year to finish an unexpired term; he earned a *Democrat-Gazette* endorsement and the support of the Chamber of Commerce. But he lacked tact and diplomacy. "He called the teachers ['horses' behinds'] in a board meeting," says Brantley, "and it set the black community on fire. It mobilized them. . . . I've never seen anything like it in a school election." Despite or perhaps because of a drumbeat of editorials endorsing Brock, Dianne Curry, an African American woman, defeated him 903 to 542, giving the school board its first black majority, a historic transfer that qualified as international news, given Little Rock's history.

After that outcome, the business interests saw Daugherty's seat, which was up in the fall of 2007, as a way to regain control. "Daugherty wasn't a guy who was friendly with Walker," Brantley said, but the African American constituency of Little Rock decided to make common cause to retain their majority on the board.

In the 2007 election, Anna Swaim got the mixed blessing of the endorsement of the *Democrat-Gazette*, which managed to be both fulsome and condescending by calling her a "lady" four times in the endorsement editorial and declaring that she "restores hope. And faith. And most of all, perspective." By all accounts a concerned, thoughtful citizen with two children in the district (the only candidate who could claim that), she was soon painted by the opposition as a pawn of the business community. If she was to win in Zone 2, she would need the support of a good number of black voters, since they were in the majority in the zone. To that end, the endorsement of the newspaper may have done her more harm than good. As Daugherty's campaign literature put it, "Don't be fooled by the newspaper!"

The election had generated a tidal wave of commentary about each candidate on the Arkansas Blog of the *Times*, moderated by Brantley. "It seems that the Democrat-Gazette endorsement is the kiss of death for Swaim due to their heavy-handed treatment of the black members of the school board ('Gang of Four' was the worst label they could've picked)," wrote one poster called Jake da Snake. Though the many-sided online dialogue often degenerated into nasty ad hominem attacks and personal innuendo (unsurprising for blog commentary), some of the more thoughtful posts addressed the issues reasonably.

"This should not be about race," wrote tiredofbs. "It isn't in my household. It's about making smart decisions to benefit all students of the district. . . . Why does the color of our skin even need to come into this? . . . I want this community to work together, but the current board majority doesn't seem interested. I realize there have been wrongs in the past, but do more wrongs make a right?"

"True," replied Jake to the assertion that it shouldn't be about race, "but that message seems to have escaped the Democrat-Gazette editorial writers and how their responses to the situation were perceived by the black community. It is also not about teacher unions running the district or John Walker making puppets out of school board members, which are two other myths perpetrated by the Democrat-Gazette and company. In the final analysis, each school board member has been representing the citizens of their district and their desires."

"Jake," wrote tiredofbs, "thanks for your thoughts. I do like to try and see things from many perspectives. Some people whose outlook differs from yours see a lot of John Walker's heavy hand in this issue as well. Why not get all heavy hands out, and let things run as they might without undue influence from Walker, unions and Hussman? Novel idea—I think Anna Swaim could be the answer there. I know she got lots of money from big-money people but in talking to her, I found her to be a free thinker open to all sides. . . . I personally just want to feel comfortable to be able to leave my kids in LRSD. I feel they learn so much from the diversity of the student body."

IABL1969 chimed in with this: "Wow, I just never really knew that so many people actually took the time to fight through the Dem-Gazette editorials. I try on occasion but about 4 sentences into it some mental block takes hold and I can't read on." Then the poster took up the topic more seriously: "Look here's the thing, if I may. If your kid is growing up in a literate [household] . . . where technology is incorporated into their life, [and] they get some . . . decent teachers and [a] few great ones . . . and they can read on a very proficient level and integrate material and information across disciplines and 'learn how to learn' all of their lives, then your kid is ok.

"If not, well, really, based on the knowledge demands for great jobs, for competing in larger markets, for attaining advanced degrees, for having the chance at being the master of your destiny and not being at the mercy of the dictates of the fads of the marketplace, your kid is not getting the education he or she needs. Simple to me, really.

"Is the school board election today going to change that? Not a chance. It starts at home and it is profoundly influenced at home and then the school does what it can. Which in my opinion, in many, but not all cases, is not much. . . .

"I'm down on public school. I'll be honest. My kids don't go there for one main reason: Because I feel they will get a better education outside of it. (I know, don't say it. There are great success stories in LR School District. I get that.)

"Is the school board going to change that? I don't think so. Is today's winner going to matter in the actual 'classroom' life of your kids? I doubt it. It's already set in motion. The school they go to either 'gets it,' that is what these kids really need today, and delivers it, or they don't get it and don't deliver it."

In the end, when the voters of Zone 2 went to the polls, there was no winner. The tally: Daugherty 811, Swaim 806, Nellums 187, Pritt 8. The percentage breakdown for Daugherty and Swaim was 44.76 to 44.48 percent, dictating a runoff. The voters would have to wait another three weeks to find out who their representative would be.

IIIIIIIIIIIIIIIIIIIIIIIIIIIIIIIIIIIIIIIII

That week, as it had fifty years before, the nation was turning its eyes toward Little Rock, in a spasm of anniversary journalism. *Newsweek, Time,* the *New York Times,* the *Washington Post,* NPR, PBS, the three major TV networks, and many, many others ran retrospective stories, interviews, and essays. In a *Newsweek* column by Ellis Cose, Ralph Brodie numbered the "problem students" during the crisis year at twenty-five, while Little Rock Nine member Ernest Green put the number at closer to "a couple hundred." The old, elegantly landscaped ground in front of the gargantuan school was still being trod by writers with history on their minds, while in the back of the school the "good ground of Central High," as one former player had termed the practice fields in his memoir of Tiger football under coach Wilson Matthews, was being plowed as it had been for a hundred years by the cleats of the young men in pads, representing their school. In the earlier forum at the church on Asher Avenue, Angelo Ancheta, a law professor at Santa Clara University and an expert in civil rights litigation who was in town for the week, noted that recent "amazing" Supreme Court decision concerning the Seattle and Louisville school districts had taken a "strong stance saying that *Brown v. Board* doesn't stand for an ideal." He reminded the audience that "we have to combine both idealism and realism" and said that when he had visited Central High earlier in that week, "There was a football practice going on. It's a functioning high school."

Before the game on Friday night, Bill Hicks stopped by the coaches' office. He had been a lineman on the 1957 team and was named a high school All-American by *Teen* magazine that season. He'd gone on to play at Baylor University as a center and linebacker and followed that with a college coaching career as an assistant at West Virginia University, Baylor, and the University of Texas; as the head coach at Howard Payne University; and recently had retired after a decade coaching and teaching at Amarillo High School. A rangy and fit sixtysomething, he had the weathered, craggy face of a character from a Larry McMurtry novel.

It was the first time he'd been back at Quigley Stadium for a game since he had stood on the field as a player, because he was always on the sidelines of whatever team he was coaching. He looked around the small room and recalled that it was the very one where he'd watched film with Wilson Matthews manning the Kodak Analyst film projector with the clicker that could rewind the film for close review. Once, Matthews pointed out that Hicks had missed a block, and Hicks, who "wouldn't have said this when I was a sophomore or junior but I was a senior and full of myself," told Matthews, "I think that was the only one I missed." Matthews stared him down and then just kept clicking the film back and forth to repeat the play while saying, "There's one you missed. You missed that one."

Soon after Hicks's visit, the Tiger offense crowded into the coaches' office for the pregame meeting. Callaway asked them, "We got how many days of Fox in a Box this week?"

"Three," they answered.

"We're going to drive off the line," Callaway said. "We're going to stay with our blocks."

Running the bleachers at Quigley Stadium, shown here during August two-a-days in 2007, is a Central High Tiger tradition and a staple of coach Bernie Cox's training methods. *(Photo by Barry Gutierrez)*

The Tigers opened the season against West Memphis as the No. 1 ranked team in the state. *(Photo by Tommy Walker)*

The construction of Little Rock High School, later Central High (shown here nearing completion in 1927), cost $1.5 million and was a source of great pride for the community. *(Photo courtesy National Park Service, Little Rock Central High School National Historic Site)*

The same year the school was built, John Carter was lynched for allegedly assaulting two women in 1927; a mob hanged him from a telephone pole, then dragged his body through town and burned it on Main Street. *(Photo courtesy Butler Center for Arkansas Studies, Central Arkansas Library System)*

On the Central sidelines, from left, head coach Bernie Cox, offensive assistant Clarence Finley, and first–year assistant Adam Acklin react to a play. *(Photo by Tommy Walker)*

The Cabot defense converges on Tiger running back Bo Dillon. *(Photo by Tommy Walker)*

During the 1957–58 school year, the nine black students who chose to attend Central were under the protection of federal troops but still suffered various forms of harassment. *(Photo courtesy National Park Service, Little Rock Central High School National Historic Site)*

The Little Rock Nine reunited in September 2007 at the fiftieth anniversary of their integration of the school: from left, Melba Pattillo Beals, Thelma Mothershed Wair (seated), Minnijean Brown Trickey, Elizabeth Eckford, Terrence Roberts, Carlotta Walls LaNier, Gloria Ray Karlmark, Jefferson Thomas, and Ernest Green. *(Photo by Julie Davis/courtesy Little Rock School District)*

Longtime coach Clyde Horton, who starred for the Tigers in the mid-1940s, returned for one more season on the sidelines to coach defensive tackle Jared Green, the eventual Metro Defensive Player of the Year. *(Photo by Tommy Walker)*

Speedy running back Tim Dunn carries the ball against North Little Rock High, from which he'd transferred the previous spring. *(Photo by Tommy Walker)*

Above: Senior Kaelon Kelleybrew had not played in the offensive backfield all season until Bernie Cox inserted him at tailback against archrival Catholic High. *(Photo by Tommy Walker)*

Left: Defensive coach Darrell Seward makes a point to junior Damien Lee, the sure-handed tight end who also made some crucial plays on defense during the season. *(Photo by Tommy Walker)*

Below: Fullback William Bennett and quarterback Randy Rankin celebrate Damien Lee's touchdown catch in the fourth quarter against Catholic High. *(Photo by Tommy Walker)*

Shown here after it was just completed in 1985, Interstate 630 bisects Little Rock; Dr. Jay Barth of Hendrix College has studied its effect as a "barrier" between black and white neighborhoods. *(Photo by Johnnie Gray/courtesy Arkansas State Highway and Transportation Department)*

Little Rock school superintendent Roy Brooks sits stoically as school board members, from left, Katherine Mitchell, Micheal Daugherty, and Dianne Curry file out after a board majority voted to buy out his contract in 2007. *(Photo by Brian Chilson/courtesy* Arkansas Times*)*

A plaque in Quigley Stadium honoring Bernie Cox reads: "A man of high moral character, he has been a great teacher of life's lessons to his players." *(Photo by Tommy Walker)*

After they filed out, Clyde Horton asked Callaway, "Are they ready, Coach?"

"I don't know," said Callaway. "They just look at you." He shrugged and added, "I asked them three or four questions and they knew the answers."

Cox spoke very calmly to the team about effort and facing challenges. "I don't want to see you in five years just getting by," he said. "I want to see you, whatever you're doing, your life's work—be able to say that you're doing the best you can do."

As a tribute to A. J. Williams, many of the players had used a Sharpie pen to ink his initials or name or jersey number on their shoes or the tape around their wrists. "I have reservations about that," Cox said, suddenly more passionate. "Why did you do that? Did you do it because it's something they do on TV? I want to know. I need some answers right now. That's no reason to do it. Are you trying to honor someone?"

"Yes, sir."

"That's the right reason. You want to honor someone. Here's my problem with that. Did you do everything you possibly could this week, physically and mentally, to meet this challenge? If you did everything you could between the time A.J. was hurt Friday night leading up to right now at this moment in time, you have every right to wear that. But if you go out there and fart around, if you let someone return a punt for a touchdown, are you honoring him?"

"No, sir."

"He was new to this program, but he was the epitome of this program, and I've been here for thirty-six years. He worked his tail off and he performed. If you're going to wear a piece of tape with his number on it, you be doggone sure you honor him and don't dishonor him. I really wish you'd think seriously about it, because it's important to me. If you're ready to play and you prepared and you got in Fox in a Box, and you blocked hard every time, and you didn't step away from any contact and you didn't step away from any challenge, you ran every bleacher hard, you ran every wind sprint hard after practice, and you prepared physically, mentally, and emotionally, then you keep it on your wrist. The only mistakes we'll accept are ones made going one hundred percent. If you're going to honor somebody, you think about that."

On the field, when the team broke the huddle after warmups, the Tigers chanted, "One-two-three A.J.!"

In the first half, the offense seemed to get in a groove for the first time all season. Bo Dillon at tailback was biting off yardage in six-, nine-, and eleven-yard chunks running the tried-and-true off-tackle forty-two. The former Tiger players from all eras who had gathered in the stands, in attendance for the 1957 squad's ceremony at halftime or in town for the following Tuesday's Little Rock Nine ceremony, saw a very familiar Tiger team, one that dominated the line of scrimmage on defense and ran the ball relentlessly. Dillon scored on the Tigers' first possession on an eleven-yard sweep, then again in the second quarter, carrying seven times on a ten-play, forty-six-yard drive to put the Tigers up 14–0. On the sidelines, Tim Dunn, with whom Dillon usually alternated, seemed upset that he wasn't getting in the game as much as usual, but Finley told him sharply, "He's in rhythm. When you get it done, I'll leave you in there. I don't like your body language." Dunn was mollified soon enough when he also scored a touchdown in the second quarter to give Central a 21–7 lead at halftime.

At halftime, during the ceremony for the 1957 team, the PA announcer recited its accomplishments—an undefeated season, national Player of the Year honors for running back Bruce Fullerton, one of the top twelve high school teams of all time according to one magazine—and the crowd met each with applause that sounded over the usual low din of distracted teenage activity. As their names were intoned, the men who had blocked and tackled and scored and celebrated on that turf as invincible sixteen- and seventeen- and eighteen-year-olds now hobbled or limped or wheeled themselves or, in a few cases, still confidently strode across that same ground. The stands they looked up to now—the ones that in their day had held members of the 101st Airborne who'd come to cheer for "Fort Central," as some called it, the bleachers they'd scanned for girlfriends or family—that spring would seat classmate Ernest Green, like them in his cap and gown, the first black student to graduate from Central High. Back then, he was the only senior boy to process alone; the others had all been paired with a female classmate. That day, the Tigers' Bill Hicks had made one last block in Quigley Stadium. He had stopped someone who was suspiciously carrying a package of eggs, surely intended for Ernest Green.

In the second half, Tiger fans young and old, white and black, had more to cheer as the team rolled to a 43–19 win. Bo Dillon ended with 249 yards rushing on thirty-two carries. Central's defense dropped the Zebras for a total of minus-ten yards on nineteen rushing plays, but the secondary, without its two best players, still looked weak, allowing three touchdown passes and two completions over forty yards. In the third quarter, coach Adam Acklin had said to Finley, "We need something like this."

"Don't tell nobody else they're horrible," Finley had replied.

The following morning, the Saturday rituals were under way by 8:00 a.m. Workers with leaf blowers moved the debris in the bleachers to the aisles for collection. Seward clipped articles from the newspaper to post on the bulletin board in the locker room. Siegel and Callaway were discussing the fauna of Quigley Stadium.

"There was a big old rat back there," Siegel said of the equipment room. "He was wearing shoulder pads."

"One last night, he ran right along that pipe," said Callaway, pointing to the exposed infrastructure of the office.

On his way to the stadium that Saturday morning, Finley had noticed that at the corner of Jones Street and Daisy Bates, the fading lettering on the stadium wall indicating "EAST STAND" and "WEST STAND" and the arrows under them had been freshly painted as part of the cosmetic improvements for the commemoration ceremony. "They hadn't ever been painted before," he said.

|||||||||||||||||||||||||||||||||||||||||||

The lawn in front of Central High was crowded with people, as it had been fifty years before, and, also as then, nine African Americans were the focus of their attention. This time, there were no epithets or signs, only admiring looks and praise. As had their white classmates from the football team on Friday night at Quigley Stadium, they hobbled or limped or were wheeled or strode confidently onto the stage in front of the school, which, as Ernest Green had said the day before in a breakfast speech at the governor's mansion, "is still a tremendous edifice." They were all here, for the first time in ten years, since the fortieth anniversary: Ernest Green, Elizabeth Eckford, Melba Pattillo Beals, Gloria Ray Karlmark, Minnijean Brown Trickey, Jefferson Thomas, Terrence Roberts, Carlotta Walls LaNier, and Thelma Mothershed Wair.

The surnames appended to the teenage names that had identified them in newspaper captions around the world testified to their lives beyond the confines of the school: marriages (and divorces), like everybody else. They pursued careers and had children and changed jobs and moved to new towns, like everybody else. Though they hadn't seen each other in a decade, once more traveling from far-flung places (Norway, California) to reunite in the same city where they'd grown up, at the very site that had made them *them* (but would never fully define them as individuals), they still felt a bond. They were a team.

"The best defense against my tormentors was to stay there," said Ernest Green at a press conference. "We supported each other. . . . 'Covering one's back,' we learned what that meant very well." None of them was allowed to play on a sports team at Central; they were forbidden by the rules of their admission from participating in any extracurricular activities. Two star football players at Horace Mann, the new black high school, who had wanted to transfer to Central were denied admission for that reason. Green, who as a member of the marching band at Dunbar Junior High had performed on the Quigley Stadium field on Saturday mornings, when the black schools in Little Rock were allowed to use the stadium, had to put away his instrument for the year. Jefferson Thomas, a track athlete at Dunbar, couldn't run on Central's track or get the benefit of being coached by Clyde Hart, who later spent forty-two years at Baylor University and coached Olympic gold medal sprinter Michael Johnson. For her part, Carlotta Walls had been captain of the girls' basketball team in junior high and had also been excited by the thought of cheering for Central's football team: "I could just imagine myself in the stands in Central's college-size football stadium, cheering and chanting for the Tigers, bursting with school spirit and pride."

In the days before they knew how bad it might be for them at Central, Walls and the others had allowed themselves to envision a relatively normal high school experience. "We had every reason to believe we would be accepted," Ernest Green said. But in the early weeks of their attendance, when it became clear how unwelcome they were, a pep rally was not a highly anticipated expression of school spirit, but rather something more sinister, as the 1,990 students in the school filed into that immense, ornate auditorium and were whipped into a sanctioned frenzy in the name of the Tigers. Melba Pattillo Beals wrote in her memoir, *Warriors Don't Cry*, that "going to a pep rally was rather like being thrown in with the lions to see how long we could survive"; she particularly remembered students shooting smirking looks at her when they sang the last word in the alma mater's line "Hail to the old gold, hail to the black." At the commemoration ceremony in 2007, Jefferson Thomas recalled getting caught up in the fervor of the rally as the band played what he assumed was a fight song while students waved a large flag back and forth. He was cheering, jumping up and down, and clapping along with the music until he looked a few rows ahead and saw Carlotta Walls staring bullets at him and then noticed even some of the white students looking at him strangely. The fight song he'd been cheering along with was "Dixie" and the flag, the Confederate battle flag.

Thomas's story was the lightest moment in the ceremony, held on a dim, damp Tuesday. Darrell Seward, Keith Richardson, and Stan Williams were all sitting together about halfway between the stage and Park Street. The seniors were given preferential seating, on risers to the right and behind the main stage, which was set up under the "LITTLE ROCK CENTRAL HIGH SCHOOL" letters that had been featured on the cover of *Life* magazine in 1957. Jared Green and Reed Caradine had front-row seats. The program promised to be a long one, with the collection of politicians and all of the nine scheduled to speak.

Because Bill Clinton was on the dais and because Hillary Rodham Clinton, then a candidate for the Democratic nomination, and Mike Huckabee, a Republican candidate, were also in attendance, security was tight. The free tickets required for entrance had long been spoken for, but by the time the program began at 10:00 a.m., the audience filled only three-quarters of the five thousand seats. The spitting rain was in part to blame for the low attendance, as was the anticipated crush of people, traffic, and security that for weeks the media had warned attendees to prepare for. But there were other reasons for the empty seats.

The corrosive racial climate the school board battles had fostered, along with the perception that the ceremony was just political theater (always a danger, in some minds, when the Clintons were involved), had left many whites feeling alienated by the events. The ovation for school board president Katherine Mitchell was equal to that for any of the Little Rock Nine, an indication of both the racial composition of the crowd and the degree to which African Americans in Little Rock still felt embattled. Hopes that the commemoration might be an occasion for expiation were never high, a note sounded by Elizabeth Eckford, who had returned to Little Rock in 1974 after an early career in the military. "I can forgive because it lifts a burden from my heart," she said. "I know the difference between an apology and someone who is just trying to make themselves feel good. If you can't name what you did, it's not an apology."

One of the enduring questions about the events of 1957 was how many in the mob gathered outside the school were from Little Rock. On the Friday before the anniversary, at one of a series of forums held at the University of Arkansas at Little Rock (UALR) Law School, Katherine Mitchell rose from the audience to ask a question. She had become a familiar face to those in the room and the community over the past few months. Her picture had often appeared on the front page of the *Democrat-Gazette* during the time leading up to the dismissal of Roy Brooks.

The speakers at the forum were two historians who had long studied the integration crisis, Johanna Miller Lewis, a professor at UALR, and Elizabeth Jacoway, whose book about the Central crisis had just been published. "In your research," Mitchell asked them, "have you found that many of the people [in the mob outside the school] were from Little Rock? *It Happened in Little Rock* [a play produced by the Arkansas Repertory Theater as part of the anniversary] implied that they weren't."

"Most of them were from here," answered Miller Lewis.

"There were many, many people from out of town," said Jacoway. "Daisy Bates even said that she knew Little Rock people and didn't recognize a lot of them."

There were lingering doubts in the black community about the degree to which Little Rock's white citizens were willing, or have ever been willing, to accept responsibility for the historic, and the continuing, divisiveness in the city. The school board conflict of 2007 did not arise sui generis, but could be traced back not only to the 1957 crisis, but also to the lynching of John Carter in 1927 and, perhaps most important, to thousands and thousands of other indignities over the decades, legal and extralegal, mundane and significant, thoughtless and intentional.

This history, both recorded and silent, gave a foundation to John Walker's assertion, in a panel on the judicial effects of the 1957 crisis, that "the thing we do have now is a voice, but it is the voice that is still being suppressed by those same forces that suppressed it then."

At a press conference with the nine the day before the main ceremony, a reporter asked the group to name the biggest "myths" about the crisis. Carlotta Walls answered without hesitation: "That members of the mob weren't from Little Rock." Terrence Roberts's book described an encounter he had with a man in the Little Rock airport who told Roberts they had been in gym class together and then apologized for not doing anything to stop the harassment Roberts endured. "He asked for forgiveness and offered his hand in friendship," wrote Roberts. "Unfortunately that kind of encounter is rare. Most of those feelings go unspoken and so remain unresolved." On the dais on that cloudy morning, the division in the city didn't go unrecognized. Mayor Mark Stodola pointed out that "too many neighborhoods south of 630 remain blighted" and cited the "still pervasive feeling that we are two cities."

Nevertheless, the nine expressed affection for the place they'd once called home as adolescents. Roberts said at the ceremony that he felt "fortunate to have been raised in this town of Little Rock." And Carlotta Walls LaNier said that she was "very, very proud to be a graduate of this institution." Gloria Ray

Karlmark began to break down as she said, "Standing here at Central High School with the memory of what happened in this school, to me and to my fellow Little Rock Nine, forever permeating my bones, I can only hope that today's wonderful student body of all cultural origins will not forget from whence they came."

Two days later, the *Democrat-Gazette* editorial page even praised long-time nemesis Bill Clinton for his remarks at the ceremony about the need for educational excellence: "Bill Clinton raised the question that should be at the heart of the next civil rights revolution: What does an equal opportunity for an education mean if that education is only mediocre?" But the paper couldn't help itself in the end, venturing another dig at the school board and its "perks and power and patronage."

CHAPTER 8

CHEMISTRY AND CONSEQUENCES

"SECURITY WASN'T NEARLY AS TIGHT AS IT WAS TEN YEARS when Clinton was here as president," said Larry Siegel in the coaches' office. "You could've gotten in today without a ticket, easy. . . . I saw Bush was at the UN and I said, 'He's not coming.' If he was running for reelection, he would have been here. He hasn't got anything to gain by coming or lose by coming. In fact, if he had come, there probably would have been a lot of war protesters."

The phone rang, and the usual predictions about the voice on the other end began.

"'I can't make it to practice,'" said Stan Williams.

"'I missed the bus,'" said Norman Callaway in his high-pitched imitating-a-student voice.

On the field, with rain still threatening, Finley was working with the defensive linemen, teaching pass rush moves called the Club, the Snake, and the Windshield Wiper, where a defensive player sweeps his arm from low to high in front of his body to free himself from the grip of a pass-blocking offensive lineman with extended arms. Cox had warned the team at practice the day before that Russellville was going to throw the ball seven out of ten plays.

Jared Green lined up for a one-on-one drill against underclassman Eric Fears, and Callaway joked, "Fears, you got your insurance paid up?" Green would be tested on Friday. The tackle he'd be facing for Russellville was six foot nine and three hundred pounds and had committed to the University of Arkansas as a junior. If he could keep Green out of the backfield, they'd have time to pass.

Seward told his defensive backs, "They're very quick and shifty. They'll stop on a dime and change directions. . . . They're counting on us not tackling."

Cox made the most of the day. The ceremony was over by noon and classes were out for the entire afternoon, so he kept the team at practice for three hours and forty-two minutes, running through every drill they had: punt team, Fox in a Box, the Chute (blocking under a low structure to encourage driving off the ball), two-minute offense, groups, goal line, etc. In order to keep the players on the sidelines active while the first team was running plays, he had the bystanders do five pushups for every snap.

The coaches ripped into Damien Lee during the Chute, but after a brief flare of anger, he was philosophical. "You try getting under that chute when you're six-two," he said. "It's all good, though. They're just trying to get into my head."

"We're trying to establish ourselves as a physical football team," Cox told them at the end of the day.

On Thursday, Kaelon Kelleybrew was back at practice. He'd served his ten-day suspension, and Cox, after meeting with him and his mother, Katrina, shortly after the suspension, had allowed him to rejoin the team. At the beginning of the school year, he'd told the Tiger football parents in the auditorium that there was right and wrong and not a lot of gray area, but there was perhaps more gray to Bernie Cox than he chose to admit. He didn't have many regrets in his career, but those he'd articulated involved taking football away from a young man who might have needed it more than another player who followed every rule. For some, and maybe Kelleybrew was one of them and maybe he wasn't, playing football might mean getting a college scholarship, and that was no small thing. But Cox knew for sure that it meant the difference between being a part of a team and being cast adrift, between finding yourself with your peers chafing under the discipline of a cruel old man named Cox and being loosed upon a ruleless world. There were numbers to back him up: The Arkansas Activities Association had commissioned a survey of 24,000 students in Arkansas (including ones from Central) comparing performance of athletes and nonathletes and found that athletes performed better in grade point and graduation rate and had a drop-out rate that was a startling 1 percent of the nonathlete population. "I think me and my son both were nervous," Katrina said about that meeting. "[Coach Cox] was just like, 'All right, we'll see you when you get back.'"

The Tigers, in shorts and shoulder pads, were in the stadium for the normal light workout the day before a game. On the first play, the offensive line blew an assignment, allowing two stunting linemen from the defense to reach the quarterback unabated.

"First play!" yelled Cox. "It's Thursday!"

"We turn two people loose!" bellowed Callaway.

William Bennett, the big defensive end and sometime fullback who had his jersey number, 34, shaved into his hair, joined in: "C'mon! It's Thursday, fellas!"

At the end of practice, Cox covered the schedule for the trip to Russell-ville, seventy-five miles northwest of Little Rock. He explained that if they were ready to go at 2:15—and if they weren't they would be left behind—the bus driver promised them they'd be eating their pregame meal at Ryan's in Russellville by 3:30. "We've got a tight schedule to keep because I'm old-fashioned and I don't want to get you out of class [earlier]," he said. "I believe in education and want you sitting your fat butt in that class and learning something for an hour."

In reciting some of the minutest details of these pregame preparations, Cox was very funny, but he didn't crack a smile. It was as if he were doing a parody of himself for the entertainment of the team.

"We'll have a meal just like we had when we went to Texarkana," he began, "chopped steak, roll, baked potato, side salad, water. . . . One trip to the ice cream bar. Guys, when we went down to Texarkana, you made one trip, all right." The team began to chuckle. "We're going to qualify that one trip tomorrow. One trip: Guess how many bowls you get?" More titters.

"You get one bowl, average human-being size." They howled, and he continued to spool out rules. "Not two bowls. And you don't see how many gallons you can try to put on there. Just get a normal-size serving of ice cream. If you want to doctor it up, then doctor it up . . . but don't spill things all over the floor." The laughter had subsided by then, and he could then drive home his point about how when you were out in public at a restaurant with a game jersey on with TIGERS across the chest, you were going to behave correctly. By then they'd laughed at themselves and they'd laughed at him and if he hadn't exactly laughed at himself he'd at least kind of made fun of himself and that made them more of a team, gave them something to bond around: They were all going to be subject to Coach Cox's draconian ice cream rules.

"Guys, I've got 3:55," he continued. "We're getting through early." He paused and reflected on the practice: "We had a screwup on the very frigging first snap, didn't know what to do. That bothered me. I wish it would bother you. It bothers Coach Finley. Coach Callaway's screaming because it bothers him. It doesn't bother you at all. . . . You guys do not understand the speed of the game when you get to Russellville. . . . Their defense plays a fast game. I've heard coaches tell you several times this week that they get down in a sprinter's stance and they *come!* We didn't get your attention, obviously. . . . You're not stepping down, closing the gap, but you don't care. I wish all of you cared as much as three or four of you do.

"Now, the most important thing on our list for you gutbuckets. You know what a gutbucket is? Somebody that's always what? Hungry." He told them that a local TV station had selected them—"for what reason I do not know"—to receive a burger, fries, and drink from Wendy's after today's practice. "Ketchup, straws, napkins—you guys won't use napkins, but they bring them." They were laughing again. "And what do we do with our trash? Let's just throw it around anywhere you want to, right?"

"No, sir!" they thundered.

"Any questions?"

"No, sir!" they said again, anxious to get to their burgers.

He was ready to dismiss them, but a small voice spoke up from the back.

"Coach, I've got something I want to say." It was Kelleybrew.

"Go ahead," Cox said.

"Uh, I just want to stand up here and apologize to the team and the coaches, for letting y'all down. I know I made a bad choice in what I decided to do. But consequences come with everything. And the consequences I had was that I let y'all down. We lost our perfect season. I think I had something to do with that. But I'm hoping that y'all can forgive me and give me another chance to redeem myself to the players and coaches, and just let me be a part of the team."

Standing next to him, Aaron Nichols, his defensive backfield mate, threw his arm around Kelleybrew's neck.

"You straight, bro," he said.

At that, the other players applauded, and Cox moved toward him and gave him a hug. "Thank you, son. I appreciate you very much," he said.

The moment seemed to soften Cox. There was nothing that touched him more than a player standing up in front of his teammates and taking responsibility for his actions, using words like "consequences" and "forgive." He said, "Guys, tomorrow . . . " Then he paused. "You guys who went to Texarkana, you traveled great. I was proud of you guys. Everybody you came in contact with was proud of you guys. To see young men, some of you sixteen, seventeen, maybe eighteen years old, acting like you did. . . . " Nothing else mattered at this point, not the ice cream sprinkles on the floor of the restaurant in Hope, not the punt returns for touchdowns, not the missed blocks on the first play of the Thursday run-through before a game. No, this was what he coached football for. "Now, you guys who were having a problem picking up the stunts, you sit together on the bus and talk about your assignments. . . . "

||||||||||||||||||||||||||||||||||||||

If there was no coach more respected in central Arkansas than Cox, there was probably none more beloved than Clyde Horton. His association with Central began in 1944, when he was a sophomore halfback on a team that went 10-1 and won the state championship. Two days before the opener for his junior season, he broke his leg and missed the entire year. But during the first game of his senior season in 1946, before nine thousand fans at Quigley, he immediately proved that he was back at full strength, ripping off a forty-five-yard touchdown run in a 31–6 win over Fordyce. After another leg injury in his senior year, he missed playing in the team's victory in the Toy Bowl, a game against Warren Easton High of New Orleans, which Central won 21-7, finishing the season at 14-0. No team that season scored more than seven points on the defense, and Central won eight in shutouts, while the offense averaged forty-one points per game. Thirty-three of the forty-six players earned football scholarships.

After the season, Horton, as he told it, "haystacked"—hitched a ride—from Little Rock to the University of Alabama on an eighteen-wheeler, where he joined the summer session. Suiting up the morning after the all-night trip, he scored five touchdowns in practice. By the end of that year he was a starter on the freshman team, and the third-team right halfback, which was good enough to travel with the Crimson Tide to the 1948 Sugar Bowl.

In the fall of '48, however, Horton, a solid six feet tall and 197 pounds, pulled a muscle in the middle of the season. "I ran hard," he said of his style, "but I wasn't real shifty," so his runs usually ended in collisions and made him prone to injury. He could also see that because of Alabama's offense, he was destined to be a blocking back, not a ball carrier. So he packed his bags and headed back to Arkansas, where he joined his old Little Rock High School coach, Raymond Burnett, who had taken a job at Arkansas Polytechnic College in Russellville and brought seven of Horton's old Tiger teammates with him. There, Horton had a stellar career, setting the Arkansas Intercollegiate Conference record for touchdowns in a game, making five on two different occasions. He received a letter from the Los Angeles Rams about a tryout (if he made the team, he'd get $5,000, a princely sum in those days), but in his penultimate game at Tech, he took a knee in the kidney, an injury bad enough that he knew his football career was over. He turned to coaching instead.

After four years in Fort Smith, where he began supervising track too, he took a job as the head football coach at Russellville High School in 1956, the hometown of his wife, Mary Jo. Back then, it was a tiny town of a little more than eight thousand, before I-40 brought more traffic and industry, and before the McClellan-Kerr river project dammed the Arkansas and created Lake Dardanelle for fishing and boating, and before the nuclear power plant, Arkansas Nuclear One, rose from the banks of the lake and went online in 1974. After three seasons there, he got a call in 1960 to join his old Tiger backfield mate and now Central head coach, Gene Hall, as an assistant; Hall had taken over for Wilson Matthews in 1958, the strange year when the team played while the schools were closed.

Horton spent the next twenty-seven years on the payroll at Central and another six years as a volunteer coach. He became a legend at the school not so much for football, but as head coach of the track team, which he took over in 1963. His teams won eight state track-and-field championships and fourteen state cross-country titles, and he was named the state track coach of the year four times, particularly for his work with hurdlers. Those accomplishments earned him a place in the Arkansas Sports Hall of Fame and the National High School Athletic Coaches Hall of Fame, but Bernie Cox thought he was just as good a football coach. Horton had a friendly drawl and a passionate personality that made him both authoritative and unthreatening. He was a diligent student of the game, but came across as knowledgeable without being autocratic. What made him beloved, what endeared him to his players and their parents, was his philosophy that coaching was a two-way street. "Everybody you coach you learn something from," he said.

Before the Russellville game in 2007, he'd spent some fifteen hours breaking down film and preparing scouting reports for Cox. Some of the best defensive linemen to play at Central had benefited from his tutelage, and this season, at age seventy-seven, he was still sweating out the 100°F Arkansas days to work with Jared Green.

That he was standing on Central's good ground and not residing under the ground somewhere was the biggest surprise. "This guy should have died," said Ron Hardin, a gastroenterologist in Little Rock who treated Horton. In 1997, Horton had become very ill with a mysterious malady that left him, he said, "bleeding three different ways"—urine, stool, and nose—and unable to eat. He went to see a dozen doctors over the next few months, at the same time "losing a pound a day," said Mary Jo. Nothing they suspected checked out: cancer, lupus, severe allergies. Late that year, he was hospitalized in Little Rock for a week after having dropped sixty pounds, the tough halfback who had ended every run with a collision now down to 127.

By early 1998, the Hortons and their doctors contacted the Mayo Clinic to see if its diagnosticians could give it a shot. The branch of the clinic that had the soonest opening was in Jacksonville, Florida, and off he went for tests and more tests. Over the next two weeks, the doctors were still scratching their heads until the file landed on the desk of an interventional pathologist, Dr. Kenneth Batts, at the main Mayo Clinic in Rochester, Minnesota, who determined that Horton had a rare condition called Cronkhite-Canada syndrome, named after the original discoverers and marked by the emergence of polyps in the intestinal tract and various skin problems.

Mary Jo remembered the doctors' excitement back in Florida when they came in with the diagnosis: "It was like they won the Super Bowl." That success was tempered by the next piece of information, the syndrome's "progressive course and thus poor prognosis," as one textbook put it. Horton's case was only the third Mayo had ever seen, and the other two who'd been afflicted had died.

There was no cure, and what little treatment they could give him included removing the polyps during colonoscopies and supplying the nutrients that the growths had prevented Horton's body from absorbing. When he was out of immediate danger, he returned to Little Rock and for much of the next two years subsisted on a diet of Ensure and Wendy's Frosty desserts. There were dangerous recurrences along the way, the most serious, late in 1998, requiring a return trip to Jacksonville for a splenectomy after another period of dramatic weight loss. For nearly two years after the onset, he was too weak to do more than move from bed to recliner to bathroom, and he was often hospitalized in Little Rock. During one admission, he reviewed his will from his bed. "They really felt I was about to go," he said. Though Horton was supposed to see only family, when Bernie Cox heard of his dire condition, he sneaked into the intensive care unit to say a final good-bye to his longtime friend and colleague: Horton had been at Central when Cox came to the school in 1972 as an assistant and had stood at his side through the five state championships the Tigers had won to that point.

Clyde Horton survived that scare. Slowly, he began to recover his strength, though he still required repeated trips to Jacksonville for colonos-copies and removal of the polyps, none of which were cancerous. His immune system had been compromised by his body's failure to absorb nutri-ents, and his bone density was low, necessitating continual monitoring of his protein and vitamin levels.

Encouraged and supported by his family, friends, and church, he emerged by degrees from the prison of the disease. He started taking short walks around the neighborhood by the beginning of 2000. Then in 2001, he told Mary Jo he wanted to start playing golf again, and though she was wary, she'd heard from the doctors that his hardheadedness had aided his recovery, so she didn't see any reason to hold him back. By 2003, he was on the golf course every morning with his longtime friends from the old Tiger teams of the '40s, and in the afternoons he was again helping the current Tigers as a volunteer assistant. He celebrated with the back-to-back state championship squads of 2003 and 2004, tutoring defensive line players who would earn all-state honors and football scholarships. Though he was thinking that he might want to take himself off the sidelines once again, he decided to stick it out through 2007 to see Jared Green through his senior season.

As the bus pulled off Interstate 40 into Ryan's in Russellville, Horton still marveled at the growth of the town and said, "Used to have just a dairy" here in town. The hourglass-shaped tower of the nuclear plant loomed in the distance, sucking up water from Lake Dardanelle for the cooling process and making Russellville a real-world analogue to the Springfield of *Simpsons* TV fame. The stadium's bucolic setting—a wooded stream ran behind the visitors' stands—featured expert topiary in the south end zone, hedges shaped into the word CYCLONES. An angry cartoon twister also adorned the press box, raising the question of why a nuclear plant might be located in purported cyclone country. Ringing the field was an eight-lane track that, like the one at Texarkana, filled Clyde Horton with envy. He never failed to lament the state of the track at Quigley: First, its cinders had been covered in asphalt in the name of maintenance, and then more recently it had been reduced from six lanes to four by the expansion of the field for soccer. The track was not fit for running anymore, and it grieved him.

The racial makeup of Russellville High School, about 80 percent white, 10 percent Hispanic, and 6 percent black, mirrored the town, but the pre-game crowd in the student parking lot, overwhelmingly white, was all about "getting ratchet" with Louisiana rapper Hurricane Chris's infectious song "A Bay Bay," one of the big hits of 2007.

The next day, Hurricane Chris would appear with a host of rap stars at a benefit in Birmingham, Alabama, for the Jena Six, a group of black high school students from Jena, Louisiana, who had been charged in a fight the previous year. It began when black students sat under a tree that was usually a gathering place for white students, and nooses were subsequently hung from its branches. A series of racial conflicts followed, ending with an attack on a white student, who was not badly hurt (he appeared at a school function that night), but six black teenagers were charged as adults with attempted murder. The charges drew outrage nationally from the African American community, and the week before the Little Rock Nine commemoration, one of the largest civil rights rallies in recent years in Jena had drawn ten thousand people. The charges also dovetailed with John Walker's repeated assertion that blacks in the court system often got due process but not equal protection. In Little Rock that week, Harvard Law School professor Charles Ogletree, the author of *With All Deliberate Speed*, a book about the *Brown* decision, said that he thought the rally represented "the rebirth of the civil rights movement." Democratic presidential candidate Barack Obama issued a statement saying, "When a noose hangs from a schoolyard tree in the 21st century and young men are treated in a way that is not equal nor just, it is not just an offense to the people of Jena or to the African-American community, it is an offense to the ideals we hold as Americans." Hillary Clinton similarly decried the treatment of the black students in a statement: "Situations like this one remind us that we all have a responsibility to confront racial injustice and intolerance." At the time, Clinton was leading Obama in the polls among African Americans, 51 percent to 38 percent.

Minnijean Brown Trickey, the day before the commemoration of her integration of Central, took time to do an interview with CBC/Radio-Canada addressing parallels between the Jena Six and the Little Rock Nine. What troubled her most was the effort by local officials in Louisiana to gloss over the conflict. "I heard this script," she said, "'We're fine . . . there's no racism here. It's outside agitators.' . . . That just rang really resonant with me, because that was the sort of script used in the '50s and '60s regarding desegregation. . . . Obviously this is a complex situation and I'm not there but those voices denying the problem made me shudder. . . . The work that needed to be done to dismantle racism never happened and young people are still living segregated lives, in the entire nation, as a matter of fact. I feel like this is a flare-up based on a smoldering problem. The sad part is that it only catches our attention when there's a flare-up."

(The Jena case ended in 2009 with five of the black students pleading no contest to misdemeanor simple battery and being sentenced to seven days' probation and fined $500 plus court costs; the other student had earlier pleaded guilty to second-degree battery and was sentenced to eighteen months in jail. The original judge was removed against his will from the case when he called the students "troublemakers.")

Closer to game time, the rap from students' cars gave way to music from the marching band, the setting sun glinting off the brass. "We're a large school with a small-town atmosphere," Russellville coach Jeff Holt said later. "If you've ever been a part of small-town football, you know—the town kind of lives around that."

After Central kicked off, Russellville put the ball in play from its own 21-yard line. Quarterback Blake Humphrey threw a quick pass behind the line of scrimmage to wide receiver Derek Owens, who first evaded safety Aaron Nichols and then headed up the sideline, ultimately dashing past Kameron Finney for a seventy-nine-yard touchdown with only forty-six seconds gone in the game.

Up in the Central stands, Kaelon Kelleybrew dropped his head into his hands. Finney was playing in his spot, as safety. Kelleybrew's suspension was over and he'd practiced on Thursday, and the apology he had made to the coaches and team "lifted so much off my shoulders," he said, but he was still suffering the consequences of his actions—Cox kept him out of the game because he'd been there for only one day of practice that week. If he'd been able to come to practice on Wednesday, he could have played. Instead, after making certain it was okay with principal Nancy Rousseau for him to attend the game, he'd driven to Russellville and sat in the stands. Now this, just like at Texarkana: a long touchdown play to put them behind early. He knew that nobody on Russellville's team could have outrun him. With him in the game, there would have been no touchdown on the first play. He would have taken the right angle.

But here he was in the stands and there was A.J. on the sidelines on crutches—two leaders of the best defense in the state wearing jeans on game night. It wasn't right. Even missing two starters, Central's defense could usually keep the team in any game, but with the erratic offense, it wasn't going to be easy to claw back into a game after they'd fallen behind.

Throughout the first quarter, the offense was doing the usual sputtering, and tempers were igniting. De'Arius Hudson, the left offensive tackle, came off the field yelling, "He can't talk to me like that!" and Stan Williams tried to calm him down. After receiver Lamont Lacefield was tackled in the end zone on a reverse for a safety, making the score 9–0 as the first quarter ended, he came to the sidelines upset, and Finley had to pull him aside and reassure him, "It wasn't your fault, it's our fault."

In the second quarter, an interception by safety Aaron Nichols, along with a nifty, twisting thirty-two-yard runback, gave the Tigers a lift and put them into Russellville territory, but again the offense stalled. Rankin's punt on fourth down rolled out of bounds at the 1, and the Tiger defense dug in. Even if the offense couldn't score, maybe the defense could get that safety back, or at least give the offense some good field position. The Cyclones' quarterback sneaked for one yard on first down. On the next play he dropped back, and his line closed down the Central rush and allowed him to heave the ball thirty yards downfield behind the surprised secondary. Receiver Josh Cloud caught the ball in stride and outran pursuers for a ninety-eight-yard touchdown and a 16–0 lead. "We were just looking for a place to punt," Russellville coach Jeff Holt said later. "But then I said, 'You know, that's not us.' We're going to try to attack no matter where we're at."

At halftime in the visitors' locker room of the field house, which was much nicer than Quigley's home locker room, Cox told them, "Your lack of character is showing. . . . We're not coming together to change anything. We don't have eleven people who want to be a team, who want to be a unit, who want to be together. Yesterday, first play, you didn't block anybody. When is it going to happen?

"You're missing to me one of the greatest things about athletics. And that's about loving and respecting and caring about one another. You should be learning this in this program. I've failed you in that respect. I don't see that, and that bothers me more than anything else, more than the score on the scoreboard at Cyclone Stadium."

After halftime, nothing changed. In the third quarter, the Cyclones scored on a twenty-five-yard touchdown pass, and the ineptitude of the Tiger offense all but ensured that the 23–0 lead was insurmountable. After Russellville's kickoff, on first down the Central center sent the ball flying over Rankin's head, creating a second and thirty-three. The frustration and lack of unity that Cox had identified at halftime infected the fans; a fight was brewing in the Tiger stands.

Even as tight end Damien Lee was finishing one of the best Central plays of the night, taking a pass from Rankin and running over two Russellville players for a twenty-three-yard gain, one player's mother was addressing two men sitting behind her who had apparently been complaining about the team's performance.

"We have children out there, and you've been talking smack the entire game," she said to them.

After a heated back and forth, a father marched up the bleachers from a few rows below and confronted them. "Stop," he said, looming over the two men, "or I'm going to come back up here and kick your goddamn ass."

"You are?"

"Yes, I sure as hell am. Shut your damn mouth!"

All three men were wearing caps with the Central logo.

It didn't seem that things could get worse, but they did.

In the fourth quarter, a Russellville player caught a pass at midfield along the Central sideline, then stopped and started to avoid a tackler before William Bennett, the relentless 235-pound defensive end, caught up with him at a full run and they tumbled out of bounds, a four-hundred-pound mass of momentum, right into Clyde Horton.

The coach tried to get out of the way, but the players rolled into his legs, snapping his body down like the sprung arm of a mousetrap. His head struck the ground. Two Tiger players bent over him and tried to help him up, but trainer Brian Cox rushed over to stop them. Horton staggered a bit to one knee as Brian questioned him. Larry Siegel arrived, and before anybody else knew what was going on, as the Central band continued playing and the cheerleaders ran through their routine, Horton was back on his feet, seemingly unhurt.

It was exactly the kind of hit that had fractured both bones in A. J. Williams's lower leg, yet Horton popped back up as if he were playing for Central in 1946. And it was just what Mary Jo had feared when he had returned to the sidelines, that the bones made brittle by Cronkhite-Canada might meet a force that would shatter them. Yet somehow they had held firm and Clyde Horton stood on the sidelines for the sad, sorry end of the game, as he had so often for so many wins and very few of these kinds of losses since he started coaching right there at Russellville High in 1956. It was the first time Central had failed to score in ten years.

The game ended, and the Tigers, Horton included, boarded the bus home.

The postmortem among the coaches focused on the lack of chemistry. The team seemed listless from the beginning of the game, emotionally absent. Cox narrowed it down to a "tremendous communication problem" between players themselves and between coaches and players. Seward added, "You've got people blaming each other."

In the aftermath of a bad loss, after a long bus ride late on Friday night, Callaway saw only disorder and need everywhere he looked. He lamented the youth of the offensive line and thought back wistfully to Central's stable of excellent running backs from previous years. "Bo's okay," he said, "but he's no Charles Clay or Mickey Dean or Dedrick Poole." He glanced at the all-state plaques and pictures haphazardly hung on the office walls with those past players' names etched on them. Then his eyes seemed to range over the dingy yellow paint, stained ceiling tiles, and cheek-by-jowl desks. "This is the pits here," he said. "When you've got a place the kids appreciate, they're going to come up there and use it."

Finley wasn't so sure. "Different kids, different program," he said. "They just don't love it. We can't give up on them, but they don't love football." He didn't think the situation was hopeless, though, and he threw the responsibility right back on himself and the coaches. "They need us bad, now. When they panic, we can't panic," he continued, and he cited one player's sidelines diatribe against a teammate. "He was panicking, and he was asking for help. You've got to read them."

"Our kids were never emotionally in that ball game," Cox said.

On Monday, the team spent an hour watching game film, and the coaches tried to address specific things the players were doing wrong. "I want you to accept this in the spirit it's offered," said Cox to the team. The next game was homecoming against Conway, one of the weaker teams in the conference, but Finley wasn't going to wait to see if that fact would inspire them. During the film viewing in the locker room, at one point Finley rushed the screen and pointed to Russellville's players. "I want you to look at something," he told them. "Look at the body language of that stance." Just as Cox had told them before the game, every Cyclone was in a sprinter's stance, ready to fire off the line. "I'm gonna need some leaders," Finley said. "I've failed you because I knew in the spring we needed that, and I didn't get on you."

The practice was brisk and had a sense of newness about it. The school spirit leaders had adopted a blackout theme for the game and encouraged all the fans to wear black clothing. When the players broke their huddles on Monday, their chant was "Blackout!" There were personnel changes as well.

Jared Green and nose guard Quinton Brown had come to Cox more than once during the year and told him that if he needed them to play offense too, they were ready to do it. For Conway, Cox was convinced he needed to keep his best athletes out there, so he told the coaches that Kelleybrew was starting at split end and Brown at left guard. (Green had hurt his shoulder, so he was going to be kept out of contact for the week of practice and continue to play only defense.)

At the end of the day Cox gave a short speech, saying that he hoped they'd all taken any criticism in the way it had been intended, which was . . .

"To make us better," they answered.

When Cox asked the usual pro forma "Any questions?" lineman Kyle Temple spoke up.

"How's Coach Horton?" he asked.

"Coach Horton is bruised up," Cox said. "His knee is swollen. His head hit a pretty good lick, but it's his knee and ankle more than anything. He hopes to be out here tomorrow, but I don't know. . . . He's in good spirits, though."

Coach Horton didn't show up the rest of the week. He was getting around with a cane, but Cox didn't want him anywhere close to the action to risk getting hurt again.

Before the game on Friday, Cox told the other coaches that the team was at a critical point. "I want to be positive tonight," he said. "I'm the first one to be negative, Callaway's the second, but I want to be positive tonight." He had adopted Finley's theme: "If we panic, then they do."

Seward tried to fire up the defense. "Guys," he told them, "we let you down last week. The coaches sat down here on Saturday and said, 'They don't look like they're having fun.' You looked miserable. You cannot win a football game when you're in misery. . . . I'd love to see you be vicious and violent tonight. I'd love to see you play with viciousness in your heart—not breaking the rules, but defense is passion!"

Cox closed off the pregame talk by encouraging them to "play hard and have fun."

Finley was making sure the sidelines were engaged with the game. Addressing sophomore running back Tim "T.T." Campbell, he said, "T.T., watch the running backs." And to the other backups: "I want offense down at this end and defense there—watching and talking. You're going to help me tonight, or I'm going to send you in [to the locker room]. Your mama comes down here and doesn't help out, I'm gonna send her in. And your daddy, too. And if Mrs. Rousseau comes down here and doesn't help out, I'm going to send her in, too."

Early in the game, Ryan Conley, a junior starting for the first time at defensive end, took up Seward's call for viciousness and, on the opening Conway offensive series, laid out the quarterback on an incomplete pass. Larry Siegel had told them earlier that the QB was a second or third stringer playing for the first time in Quigley and he wanted to send him a message: "Nothing illegal—no flags, no late hits—but I want to get his attention early." Linebacker Hunter Sinele followed up with a perfectly timed pop on him as he scrambled out of bounds at the Central sideline, drawing "Ooooo"s from the black-clad crowd.

On offense Rankin fumbled at the Conway 30 after a seven-play drive, but didn't seem in a funk about it. When Central next got the ball back, he hit Kelleybrew on a slant that the receiver turned back toward the sideline for a thirty-three-yard gain. Five straight runs by Tim Dunn took the ball to the 1, where Rankin sneaked over.

On the sidelines, the backup players were chanting "Deee-fense" along with the crowd. And when Central got the ball back, Rankin threw a quick hitch to Kelleybrew, who outran the Conway secondary down the sideline for a sixty-seven-yard touchdown that was almost an exact replica of one of Russellville's touchdowns of the week before. Kelleybrew seemed to own the game when he scooped up a fumble to set up another Rankin touchdown pass, this time to tight end Damien Lee, who caught the ball at the 10 and put a spin move on the defender for a score. Even though Conway returned the following kickoff for a touchdown and then picked off a Rankin pass and returned it for another six with only a minute left in the half to make the score 21–14, the buoyant, confident mood of the Tigers wasn't stanched.

At halftime the players were joking around and laughing—lineman Taylor James-Lightner was showing fullback Will Rollins how to execute a proper stiff arm—and a couple of the players from the 2003 and 2004 championship teams were in the locker room, having returned for homecoming. Cox would ordinarily have fumed and raged about how they let Conway back into the game with two stupid mistakes, but this time, as difficult as it was for him, he held his tongue. After all, he'd told them to play hard and have fun and they were certainly doing that. He gave no halftime speech.

In the fourth quarter Conway's last threat to score stalled at the Central 39 with fifty-four seconds left in the game, and Central had its homecoming game victory to go 2-1 in the conference and 4-2 overall. Though the offense moved the ball fairly easily, the fumbles—especially the two by Dunn, one lost at the 6-yard line—were troubling. But it was sure nice to have Kelleybrew back. As Finley said on the sidelines at one point in the third quarter: "If we throw the ball, we're going to throw it downfield where Kelleybrew can go up and get it."

Back in the corner of the coaches' office where the plaster tiger silently roared, its head piled with hats and its mouth holding coat hangers, Larry Siegel said, "It was like old times." He meant all kinds of things: the players from those title teams were back in the locker room, Central ran the ball with authority, the defense shut down the opponent, the fans were excited, there was real teamwork both on the field and on the sidelines, the players were having fun, and the Tigers won.

"I thought the attitude on the sidelines was great from the start," said Cox, but he couldn't help looking ahead warily to next week and the Cabot Panthers. "We'll have as tough a game next week as we'll have all year."

"Same old Cabot?" Siegel asked, referring to the Panthers' relentless run game.

Finley answered with one surprising fact. "They've got this black nose guard . . . "

"Really?" said Siegel.

CHAPTER 9

ON THE OFFENSIVE

THE WEEK OF THE CABOT GAME, the runoff between Micheal Daugherty and Anna Swaim for the school board seat from Zone 2 was nearing its combative conclusion. The three weeks since the last race had seen an outpouring of invective, not necessarily from the candidates, but from their supporters.

Lining up behind Swaim was the poison pen of the *Democrat-Gazette*'s editorial page, which continued to hammer Daugherty and the other members of the "Gang of Four" on the board for "putting education last," behind "patronage, ill-feelings, and the lawyers seeking an easy payday at the taxpayer's expense." The paper never failed to write a story about Daugherty, either in the news sections or on the editorial page, that didn't include a reference to his failure to speak to the paper, the decade-old controversy about his academic degrees, or tax liens on his business. Even Swaim, while not disowning the importance of the paper's endorsement, called its "Gang of Four" label for the black board members and other statements "unreasonably nasty editorial comments." Despite Swaim's attempt to tiptoe around the paper's support, its editorials' cheerleading on her behalf served only to unify the opposition against her.

Not many people could find harsh things to say about Anna Swaim, but on his blog longtime local commentator Pat Lynch dubbed her the "darling of the downtown business elites and professional mouthpiece for greedy corporate special interests," that is, the Arkansas Forestry Association, where she was communications director. The group counted among its members companies like Deltic Timber, the force behind the booming Chenal neighborhood in west Little Rock, and International Paper. The *Democrat-Gazette* had also reported that contributors to her campaign included big real estate developers and bank presidents. As for Daugherty's money sources, the *Democrat-Gazette* led with a bit of code easily discernible by longtime Little Rock residents: "The first contribution listed on Daugherty's campaign contribution report is $100 from the Sandpiper Club, a local private nightclub." Located on Asher Avenue, the club had often been the site of trouble, and on September 29, eleven days before the election, Little Rock's thirty-fifth homicide of the year had taken place in the parking lot. Five days before the election, the city filed suit under a nuisance law to have the club shut down.

Neither Daugherty nor Swaim was as dogmatically ideological or bought-and-sold by his or her respective special interests as opponents painted them. The year before, Daugherty had voted for extending to five schools in the district the Achievement Challenge merit-pay program, which was funded by, among others, the Hussman Foundation, the charitable arm of the family of Walter Hussman Jr., the *Democrat-Gazette*'s publisher. (A fellow "Gang" member, Katherine Mitchell, had cast a dissenting vote.) Swaim had said she preferred awarding merit pay based on the Milken Family Foundation's Teacher Advancement Program, which advocates basing compensation on a combination of professional development and student achievement, and supported permitting collective bargaining with the Classroom Teachers Association, contrary to the newspaper's strong antiunion stand. After weighing both candidates' qualifications and qualities, even as liberal a voice as Max Brantley and the *Arkansas Times* came down slightly on the side of Swaim, who, he said in an editorial, "can't win without biracial support. Should she achieve that, her election would be a hugely hopeful sign. I also wouldn't fear Daugherty's re-election if the less predictable Daugherty of earlier years reemerged. That's unlikely, however, if his victory is a product of racially polarized voting. Then, the 4-3 division will continue. And all will pay a price."

The continuing desegregation case dogged the election. A week before the runoff, John Walker had filed his appeal of the district court's February decision that the school district was unitary. Earlier that year, the board had voted, by the four-to-three vote that was inevitably termed "racially divided," to mediate the case in order to forestall an appeal—that is, to negotiate with Walker even though he had lost. The board's counsel, Chris Heller, saw no reason to undertake mediation; the district had already been declared unitary, he reasoned, so let Walker take his chances with the court on appeal (even though Walker had enjoyed much success in the Eighth Circuit over the years). Swaim also had declared that she was not in favor of mediation, though she added that she would "approach [Walker's] involvement with an open mind." Daugherty said that court supervision during the years of Walker's desegregation litigation had made the district "much better suited to deal with the edicts of No Child Left Behind" and that "every child in the LRSD has benefited in some way from the actions of Mr. Walker and the Joshua Intervenors." Thus, mediation, he seemed to imply, might lock in those achievement improvements Walker had long argued for.

The runoff turnout exceeded the general election's by 50 percent, and when the results came in to the Daugherty watch party on John Barrow Road, he had been reelected 1,449 to 1,256, allowing the board to retain its "historic majority," as a local newscaster reported. Daugherty—and almost everyone else—seemed ready to leave the contest and its racially charged rhetoric behind. He told a local TV station: "It'll be a collaborative effort between the board—the whole board—as to where we want to go. . . . I hope it's not an adversarial type of thing; . . . at this point I envision the district trying to heal itself." Skip Rutherford, a former school board member and dean of the University of Arkansas's Clinton School of Public Service, said, "When the election is over, you start governing, and this election is over." But not without one more swipe by the paper: The paper's election-day roundup once again reviewed the candidates' financial support and ended the story with this line about Daugherty's funding sources: "The Sandpiper Club also was a contributor."

|||||||||||||||||||||||||||||||||||||||||

That week, Cabot's citizens were preparing for two of the biggest events of the fall: the homecoming game against Central on Friday night and the start of deer muzzleloader season on Saturday. Many of the fans were plotting their weekend with military precision and stocking their trucks for an immediate getaway after the game on Friday. In the stands, plenty of camouflage mixed with the Panther red and white.

Cabot is a booming community twenty-five miles northeast of Little Rock, off the main artery for that area, Arkansas Highway 67/167. The *WPA Guide to 1930s Arkansas* listed the town's population as only 741, and its most notable feature (the only one cited) was that it was the hometown of Roark Bradford, who as a youth spent his "Saturdays loafing around the cotton gin, absorbing patterns of Negro thought and details of Negro phraseology." He later wrote a book that became the basis for the play and film *The Green Pastures*. Enormously popular with both black and white Southern audiences of the 1930s (in segregated theaters), the musical was a retelling of the Bible in African American dialect and rousing gospel songs. Both Bradford and the play's author, Marc Connelly, who won a Pulitzer Prize for drama for the stage adaptation, were white.

Bradford might have a hard time finding inspiration in Cabot these days. By the 2000 census, the population had grown to 15,261, of whom fifty were black, totaling 0.3 percent. That number was exceeded by all other ethnic minorities except residents of "Native Hawaiian and Other Pacific Islander" origin. The town's population had almost doubled since 1990 (when black Cabotites had numbered seventeen). Over the past twenty years, the town, which is just across the Pulaski County border in Lonoke County, had gained a reputation as a "white flight" community where residents might commute into Little Rock, but find reasonable real estate prices and good public schools that were not subject to the desegregation turmoil that was roiling Little Rock and its fellow districts in the county.

In 2006 a Brookings Institution study, relying on 2000 census data, determined that the Little Rock metropolitan area ranked second in the United States in exurban population; it defined an "exurban" community purely in demographic terms as one that was connected to an urban area, exhibited low housing density, and was experiencing explosive growth. Bryant, south of Little Rock in Saline County, was another of the communities outside Pulaski County that contributed to Little Rock's high ranking. Movement to areas outside the county, according to Hendrix professor Jay Barth, stemmed largely from the effects of Judge Henry Woods's 1984 decision ordering that all three Pulaski County school districts merge. In order to desegregate the entire county, it had been expected that widespread busing would be the remedy. The decision was overturned a year later, but not before jump-starting the exodus as well as spurring the creation of a host of private schools.

"At the dawn of the twenty-first century," wrote Kevin M. Kruse in his book *White Flight*, "white flight had spread from the city through the suburbs to a new exurban frontier, with no signs of slowing down." Although Kruse was speaking of Atlanta, his conclusions were applicable to Little Rock and many other southern cities. A 2007 census study bore out his prediction for Cabot and other exurban towns: While Little Rock had grown less than 1 percent since 2000 and North Little Rock's population had declined by 2.5 percent, Cabot had expanded by 43.5 percent. Kruse identified in these new communities an obscure or *obscured* foundation in the segregationist beliefs that originally drove the growth of the suburbs. What he calls the "modern suburban conservative agenda"—a "secessionist stance" toward the cities, a demand for individual rights, "fervent faith" in free enterprise, and objection to federal meddling—"was, in fact, first advanced and articulated in the resistance of southern whites to desegregation."

Anecdotal evidence of racial intolerance in Cabot was not hard to find, even with so few targets in residence. In 1995, for the homecoming parade, a group of students had adorned a float with a Confederate flag and a hangman's noose, which held a representation of a cougar, the mascot for the predominantly black team they were playing from Helena, Arkansas. School administrators disciplined the students, who denied there was a racial component to the display. More recently, in January of 2007, Marcel Williams, an African American woman whose husband was in Iraq and who had moved to Cabot the previous May, found "move nigga" spray-painted on her garage door. She called 911, the mayor came to her house and painted over it himself, and the Federal Bureau of Investigation was looking into it as a potential hate crime. Williams told the local paper that she liked her house and neighborhood and that it "doesn't make me have second thoughts about living in Cabot." At the time, Internet discussion boards like those on City-data.com often heatedly debated the idea of whether or not Cabot was a racist place, but few denied that its homogenous population sometimes left it open to such charges, including one about the football team. "Ask the kids that play football against Cabot High if they think Cabot is racist," said one poster called North Pulaski Player. "Let's be honest—If you have too much melanin in your skin, then Cabot is not the place for you."

Thus, when Finley broke the news to Larry Siegel that Cabot had a black nose guard, he was surprised. The player in question was T. J. Bertrand, a sophomore who had been forced north with his family after Hurricane Katrina.

Coach Mike Malham had led the Cabot Panthers football team for twenty-seven years. He'd been a star quarterback and linebacker at McClellan High in the 1970s and then at Arkansas State University in Jonesboro, playing for his father at both schools. He was drafted by the Chicago Bears after college, but a broken arm had kept him from pursuing a pro career. After a couple of years as an assistant at Jacksonville High, the head job opened up at Cabot, he got it, and he'd been there ever since, amassing a record, up to the Central game, of 216 wins, 88 losses, and 4 ties, including two state championships. He was an old-school disciplinarian. "He'll get so excited on the sideline," Norman Callaway said, "he'll go crazy."

His system was predicated on getting the most out of limited talent: He lined up his players in a Dead T formation and ran dives up the middle or off tackle, with misdirection and option plays thrown in for unpredictability. In 2007, sophomore fullback Michael James, number 14, a straight-ahead runner who might carry thirty times a game, was the key. Cox told the Tigers that week that they shouldn't get cocky when looking at the 165-pound linemen across from them. "We've got better athletes than they do," he said. "They're a whole lot better disciplined than we are." One of the coaching advantages of being in a single-high-school district like Cabot was that you knew exactly who your players were going to be years in advance.

Without exaggeration, the Central coaches talked about how Cabot players had been learning the offense they were going to run in high school since the third grade.

"They will play forty-eight minutes," Cox added. "You don't think their little sophomore quarterback can beat you? You have to prove that he can't."

To counter Cabot's running game, Cox had decided to go to an eight-man front. "If they throw," he said, "it will be play action."

"They run that wraparound draw," Seward added. "It went for about twenty yards against Catholic," which had handed Cabot its only loss of the year two weeks earlier. "They ran it twice against us last year."

"I think we can man up on them," said Siegel.

"They wore our butts out last year," Cox said, though Central had won in a close game at Quigley. "We're going to gamble rather than have them knock us off the ball."

"We're going to have to play the best technique football we can play," said Callaway.

On offense Cox boiled down the execution to one simple rule: "We're going to commit to getting the ball to Kelleybrew."

On Tuesday at practice, Siegel had drawn up an eight-man defensive front on a manila folder. Cox wanted to use Jared Green on offense in addition to defense, but wasn't sure his injured shoulder could take the pounding of going both ways. Damien Lee, the tight end, was also getting some reps on defense and was having a good week of practice. He'd earned praise from Cox for trying to get the offense in the right formation during one series.

Of course, they should have been in the right formation from the start, but the offense was still showing signs of dysfunction. Finley was lamenting the lack of a breakaway back. Bo Dillon was solid, but he was not going to outrun anybody, and Dunn had the straight-line speed, but Finley thought his running was "mechanical." During a sweep play in practice, Finley held an imaginary Xbox controller in his hands and moved his thumbs over it frantically. "I want somebody to hit that turbo or X button or whatever it is," he told the offense.

"Sprint," Damien Lee said. "On Madden, it's sprint."

Worse, the backs were still putting the ball on the ground, fumbling far too often. Cox sent the whole team to the bleachers as punishment. For linebacker Hunter Sinele, the fumbling was a symptom of attitude: "We should be able to beat anybody. We have the talent. We just don't have enough guys who really care." One of those guys who did was Green, who got in Tim Dunn's face over his miscues. "You fumbled three times today," Green said. "Somebody's got to say something to you!" Cox echoed Sinele's sentiment at the end of one practice when he held up his open hand and said that there were only five guys on the team "who will come out here and work hard and bust their butts the entire day. Quinton Brown doesn't care who gets the job done, he just wants the job done—he's one of those five."

Returning to one of his themes of the year—the reluctance to admit mistakes—he referred to a sign he kept on his desk that read, "It's amazing what can be accomplished when no one cares who gets the credit." But of most of them, he said, "You go home and you look in that mirror for an hour and tell that mirror how great you are: 'Me, I did this, I did that. Those coaches don't know anything. Coach Cox is so foolish. He screams and hollers at me, and I'm doing everything perfect, because I'm a perfect human being. Tell me I am, Mirror, tell me I am.'"

He pleaded with them to encourage each other and not just be concerned about themselves. "We're not a family, we're afraid to be a family, you're afraid to touch the kid next to you. You're afraid to hug somebody's neck. You're afraid to say 'I love you' if you're a male. If it's not a sixteen-year-old girl, you won't say that. . . . There's nothing wrong with the word 'love.' . . . Let's care about each other. I wish it would go beyond this football field, I wish it would go beyond school, I wish you guys would get to be close and be friends and care about each other. . . . Learn to stand together."

The night before the Cabot game, several players met at Aaron Nichols's house to watch film of the Cabot-Catholic game. The living room of the tidy, modest ranch in southwest Little Rock was furnished with a couple of overstuffed sofas oriented toward a fifty-two-inch flat-screen television on the wall. The group studying the film included Rickey Hicks; Quinton

Brown; Jared Green and his twin brother, Johnathan; Tim Dunn; Aaron Nichols; Denzel Harris; and a few others. Though an invitation had been extended widely after practice, no white players were there. Cheese dip and chips were the foods of choice.

The players stopped and started the tape and commented on Cabot's team.

"Need to turn that option up," Denzel Harris said after one Cabot play.

"How big is 14?" said Hicks, a defensive lineman, referring to Cabot's fullback, Michael James.

"Not big at all," said Aaron Nichols.

"They look extremely slow," said Hicks.

In play after play, as James pounded the middle for Cabot, his powerful running style won grudging admiration and comparisons with Razorbacks fullback Peyton Hillis, a Conway graduate.

"That dude is a player," said Nichols of James.

"Their center is X-rated," said Hicks. "He got in a four-point stance and he hit that linebacker. Look at him knock that linebacker off, every time."

Firm analysis soon turned to insult, needle, and boast.

"Number 72 looks like a white Rickey," said Harris.

"You saw a neck roll and you said that, that's it," said Hicks.

"He's got the arm pads and he's got the neck roll," said Harris.

"My arm pads come from here to here and they say, 'Under Armour,'" Hicks countered. "He ain't got nothing from here to here."

"His say . . . D-1," quipped Harris.

"He can go to D-1, that's fine," said Hicks, "but he don't look like me. So he won't look good going to D-1."

"That tackle on my side," said Jared Green, "is not firing off the ball and he will regret it." He then got up to go into the kitchen.

"Are you going to get me a drink?" Hicks said.

"No, you ain't talking to me like that," Green responded.

"Jared, will you please get me a drink? Thank you, my best friend in the world. You know I love you. See, Coach Cox said we don't tell each other we love each other, but we tell each other we love each other all the time."

After half an hour, the game film gave way to Madden NFL 07, and the players became raucous, high-fiving and whooping with abandon. Jared Green took over the controls as the Kansas City Chiefs while his brother, Johnathan, manipulated the Atlanta Falcons, with Michael Vick at quarterback.

"You're an idiot!"

"Go back, go back!"

"You got caught inside!"

"Up the middle, up the middle!"

"Michael Vick can't run on me!"

"Way to put a hurt on somebody!"

After one good defensive play, Jared, serving as his own commentator in the broadcast booth of his mind, cried, "Jared Green with the tackle! He is a beast! That dude is a beast!"

"He is obese!" came a comment from the couch in imitation of the 285-pound Green. It was junior defensive back Cherard Grant, who smiled widely at his own wordplay, showing the braces on his teeth. The others howled with laughter and repeated the line a half-dozen times.

"Did you hear what he said? 'He is obese!'"

"That was a good one."

The ones who weren't playing browsed through a copy of *King* magazine and passed around a notebook computer on which they checked their Facebook pages. Eventually, Jared got tired of the Madden game and abandoned it, trailing 28–14. The gathering moved into the kitchen, where the players got into a heated discussion about the Russellville game and who was responsible for the three touchdown passes the Cyclones had thrown on the secondary. Aaron Nichols felt impugned.

"I play better," said Nichols, "when I know the whole load's not on me. Kelleybrew will be back and Ke'Won's playing better. In Russellville we started two corners and it was their first start."

Just then, Nichols's grandmother, whom everyone there called Mawmaw, spoke up.

"Everybody wants to be a star," she began, her voice strong over the noise. "Everybody stars when the whole team plays together as one, not when I'm trying to showcase and you're trying to showcase and he's trying to showcase. . . . Each of you needs to play the best that you know how to play. Everybody has their own unique abilities, right?"

Someone made a comment under his breath and Rickey Hicks made a move in that direction before Mawmaw raised her hand to stop him.

"I'm not playing," said Mawmaw to Hicks. "Sit down."

"Did you hear what he said?" Hicks asked. "He said that my best ability is *eating*, so if I hit him in the face with this water bottle, you're going to let that slide, right? Why don't you grow up, man, we're trying to be serious."

"Now, look, Rickey," she said. "You can't let people get in your head. Right now, the business at hand is to win. . . . We want to see a W and we can't win if everybody is pulling apart, everybody pulling in their own direction. . . . Now, you listen to Coach Cox because when you listen to an authority figure, God honors that"—suddenly the laughter died down and someone sounded "Hmmm . . . " in considered agreement, and the boisterous teenagers, churchgoers all, fell silent—"and you have to honor what God honors.

"You've got to listen to what he tells you because Coach Cox can see things that you can't see. Believe it or not, he can. . . . You do what you're supposed to do. Do the right thing. . . . Do the best that you know how to do and you'll come off the field feeling like a winner every time. Don't tell your teammate, 'You ain't this and you can't do that.' Don't do that. That's just like me telling my son, 'You ain't nothing.' He might mess up sometimes, all of them do. But allow for weakness. The Bible says, 'The strong ought to bear the infirmities of the weak.' When Jared is weak, Johnathan can be strong. When Aaron is weak, somebody's got to have his back. That's a team."

By now they were all attentive, punctuating her pauses with "Um-hmm" and "That's right."

"You can't keep going out there, everybody pulling in his own separate way," she continued. "I don't want to see that tomorrow. That's all I've got to say."

They had listened. In a minute they were back to being loud and insulting and rowdy young men, but they had listened.

For all their pointed put-downs and high-volume crowing over the two and a half hours of the gathering, not one player had uttered a term that would have been bleeped from TV, not one player had called another player the *n* word, despite the fashion of rappers and others to do so. They were attentive when called upon to be and listened when spoken to. Like the coaches always said, they were good kids. But that might not be enough to beat Cabot.

IIIIIIIIIIIIIIIIIIIIIIIIIIIIIIIIIIIIIII

The fervor for football in Cabot was immediately apparent by the expanse and opulence of Panther Stadium: jumbo video scoreboard, artificial turf field, stadium suites, three-story athletic complex with indoor turf field and Panther Den store for fan gear. In 2006, the *Wall Street Journal* had included Cabot—along with schools in Texas, Georgia, and northwest Arkansas—in a story on the growing amount of money devoted to high school football programs. "Top teams in big football states such as Texas and Georgia say they spend $100,000 to $350,000 on their programs annually," the *Journal* reported, adding that the artificial turf field at Cabot had cost around $500,000. The Cabot Panther Education Foundation, a 501(c)(3) nonprofit formed in 2006 and independent of the school district, was absorbing some of that cost. In 2008 and again in 2009, it handed out two $1,000 scholarships and $10,000 in technology grants to teachers, but the athletic department seemed to get the panther's share of its largesse. Under the "What We Do" heading on its Web site's About Us page, the first words are "We are presently working toward retiring the debt on Panther Stadium improvements."

From 2002 through 2005, Central got used to seeing Cabot's envy-inducing facilities. During that time, instead of scheduling the usual home and home series, the Tigers agreed to play their annual game with Cabot only at Panther Stadium in exchange for a $2,500 yearly payment, which

allowed Central to supplement by more than half its district budget of
$4,500, the amount that went equally to all Little Rock School District high
school football programs. "Guarantee" money like Cabot offered is common
in college programs, where big-name schools will schedule "cupcake" opponents at home by offering them a big fee, which allows the smaller, visiting
school to prop up its athletic department's annual bottom line. Usually, that
buys a win for the home team, as when the University of Arkansas brought
the University of North Texas to Fayetteville in 2007 and sent the team back
to Denton with a 66–7 loss. Central, however, was no cupcake, and Cabot
had lost the last three in the series.

One of the undercurrents of the arrangement was the racially charged
supposition that Cabot fans wouldn't travel to the 'hood for a game at Central. In 2006, after the previous contract had ended and Cabot was moved
into Central's division, requiring the team to travel to Quigley, the visitors'
side, according to the *Arkansas Times*, had held only 150 to 200 fans apart
from the band and spirit squad. On a Friday night in Cabot, the crowd was
often five thousand people strong, or a quarter of the town's population.

As Central dressed in the locker room at Quigley before boarding the
two school buses for the half-hour trip, the limping figure of Clyde Horton
appeared before them. He was his old matter-of-fact self, talking in a deep
Arkansas drawl about how the defensive line needed to stay aggressive and
that he couldn't be there with them but knew that they could do the job they
needed to do. It didn't really matter what he said, he was there as he'd been
there in their shoes in 1944, when Quigley Stadium had been only eight
years old and face masks on helmets were still twelve years away. When he
finished speaking, the team applauded. They then left the stadium to get on
the buses waiting outside the main gate for the trip to Cabot.

Once there, two and a half hours before game time, Coach Finley
walked the field like he always did while the players got their ankles taped
and suited up. The PA at Panther Stadium was tuned to the local radio
station, where the DJ warned that it had taken him ten minutes to turn
across traffic when he was coming out of the bank and that the crowd at
the stadium was going to be larger than normal because Central was in

town. Cabot students were already flocking from the school in black T-shirts reading "Panther Pitt" on the front and "Are the Panthers gonna win this game? Well Yeah" on the back. The Mt. Carmel Baptist Church had set up a tent supplying free hot dogs. The homecoming court had arrived, dressed in kimonos.

Central's "locker room" was an auxiliary gym behind the visitors' stands. There were a few classroom desks spread around and the players were lying on the basketball court's floor or sitting outside the doors, which were propped open. It was a still, clear afternoon, warm, the temperature in the low seventies. James Giese, the injured lineman who couldn't dress out but was helping the managers, was listening to American Head Charge's "Just So You Know" on his iPod, his Mohawk identical to that of AHC's lead guitarist. Damien Lee, his braided and beaded locks pulled back into a rubber-band-bound ponytail, was listening to Dem Franchize Boyz.

In the offensive meeting, Callaway implored the backs to hold onto the ball ("We can't put it on the ground and have them recover, because we'll lose eight minutes") and the line to play Fox in a Box on every down. "How many times did they do Fox in a Box this week?" he asked. "Zero. They don't do it."

Before Cox addressed the team, Finley approached him with a pained look. "Coach, I hate to bring it up," he said, "but they might take some cheap shots. I'm not saying it *will* happen, but we should be aware of it. Bennett, and Damien Lee, [and] Jared. I'm just saying we need to mention it: They might get called the *n* word."

Nearby, Adam Acklin, the young Tigers coach who'd played against Cabot as a Central sophomore in 1997, said, "Oh, it will happen."

In the pregame talk, Cox broached the topic delicately and diplomatically.

"They're going to play until the whistle blows," he said. "You keep your head on a swivel. And the best thing to do against someone who plays until the whistle blows is . . . ?"

"Play until the whistle blows!" the players answered.

"If they say something to you, you be the better man. They may do it in the heat of the game, you be the better man. They may do it intentionally, you be the better man."

The pregame ceremonies for homecoming went on and on. The collection of "sweethearts" stretched from the 50-yard line to the goal line, and as each processed, her name was announced along with the names of her parents. There was an Astronomy Club Sweetheart, a Book Club Sweetheart, a Broadcasting Sweetheart, a Shakespeare Sweetheart, and a Skills USA Automotive Sweetheart.

Finally, the field was ceded to the teams. Central's Lamont Lacefield sent the kickoff high and deep, and Cabot started the game from its 22. Eight running plays later, Central's defense held, forcing a punt to Central's 20. Tim Dunn carried twice but gained only three yards, and Kelleybrew, split wide right, dropped a quick pass from Rankin on third down. All week Rankin had suffered from a sore knee, which was heavily wrapped for the game; as a result, sophomore Adam Meeks, also the backup quarterback, came in to punt. Coach Finley had emphasized during practice that Central could win the game with special teams. Turning the season's history on its head, he had told them, "Texarkana beat us with special teams, why can't we beat someone with special teams?" He then watched as the ball sailed over Meeks's head, bouncing behind him at the 1. The punter chased it down before any Cabot defenders could get there and alertly soccer-kicked it out of the back of his own end zone for a safety, at least preventing a Panther touchdown. The Tigers were playing from behind early in the game once again. Finley despaired on the sideline, sighing softly to himself: "If they don't fumble the ball, we can't beat them."

Returning the subsequent kickoff to their own 45, Cabot began their grinding ground game, led by James, the fullback. He bulled ahead for six, three, five, and eleven yards, always giving Tiger tacklers a good look at the white panther paws on his jersey's shoulders as he delivered a blow before going down. After twelve plays, he took it in from the 3. The extra point was good, Cabot led 9–0, and considering the way the offense was playing, it might as well have been 90–0.

But Central countered with its own ground game, in the tandem of Bo

Dillon and fullback Will Rollins. Dillon carried the ball six straight times, earning two first downs. Three more runs, two by Dillon and one by Rollins, netted nine yards, leaving Central with a fourth and one at Cabot's 28. From the sideline, Giese faced the Tiger stands and waved his arms to get the crowd going. The line opened a seam just wide enough for Dillon to dive for two yards and the first down. Dillon went for another four and Rollins for three to the 18.

That was twelve straight running plays. On third and three Rankin rolled left and lofted a perfect fade pass to the left end zone corner for tight end Justin Henderson. Cabot defensive back Zach Coy was not fooled on the play and both players went up for the ball; Henderson grabbed it first and Coy fought him for it as they both fell into the end zone. Two other Tigers, Lee and Lacefield, immediately signaled touchdown, while the Cabot defenders signaled that they had gained possession. Two officials consulted and then one waved his right hand over his head, indicating an interception and touchback. It was a borderline call, but Jared Green had warned the other players at Aaron Nichols's house that "it can't be close, because you know they'll cheat us, so we can't make it close." Finley pulled Henderson aside and emphasized that he *had* to come down with that ball, after which Henderson, upset, sat down on the bench by himself. Rankin, Lacefield, and others came by to slap him on the shoulder pads and give him encouragement.

At halftime in the steamy auxiliary gym the coaches puzzled over how the offense might score. They took some comfort in the fact that they had moved the ball on the ground, but they had to avoid turnovers.

Cox and the Tigers' offensive coaches decided not to play it safe. After taking the second-half kickoff and facing third and seven after a run and an incomplete pass, Central pitched the ball out to Bo Dillon on a sweep, and he dropped back and lofted a surprise pass to Kelleybrew for a forty-eight-yard gain. Kelleybrew might have scored had the pass been equal to his speed, but he had had to slow down to get it, allowing the Cabot defender to catch him. After an incompletion, Rankin took the ball in the shotgun and hit Lamont Lacefield downfield for a twenty-yard gain to the 1. The Tiger players on the sideline were jumping in place and chanting, "Fox in a Box! Fox in a Box!" On his third try, Dillon crossed the goal line to make the score 9–6 after Cabot blocked the extra point.

The defense stiffened, and Cabot became even more conservative with the ball, especially because their starting quarterback had injured his collarbone on a tackle by Jared Green in the second quarter. During the second half, the Panthers punted twice and twice turned the ball over on downs. Cox had determined that Cabot was attacking Central's right side—running away from Jared Green—so he put in Damien Lee at right tackle on a crucial fourth and eight to get the stop. The quarterback faked to James and tried to get around the right side of the Tiger defense, but Lee and end Reed Caradine blew up the play, allowing Green to pursue from the other side and make the tackle short of the first down. Cabot's run game, however, was keeping the clock moving, and as long as they held onto the ball, Central would get few chances.

A high punt pinned Central at its own 10-yard line with nine and a half minutes left in the game. Ninety yards of Panther turf loomed large for an offense that had failed to sustain much consistency all season, but Dillon gained a first down on two runs to get them out of the hole. Rankin scrambled for sixteen, and when Cabot had a screen pass covered, he ran again for ten to midfield. After a fifteen-yard first down run, Dillon carried three more times, leaving the Tigers with a fourth and one at the Cabot 20. The Central fans were pounding the aluminum bleachers with their feet like cymbals as the Tigers lined up in the power I, with William Bennett and Rollins in front of tailback Dillon.

Dillon took the handoff and found the middle blocked, so he broke to his left and cut sharply upfield for the first down, but as he was tackled, the ball slipped out of his grasp. Tackle Kyle Temple, hustling downfield, scooped the ball up and rolled over on his back. When his back hit the turf, the ball slipped out again and squirted downfield five yards, where a Cabot defender fell on it. The Central fans were yelling, "Down, he was down!" but the official ruled the other way, giving Cabot the ball.

On their possession, Cabot gained a couple of first downs that ran the clock down to fifty-two seconds before punting. Central took over at mid-field and lined up in a "diamond" formation that Callaway had borrowed from Russellville—four wide receivers to one side with one on the line and three from the backfield in a diamond formation. Rankin's pass was complete to Kelleybrew at the Cabot 25, but William Bennett had also lined up in the backfield, making it five players behind the line and thus earning a penalty. The Central student section began rhythmically chanting, "We got cheated! We got cheated!" Two futile incomplete passes downfield, and the Panthers had their homecoming win.

There were tears in the gym. The chance for a conference championship was gone, now that Cabot was 5-1 and Central was 2-3. Cox told the team, "I thought you guys played very hard. We can still get to the playoffs." It even pleased him to see the tears. "I'm not sorry that it hurts," he said, "because we can build on that."

They would have a long time to soak in the loss in Lonoke County before the buses left Cabot. The traffic was terrible.

When would Central return from a road game and sing the alma mater in front of the school after a win? When would the words of that song—"Let our motto be / Victory"—not ring hollow as the bus pulled away from that famous façade and around the corner to the gate in Quigley's wall?

Down in the bowels of Quigley, the rituals continued: the pants and jerseys on their respective piles, "right side out," as Cox reminded the players, who then filed out to their cars or their parents or the bus that roamed the neighborhoods of Little Rock, dropping off the tired, sad Tigers.

The coaches were never tired after a game. A win left them full of adrenaline and a loss full of worry, so they didn't mind hanging around the office and hashing out the game.

"We had our chances," said Keith Richardson when everyone had settled into their places. "I think the kids have got some resiliency now." Callaway gave him a skeptical look. "You don't think so?" Richardson continued. "I'm trying to think of a little something to build on."

"I don't think they feel one way or the other, to tell you the truth," said Callaway.

"So those were fake tears?" Richardson asked.

"No, they hurt a little bit after the game," offered Finley. "For a few minutes . . . "

"You look at it," said Seward, getting back to the game itself, "what we have given away and what we have failed to capitalize on."

"If it's a good team," said Finley, "we have struggled to score. I don't care what you say, we're going to have problems. We're not getting better offensively. We're moving the ball, but we can't score."

Brian Cox, the trainer, came in to give the injury report, running through the various nicks and pains, Rankin's knee, De'Arius Hudson's headache, Ke'Won Jones's cramping.

"And how are we mentally?" said Finley to laughter.

"What about the coaching staff? How are we mentally?" said Richardson, to more laughter.

"One thing I told Sinele," added Larry Siegel, "don't say we got cheated. Don't even go there."

"The drivers on the buses were talking about it," said Seward, "the clock, everything. . . . They went through the whole ball game talking about it: 'It's just blatant out there.'"

"That referee did not fumble the ball," said Finley.

"That's right," said Siegel.

"He didn't snap it over their heads," said Finley.

"He didn't take the ball away in the end zone," said Richardson.

"Sure didn't," said Siegel.

One of the parents had left cookies for the coaches, and Stan Williams, the coaching staff's joker, started passing them around.

"Coach Fin," he said, "you want a cookie?"

"Yeah," said Finley, "give me a couple."

Standing over Finley in his chair and looking him up and down, taking in his bulk, Williams, as wiry and kinetic as Finley was stout, deadpanned: "I'm only going to give you half of one." The rest of the staff chuckled.

Finley turned his head and looked across the desks at Siegel, who had been opposite him in that tiny space for nearly a decade. "Coach Siegel," said Finley, "give me that pistol, the one in the drawer."

Siegel opened his desk drawer and handed to Finley across the desks a gleaming silver .45. "Here, take care of him, Coach," Siegel said.

Finley pointed the gun at Williams and pulled the trigger twice, and the pin clicked twice. The room echoed with peals of laughter as Finley then threw the plastic replica on his desk. They all clearly needed that moment of release.

"Siegel, who'd we take that from?" said Williams, who in his thirty years as a teacher and coach had collected plenty of tales of real guns.

Siegel named a recent Central track star, and they discussed his fortunes: an injury in a meet, nerve damage in his leg. Richardson reported that he was now a student at UALR.

Silence. Coach Cox had been in and out of the office, attending to the usual postgame duties in the locker room—filling the big washing machine, picking up tape and debris from the locker room floor—but now he sat with his feet on his desk, lost in thought.

CHAPTER 10

THE DISTANT GOAL (CONTINUED)

THE COACHES WATCHED THE CABOT GAME TAPE on Saturday morning. When the giant TV screen went black, Cox told them, "We're not a very good football team, and a lot of it's because of the coaching staff." Nobody disagreed.

They had said it all season: They knew what kind of talent they had, they knew the kinds of kids they were working with, and they hadn't done enough to figure out how to motivate them to win.

A driving rain greeted the team at Quigley after classes on Monday, and Cox thought they'd accomplish more if they stayed inside and watched the Cabot tape, did some weight-room work, and had the receivers catch passes from the machine that fired footballs at them. As they watched the painful replay of the Cabot game, Cox told the Tigers, "I saw some emotion Friday night that I love. I did see some real tears, and there's nothing wrong with that."

Finley addressed the difference between the week of practice they'd had before Cabot and the performance in the game. "This is called game slippage," he said. "Fox in a Box, you destroyed everybody this week. That's our fault. We need to figure out something because we're not carrying it over into the game."

They tried some different things in practice later that week. Instead of standing behind the huddle, Callaway called offensive plays from the sidelines, just as he would during a game. Denzel Harris, whose quick feet offered a change of pace from both the power of Bo Dillon and the straight-ahead speed of Tim Dunn, got more time at tailback.

In truth, they didn't expect much resistance from North Little Rock, which was the weakest team in the division under its new coach. He'd installed a complex new system with multiple formations, and his players hadn't mastered it yet. The Charging Wildcats were 0-4 in the conference.

Still, it would be a nail-biter. North Little Rock's quarterback found himself harassed throughout the game and was sacked eight times, but Central couldn't score either until the fourth quarter, when Denzel Harris carried five times for forty-seven yards on a fifty-two-yard drive for a touchdown. Central's defense closed out a 7–0 win.

After the game, however, Rankin was disconsolate. When a well-wisher told him, "Good game," he replied, "I'm not going to say thanks to that. I played a terrible game. I almost got taken out of there."

Indeed, he'd completed only two of seven passes for twelve yards and thrown an interception, and in the coaches' office afterward, Cox said to the staff, "If you want Randy to play quarterback, you need to start convincing me because I've about had it."

Rankin was as hard on himself as anybody was. He had a good understanding of and a real love for the game, and he had thrived in previous years when he had a strong cast around him. But this season, his restless mind often got the better of him. The year before, said Seward, "he had Charles Clay back there as a safety valve, who could score for us. The fact that we haven't been scoring has been freaking him out." Another coach said Rankin had told him that the center was so nervous about the nose guard he was facing that his butt was shaking, and he couldn't get a good snap.

"He will freak our whole staff out if we let him," added Finley. "I don't even let him start with me."

Callaway thought the solution to focusing Rankin was as simple as playing backup quarterback Adam Meeks more often: "If you give Meeks a whole lot of snaps this week, Randy will perk his butt up."

Rankin had expressed a desire to be a football coach himself and sometimes already spoke like a coach by finely articulating ideas about the game, such as the difference between a hard-hitting football team and a "dirty" one: "There's one thing about being physical: Football's not about hitting a random person, but about executing a play. You have to be physical with the right person."

Despite how hard Cox could be on him, Rankin said of him, "I respect him more than anybody in the whole world. I'm not just saying that. I don't always necessarily like him, but he does exactly what he says he's going to do."

Cox was certainly as good as his word about Rankin and the senior's tenuous hold on the quarterback position, a risky change this late in the season with two crucial games remaining if Central hoped to make the play-offs. Meeks, a sophomore, started the week running the first team, and Rankin didn't seem to know what to do or where to stand, so he took up a position halfway between the sidelines and the huddle. At one point, a player on the sidelines called out, "Good throw, Randy!" and another corrected him, "That's Meeks."

Finley, more than any of the other coaches, seemed to be racking his brain to come up with changes that might still get the team on a roll and into the playoffs. "We've got to be more creative as a staff," he pleaded. He proposed that they practice a fake punt. He suggested from his study of Catholic's defense that they might be able to run wide. He floated the idea that they go seven on seven in practice and work on tackling in open space to prepare for Catholic's short passing game. And despite the fact that Seward had told the defense "Kaelon Kelleybrew is not the savior of this football team," Finley couldn't avoid thinking of him that way. "Might want to give Kelleybrew some touches at tailback" was his final suggestion. Cox agreed. "We have one go-to guy on this team," he said.

On that Thursday at practice within the walled confines of Quigley, Randy Rankin's father, also named Randy, was standing on the sidelines, sad but accepting of his son's demotion to second string before Senior Night, of all games. "Friday night was horrible," he said, thinking back to the errant passes against North Little Rock. "It's been a rough week." When young

Randy came in to take some snaps with the first team, Finley made sure to be encouraging. "Good job, QB," he said. "Be focused like that tomorrow night."

Soon thereafter, Cox blew up at the bickering and lack of focus and imposed on them the Bataan Death March of bleachers. The team looped around and around the stands they'd traversed now throughout their high school careers, which had just nine days remaining if they failed to make the playoffs. As they wheezed with exhaustion, Cox told them with some scorn that if they wanted to blame the probable loss to Catholic on him because he'd tired them out by making them run bleachers the day before the game, then they were free to do that. Kelleybrew, who had to run five extra bleachers with several other players because of their roles in the team's squabbling, said afterward that when he got in his car, his legs were shaking from the punishment.

In the office, Cox briefly commented on the debacle at practice. "I was somewhat embarrassed to be out on that field," he told the other coaches. "They hadn't run two plays and they were cussing at each other and hollering at each other and screaming at Meeks. It's unbelievable what our team has deteriorated to. . . . I'll tell you, we got problems. I'm glad we've just got two weeks left." Showing as much disgust as he had all season, he sat down at his desk and turned quickly to other matters.

Earlier, Pulaski Academy's athletic department had called Central, which still had two games to fill on the schedule for 2008, to see if the school would be interested in a two-game series for the next two years. Most often called simply "PA," the school had been founded in the new western Little Rock subdivision of Pleasant Valley in the 1970s in large part to give parents a way to avoid busing, like dozens of other "segregation academies" established throughout the South at that time. The years since had seen it develop into a well-respected college-preparatory prekindergarten-through-grade-twelve school, though one still lacking in meaningful diversity. Despite the contention in its "guiding principles" that it "embraces racial, ethnic and socio-economic diversity," only 4 percent of the students enrolled during the 2007–2008 school year were black.

In recent years, some of those few black students had been star football players for the Bruins' high-powered offense. Cruz Williams was a six-foot-three all-state receiver in 2007 who went on to play for Louisiana Tech, and running back Broderick Green, a senior in 2006, originally signed to play with the University of Southern California before transferring to Arkansas. (Other Little Rock–area private schools with minimal black enrollment also featured outstanding black football players: Joe Adams, a 2008 graduate of Central Arkansas Christian [CAC], became a starting receiver at the University of Arkansas, and Little Rock Christian's Michael Dyer, the top running back in ESPN's recruiting rankings for 2009, eventually committed to Auburn.)

Under coach Kevin Kelley, Pulaski Academy had developed one of the most potent and exciting offenses in the state, often employing five wide receivers in a shotgun formation and averaging more than fifty passes a game, the antithesis of Bernie Cox's hard-nosed, field-position football. Kelley had gained national publicity for some of his "mad scientist" football notions: He almost never punted, even when deep in his own territory, and he eccentrically and tactically tried onside kicks at all times of the game. Through 2007, he'd won a state championship, compiled a 46-8-1 record, and reached at least the quarterfinals of the playoffs every year.

Cox had asked Darrell Seward what he thought of the idea of playing PA, and Seward had been mulling it over. "You want to share with them what you shared with me this morning?" Cox asked.

Seward had decided he was opposed to scheduling the Bruins. "I feel pretty strongly about this thing with PA for one reason and one reason only," he began. "I could care less about the competition part of it. I'd love to play them. The thing I have a problem with is these private schools are actively going out and recruiting kids to play in their programs. . . . " "Recruiting" was a word rarely spoken so openly, since the practice was expressly forbidden by the Arkansas Activities Association (AAA), the governing body for public and private school athletics, and could lead to penalties if a school was found to have engaged in it. But coaches everywhere knew it went on in ways both subtle and overt, and they often joked about it. One public high school in the Little Rock School District was supplying practice jerseys to a junior high team, thus developing a bond with players who might choose to go there; someone got wind of the tactic and it was stopped. Summer seven-on-seven leagues, which had become ubiquitous, were another opportunity for coaches and parents to have contact with opposing players and influence them to attend different schools, whether public or private. Even as respected as Bernie Cox was among his peers, Central was not immune to charges of recruiting. After A. J. Williams had returned the interception against West Memphis for a game-winning touchdown, one coach had asked the AAA to look into his transfer from Stuttgart; no irregularities were found.

Pulaski Academy had proposed playing the two games with Central at Little Rock's War Memorial Stadium, where the Razorbacks hosted a couple of games a year. A contest between two of the premier football programs in the city would generate tremendous interest, and the take would be substantial. For the one year of the two when Central was the home team, the gate would go to the Little Rock School District's bottom line, but the next year, when it counted as a PA home game, the private school would not have to share the proceeds. "If they're going to get a $10,000 gate," Seward continued, "they're going to use that money for scholarships to offer to other kids. Now they may be taking our kids and they may not be taking our kids. I don't know how many kids on their roster are in our zone. The only reason PA would be interested in doing this is the benefit to PA. . . .

"I'm just speaking for me. That's my personal opinion about it, but I don't want to do a doggone thing to help Pulaski Academy, CAC, Little Rock Christian. It's nothing personal or against any person, it's the mind-set of the people in those schools. . . .

"This crap with the triple A and the private schools, it's getting worse and it's not going to get better—whether it's white flight or whatever the parents think, it doesn't make any difference, we're losing kids."

On a larger scale, the district as a whole was experiencing the same thing—losing kids. In 2007–2008, the Little Rock School District had an enrollment of 26,537, which was an increase of only 1,533 from 1963–1964, and that included a spike in the mid-1980s when the district boundaries had been expanded by court decree. Most of the flatlining was attributable to the growth of suburban and exurban communities, but Little Rock's private schools, as they had across the South and the country, played a part. In editorials in both Little Rock newspapers in the fall of 1971, the fact that five of the seven board members had their children in private schools, including two at Pulaski Academy, led to calls for their heads: "Resign!" was the *Gazette*'s headline, while the *Democrat* termed it a "Betrayal of Trust." From 1970 to 2000, private school enrollment in the metropolitan area grew by 157 percent. That period saw the founding of the Central Arkansas Christian Schools and Pulaski Academy in 1971, Little Rock Christian Academy in 1977, Arkansas Baptist School System in 1981, Southwest Christian Academy in 1987, Word of Outreach Christian Academy in 1989, Episcopal Collegiate School in 1997, and Lutheran High School in 1998. That increase was consistent with regional and national tides. As Duke University professor Charles T. Clotfelter writes in his book *After Brown: The Rise and Retreat of School Desegregation*, the four decades between 1960 and 2000 "witnessed two major trends in private school enrollment: a nationwide decline in Catholic parochial schools and a rise in non-Catholic private schools, particularly in the South."

The other consequence of that movement, joined to the context of greater metropolitan area housing trends, was declining white enrollment in the public schools. Little Rock's graph of white and black student enrollments in the district from the mid-1960s to the present resembled a giant X, with white enrollment plummeting and black soaring; the two crossed in the mid-1970s and then continued on their respective paths. By 2007–2008, the percentage of black students was 68.1, compared to 22.8 for whites ("other" totaled 9.0 percent).

Historian Grif Stockley has characterized that trend as an "abandonment" by whites of the public school system, yet Little Rock still ranks far above other southern cities like Atlanta; Birmingham, Alabama; Jackson, Mississippi; Memphis; and Richmond, Virginia, in white enrollment. No doubt the continuing academic excellence of Central and other magnet schools, along with the strong devotion parents have to various neighborhood elementary schools, has forestalled some departures. Nevertheless, private schools in Little Rock, and across the nation, remain starkly white. The number of blacks in private schools in Little Rock, according to the 2000 census, stood at 4 percent, while the national figure was closer to 10 percent. As Clotfelter puts it, "American private schools have historically represented islands of whiteness in comparison to neighboring public school systems."

Clotfelter bases his research on an examination of "interracial contact," taking as a starting point psychologist Gordon Allport's assertion that "contact is a necessary, but not sufficient, condition for the reduction of racial prejudice." Because of the predominantly white composition of private schools, "their very existence alters the makeup of the public schools" and therefore affects interracial contact. In overturning Henry Woods's district court ruling from 1984 that the three Pulaski County school districts should be merged, the Eighth Circuit Court of Appeals made a "final observation": "The [district] court stretches mightily to find a basis for making the boundaries of the City of Little Rock and the LRSD coterminous. This result will make the LRSD 60 percent black and 40 percent white. However, one most significant factor has been omitted from this equation. . . . In the LRSD alone, if the white students in private schools attended public schools, the district would be approximately 52 percent rather than 69 percent black. Another significant factor which is not taken into account is that the number of white students in private schools in LRSD increased by more than 1,000 between 1970 and 1980. . . . It is evident from the sharp increase in enrollment in private schools in these ten years, and the impact of these numbers on the total student population, that private choice is having a far greater segregative effect than those factors the court points to in its opinion today. This is a factor, however, that at present, and in all likelihood in the future, will pose a significant impediment to any effort to achieve desegregation within any of the three school districts."

Clotfelter gives his copious data some rigorous number crunching before determining that "private schools do appear to have contributed to racial segregation in K-12 schools, though their contribution is significantly less than that attributable to racial disparities among school districts."

Interracial contact seems most meaningful to Clotfelter, in the decades since *Brown*, outside the classroom, where the dividing line of the "two Centrals," for instance, one white and one black, is less powerful. "To be sure," he asserts, "interracial friendships remain the exception rather than the rule, but the 'loose ties' of association routinely bridge the color line. Thousands of integrated football and wrestling teams, bands, and school clubs give students . . . opportunities to know those from other racial and ethnic groups as individuals rather than as stereotypes. So, while school desegregation has been an imperfect revolution . . . it has been a revolution nonetheless."

In Little Rock and elsewhere, athletics played a big part in the decisions of parents and students about where to go to school. During the heyday of the 2003 and 2004 seasons at Central, a marginal but enthusiastic football player might have opted to attend another school, public or private, with a lesser concentration of good athletes so he might get the chance to get in a game. More rarely, as with Will Rollins, who elected to transfer to Central because the competition at Arkansas Baptist was not fulfilling him, does the current move in the other direction, toward the public school. Little Rock Christian principal Boyd Chitwood told the *Arkansas Times* in 2004 that athletics was a big draw at his school, which occupies an expansive campus in far west Little Rock. "If we didn't have athletics, we wouldn't be nearly as big as we are," he said.

Catholic High remained the private school with the strongest athletic department. And it had been Central's greatest rival over the past seven decades. The Rockets first played Little Rock High in the inaugural game at Quigley Stadium (then Tiger Stadium) in 1936. At that time, both the Tigers and the Rockets were coached by former Razorback stars early in their coaching careers: Little Rock's rookie coach was Clyde Van Sickle, who had joined the team after a successful pro career playing for the Green Bay Packers, and Catholic's Tom Murphy was in his second year as coach after being named the Southwest Conference Most Valuable Player in 1933. Late in the fourth quarter of that initial 1936 contest, Catholic led 14–13, with the Tigers driving in Rockets territory. Catholic's defense stopped the Tigers on fourth down at the 18, and the Rockets took over the ball. After a fifteen-yard penalty pushed Catholic back to its 3-yard line, Little Rock's defense mounted a stand, and Billy Edwards sacked Rockets quarterback H. A. Mayer in the end zone for a safety to give the Tigers an improbable 15–14 win.

Clyde Horton had run wild in the Tigers' 61–0 win over the Rockets in 1946, but over the years, many games with Catholic had been tense and close. In 1977 Catholic eked out a 3–0 win on a thirty-yard field goal with seven seconds left, and in 1991, Catholic scored a touchdown with eleven seconds remaining to close to within one point, 14–13, only to miss the extra point after a motion penalty moved them back. And in 1995, Central intercepted a two-point conversion attempt in the end zone in the second overtime period to take a 28–26 win that sent them to the playoffs.

The rivalry was fiercer for the close relationships between students at the schools, especially among the white players, who were often neighbors and friends and former schoolmates. In 2007, students fashioned insulting Facebook pages and T-shirts during the run-up to the game.

Bernie Cox had shared a warm relationship—as well as a philosophy of discipline and responsibility—with Father George Tribou, the longtime principal and presiding spirit of Catholic High. Catholic High students were required to have their hair cut short and to wear ties, and they often walked the halls in fear of being caught in some infraction by Father Tribou, who doled out unusual punishments like forcing students caught smoking to puff on one of his powerful cigars, which inevitably left them ill. Before Catholic-Central games, Cox and Tribou would meet on the field and talk about education and kids.

"How much longer are you going to do this, Bernie?" Tribou had once asked Cox. "You're like me. They're going to have to carry me out." He stuck by his words: Tribou remained principal of the school for thirty-four years, until December of 2000, when he was already suffering from an advanced case of cancer. He died two months later.

Central had a few surprises in store for Catholic this season, startling changes for the ninth game of the year. First, the Rockets defense would see a new starting quarterback, Adam Meeks, and a new starting tailback—

although it was not Kelleybrew. Callaway had told Cox in the pregame coaches' meeting: "I'm tempted to start Denzel this week."

"Then start him," Cox replied. "He deserves more snaps than those others." Cox was fed up with the fumbling and the lack of offensive production.

"We wouldn't have won that ball game last week if it wasn't for him," Siegel added.

As Cox walked into the main locker room and stood in front of a dry-erase board, the team of seventy-odd padded boys roused themselves from the floor, where they'd been lying down and listening to their iPods or napping or fiddling with their shoelaces and tape and arm pads. The seniors took their places on the aluminum benches facing Cox, squeezing in next to each other so their shoulder pads overlapped.

"If I could say three words and leave them with you," Cox began, "which I can't do, you know I can't say three words and shut up"—he took the marker from the board and wrote on it while saying the words—"'challenges make champions.' . . . I've been doing this a long time and I've seen it come through.

"You guys who have played against Catholic before, you know they're going to play hard. They're the epitome of what all coaches want. I'm going to tell you what I heard in the last couple of weeks. This guy I've known a long time—I'm not going to tell you who it was—he's one of the more successful high school coaches in the state of Arkansas. . . . You know what he told me he'd like to do one day? Where he'd like to coach? Guess."

"Catholic High," the players answered in unison.

"I said, 'Why?'

"'They're smart, they're strong, they're hard to beat. . . . They don't have the athletes everybody has. But they play so hard.' We've got better athletes than they do. We've got to accept the challenge. You need not think about winning the ball game if you'll play like a winner. I don't know whether you can process that or not. . . .

"I'll tell you what I would have liked to have done. . . . I'd like to have a tape of the eleven defensive starters tonight and the eleven offensive starters tonight and take all those backups who don't play. . . . I would like to have a camera on every one of you at every practice session, and then I would like Coach Seward . . . to take that tape and make a highlight tape of every single player in this room and I could show it to you. You'd all be impressed. . . . There's not a one of you guys who's playing in this game tonight who hasn't had great plays . . . not one of you, not one of you. The idea is to make those great plays out there and make them consistently. . . .

"I know you know this: Yesterday I was bitter, I was disappointed, I was frustrated. I didn't expect to see and hear what I heard on the field yesterday. Guys who have gone through what you've gone through, for three years now. Hollering at each other like that, one of you cussing another. It breaks my heart to think that I haven't done a better job than that. And I'm taking some responsibility. Obviously I'm not the model I could have been if that's the way you're acting out there.

"We've never been able to come together as a team. We're a group but not a unit. . . . Being selfish will just eat you away, eat you up. That's one of the main things I always thought athletics was so good at, was getting its participants to be unselfish, to be committed to play for each other, looking out for each other.

"I make no apologies for yesterday. I was upset. You guys may not want to hear this, but we'll always feel like you're our guys, you're our kids."

At this point he seemed to think back to all the players he'd ever coached and all the players he'd ever stood in front of in that very spot in his three-plus decades at Central, some of them now doctors and architects and convicts and welders and football coaches, but all Tigers. Clark Irwin, the unflappable quarterback of the two most recent state championship teams, who was merely holding for extra points up in Fayetteville but getting an education in coaching at the feet of Houston Nutt, his predecessor by exactly thirty years at Central. And Michael Perry, the all-state running back in 1976, who the coaches remembered always played hurt and never complained, now serving fifty years for first-degree murder. And Tommy Pearce, class of 1975, who had dropped dead of a heart attack in August, just two weeks after jogging on Central's track and recalling how Bernie Cox could out-bench-press anybody on the team when he started. And before them, all the Tigers who'd ever stood on those same hard, cold concrete floors long before he got there, back to the first time Little Rock High played Catholic High in 1936 in brand-new Tiger Stadium, soon to be Quigley Stadium. And then back to all the players who'd ever been Tigers, who had stood on the good ground under those floors when it was Kavanaugh Field, when Little Rock was not far removed from being a frontier town and it was a rare football game where a forward pass was attempted.

Bernie's son, Brian Cox, had spent years searching for the names of all those Tigers, and the lettermen listed in his book about the century of Central football took up seventeen pages, from an Abbott in 1905 whose first name is lost to history, to Kenneth Zini, who played on the 1957 undefeated national championship team. All 1,537 of them precursors to this team, all of them clad in black and old gold, just like Jared Green and Quinton Brown and Randy Rankin and Kaelon Kelleybrew.

Cox began speaking again, about another Tiger, Clyde Horton.

"He is one of the most fierce competitors that Central High has ever had," Cox continued. "He went to Alabama to play football. He wasn't very big, but he was fierce. He wouldn't back down from anyone at any time. That's the reason I believe in my heart—I would sneak into the ICU when he was in the hospital with that disease he had; I wasn't supposed to be in there, only family could go in there, but I would sneak in there when the nurses weren't watching. If you could have seen Coach Horton when I saw him in the ICU . . . ," he paused as his eyes started to well. "I said a prayer every time I saw him up there, because I thought he was gone. But he made it. You know why he made it? I believe this with all my heart. He learned to compete against any- and everyone as an athlete as a young man. Whether you know it or not, he's still that way today, seventy-nine, eighty years old . . . that's something that's in you, that never leaves you.

"That's the kind of thing we're trying to instill in you, that spirit, that power. I've told kids for years: I love to see you grab each other, I love to see you grab someone's hand, I love to see you hug someone. . . . That's not a show of weakness, that's a show of strength. That's a sharing of power and strength to me, sharing with your teammates and friends, those you respect and those you love."

He couldn't say any more and he bowed his head for the minute of silence they observed before every game.

When he raised his head, he said, "Leave it out there, now! Let's go!" The players began clapping and slapped each other on the shoulder pads and filed down the narrow hall to the steps leading out to the field, reaching up over the last doorway to touch the horseshoe that had been there for as long as anybody could remember, though nobody could remember who had put it there.

On the field for warmups, Horton took his defensive linemen as usual under the south goalpost and ran them through some basic contact drills. He was fierce, but he was not made of stone, and there were tears in his eyes from the locker room speech. His group told him that they were going to win the game for him.

"Win it for Bernie," he replied. "He needs it more than I do."

From the first play of the game, it didn't look like they were going to be winning it for anyone. Three plays netted no yards. Meeks and the offense looked confused. An errant punt with a good return left Catholic with a first down at Central's 27, and from a five-receiver set, the Rockets' quarterback threw a slant pattern over the middle and the receiver then split the safeties for a quick touchdown. Within moments once again, Central was playing from behind.

On the Tigers' second offensive series, Rankin was back at quarterback, his exile having lasted all of three plays. He fared no better than Meeks, fumbling his first snap and falling on it and, on third down, getting sacked for a thirteen-yard loss, which forced Meeks to come on and punt from his own end zone.

The defense stood its ground, and after a bad punt by the Rockets, the Tigers took over again at their own 27. On first down, Rankin dropped back and pump faked a short pass, then lofted as beautiful a rainbow as he'd thrown all year to Lamont Lacefield, streaking down the Central sideline. Lacefield took the ball in stride at the Catholic 40 and made it to the 15 before a defender wrapped up his feet from behind. Three plays later Bo Dillon scored on a sweep and freshman Walker Hawkins's extra point tied it, 7–7.

It didn't take long for Central to fall behind again, in the same way that they had been burned all season, by a long pass play. A Catholic receiver got behind Ke'Won Jones on a "wheel" route, took in the pass on the sideline, and outran the secondary for a seventy-yard touchdown. Was it too much to ask for the offense to keep up? They'd not shown an ability to come back all year.

When Central next got the ball, the coaches tried some creative ways to get the ball to Kelleybrew, sending him on a "go" route that the Catholic defender broke up with a late, one-arm stab at the ball, and handing off the ball to him on a reverse that netted twenty-six yards. The Tigers maintained the drive, with erstwhile defensive end William Bennett in at fullback and Dillon running behind him (Denzel Harris had started, but was injured in the first quarter), before the march stalled inside the 10. Hawkins came in to try a twenty-four-yard field goal, which hit the upright and caromed straight back into the field of play, no good.

Catholic scored again before the half on a fifteen-yard touchdown pass after Central had failed to make any significant yardage deep in its own territory. A missed point-after left the score 20–7 at the half, but no one point seemed significant then. The Rockets were in control.

Cox still found reason for optimism. He and defensive coordinator Larry Siegel decided to go to a four-man front with Reed Caradine in a down position to put more pressure on the elusive Catholic quarterback, Taylor Bartlett, who had scrambled his way out of trouble several times. More important, as Cox told them in the locker room, they were "playing their hearts out," and he felt like the offense could still move the ball as they had on those two sustained drives. They believed him: Kelleybrew and Rankin, the latter sipping on his usual halftime can of Red Bull, took the offensive line aside, and Kelleybrew told them, "Look, if you block for Randy, we can pass this ball, we can move this ball, we can score."

Catholic promptly took the ball to open the second half and drove seventy yards in ten plays to make the score 27–7. Three touchdowns behind?

In five of its games, Central had scored only one touchdown or less. In two of those games, only the defense had scored. But they weren't dead yet. There was Clyde Horton on the sidelines, living proof that just because you were flat on your back, it didn't mean you had flatlined.

The offense came out in the "Tiger package," two receivers split wide to each side, and Rankin, throwing from the shotgun, kept looking for Kelleybrew. He caught a quick out for six yards. He caught a swing pass and broke three tackles for a gain of nine. Rankin was clicking with other receivers as well, mainly to the sidelines, hitting Aaron Nichols and Bo Dillon, all from the Tiger formation. When he was working quickly, reacting and not allowing himself to overthink or worry, he was at his best.

But he pressed his luck one time too often when he tried to hit a well-covered Kelleybrew down the field from the 30 and the Catholic defender, Patrick Chaffin, intercepted the ball before falling back in the end zone. The only salutary thing about the play was that the official placed the ball on the 1-yard line rather than ruling the play a touchback, which would have meant it came out to the 20.

Three running plays brought the Rockets out to the 5, and they lined up for a punt. The Tigers packed the line, and when the ball was snapped, the left guard blocked down on nose guard Quinton Brown, allowing linebacker Hunter Sinele to charge straight up the middle untouched. The kick ricocheted off his chest, and coming from the left end, William Bennett fell on the ball in the end zone for the touchdown. Hawkins made the extra point to close the lead to thirteen points, 27–14, late in the third quarter.

It was too late to trade scores. Central had to have a stop. That seemed unlikely when the nifty Catholic quarterback Bartlett scrambled up the middle to midfield. Cox countered with a defensive move; he had to have his best athletes on the field, so he inserted Damien Lee at right end, replacing Johnathan Green, Jared's twin brother, who looked tired from chasing Bartlett all over the field for three quarters. On the next play, Lee bull-rushed the Catholic tackle, who had given Bartlett enough time to throw, but Bartlett pulled the ball back in and Lee, who by that time had been released inside, leapt at the quarterback, reaching him just as he was passing.

The ball popped in the air and William Bennett was there again, intercepting the short pass and rumbling down to the Rockets' 28-yard line.

Lee, never short of bravado, flexed both arms in a bodybuilder's pose as he ran off the field. Bennett and Jared Green propelled themselves in the air at each other and chest bumped. The Tigers were no longer fragile, but fierce.

The offense swaggered onto the field, and why not—four players from the already swaggering defense were now often playing offense as well: Jared Green at tackle, William Bennett at fullback, and Aaron Nichols and Kaelon Kelleybrew as receivers. Bo Dillon, on three pitch plays, made swift cuts upfield and shed tacklers to take the ball to the 9 as the third quarter ended. The teams swapped ends of the field and the offense faced the scoreboard, with its stacked names of Quigley and Cox representing 395 wins.

On the first play of the fourth quarter, Dillon, from a power I formation, took another pitch, and with the two big fullbacks, Rollins and Bennett, clearing the way, cut up again into the end zone. As he came off the field, De'Arius Hudson, the three-hundred-pound left tackle, began nodding his head up and down like a bobblehead doll. Hawkins came on again for the extra point and struck the ball low, allowing a Catholic lineman to get a finger on it, but the ball stayed straight and tumbled over the crossbar. Catholic's lead had been cut to 27–21.

When Rankin came to the sidelines after holding for the extra point, he introduced a new catchphrase that, if he'd been playing in the NFL, would have earned him a million-dollar endorsement. "The Red Bull's kicking in!" he shouted.

The Central defense came up with another three and out, and the Rockets offense was rattled. There were more than ten minutes left in the game, a world of time. On the first play after the punt, Bo Dillon once again replicated the play that had been so successful on the earlier drive. He took the pitch from Rankin, ran left toward the Central sideline, with Bennett leading, and then planted his left foot, nearly losing his balance but righting himself with his right hand. The Catholic defender slid by without touching him. As Dillon cut behind Bennett's block, a Rockets player pursuing the ball carrier from the right poked the ball out of Dillon's grasp during the tackle. The ball squirted behind Dillon, and even before he hit the ground, he brought both his hands to his helmet in anguish. Catholic's Ryan Herget fell on the ball, right in front of Clarence Finley, who looked to the heavens. On the sidelines, Kelleybrew, who was not on offense that play, turned to Norman Callaway and simply extended his hands, palms up, in the universal gesture of disgust at the harsh workings of fate.

But fate turns. Three plays later, Catholic threw the pass that Ke'Won Jones saw hanging in the lights, the ball he was able to reach up and grab, just inbounds, to finally earn the nickname he'd inked on the scrim during his stagecraft class. He had finally become Ke'Won "Shutdown" Jones.

Central still had ninety-nine yards ahead of it, with 8:12 left in the game.

The offense trotted onto the field, huddling in their own end zone. They lined up in the power I, Dillon at tailback and the two fullbacks, Rollins and Bennett, ahead of him. Rankin called good old forty-two, tailback off-tackle, the Central staple that Callaway once said the school had been running for 102 years. Dillon gained only a yard.

"Kelleybrew!" Cox yelled on the sidelines. The player was already right there, his chinstrap buckled. He knew they'd need to throw to him in the Tiger package. "Get in there at tailback!"

"What?" Kelleybrew said and hesitated. Despite all the talk from the coaches about using him as a running back, he had not run a play from that position in a game before. Oh, he'd substituted in practice for Dillon and Dunn from time to time, "when they were getting some water or something," as he described it later, but he never imagined being in a game in that position under these conditions. "It was so unexpected," he said.

He finally said, "Okay," and ran to the huddle, in for Dillon, not quite sure he knew what to do or where to go. So he told Rollins and Bennett, "Wherever you're going, I'm following y'all."

On the first play, off-tackle left, he did just that. The tight end on that side, Justin Henderson, drove his man out, Rollins and Bennett took care of the two linebackers, and Kelleybrew shot through the hole for an eight-yard gain. Now that the Tigers were out of a hole, Kelleybrew thought he would come out, but they called his number again on the same play. The defensive lineman facing left guard Eric Fears dived at his feet, so Fears simply fell on him to take him out of the play. This time, Bennett helped Henderson with the end, Rollins and tackle De'Arius Hudson took out the linebackers, and, even though one defender was left free, he wasn't used to the speed in the backfield and Kelleybrew was past him in a flash into the secondary, carrying two defensive backs another five yards after contact to the 26. He kept telling himself one thing over and over: "Hold onto the ball, hold onto the ball."

Why change what was working? No need to huddle, so they didn't. Off-tackle left again: Fears lay down on his man, the crazy diving bastard, Henderson kicked the end out, Bennett destroyed a linebacker, Rollins nailed the other one, and all Kelleybrew had to deal with was the d-back closing from his left. He stopped suddenly, let the defender's momentum carry him past and gave him a good-bye push with his left hand to help him on his way. The flailing Rocket grabbed Kelleybrew's jersey, elongating the number 7, but he couldn't hold on, and once again the runner carried two more Rockets another five yards to the 37.

Kelleybrew tried the right side for one yard, but he was spent. He'd played almost the whole game except for extra-point tries: on offense at receiver and now running back, and on defense at safety, punt and kickoff coverage, punt and kickoff return. He came out of the game, and Tim Dunn replaced him.

Dunn took a pitch right and turned at a right angle upfield, his straight-line sprinter's speed facing no resistance until he'd reached the Catholic 43, a twenty-yard pickup. Rankin gained ten on a keeper, and Dunn plowed ahead off-tackle for another seven behind the two fullbacks. Catholic bottled up a sweep left and a sweep right with Dunn and suddenly, it seemed, the down marker they hadn't had to worry about as long as they were biting off huge chunks of yardage had flipped over to four, with five yards to go from the 23.

"Kelleybrew!" Cox yelled.

In the huddle, Rankin called, "Full left, forty-one sweep."

Rankin pivoted right and pitched to Kelleybrew, who started left behind Bennett and Rollins. Left end Henderson in a two tight-end set drove his man way wide and kept driving him. Bennett delayed a shooting linebacker long enough to let Kelleybrew scoot outside him and inside Henderson, and then the fullback, whose back pad bore the letters IHOP in Sharpie for the frequent pancake blocks he delivered, went looking for another man to take out. By this time Kelleybrew was only to the line of scrimmage; he'd need five more. The unfortunate defensive back in the 235-pound Bennett's way was the five-foot-seven, 157-pound Eric Redmon, a tenth grader. Bennett treated Redmon to a pancake at the 20, two yards from a first down, but the plucky Rocket managed to reach up while on his back and throw Kelleybrew off stride. The runner stumbled another five yards before falling, making the first down as the crowd and the sidelines erupted. But Redmon had saved a certain touchdown. It was first down from the 13 with 3:10 remaining.

Kelleybrew went for two, Rankin for another two on a busted play. Dunn cut a sweep up and charged ahead to the 3-yard line for a first down. On the next play, the submarining Rocket whom Fears had laid down on for the whole drive finally got his revenge as he dived under Fears and tripped up Dunn for no gain. On second down, Kelleybrew came in again and took the ball on a sweep wide to the right; he cut it upfield too soon. Bennett was leading him around the end, and when he saw that Kelleybrew had turned it up and was stopped, he threw his hands in the air in frustration. "I should have just kept going to the outside," Kelleybrew said later. "When I got back to the huddle, I was like, 'I hope we don't lose because of this.'"

It was third down and goal from the 3-yard line with only thirty-eight seconds remaining in the game. This time Rankin faked a dive to Rollins and pitched out to Kelleybrew, who went wide left. Bennett took care of the charging linebacker, but perhaps remembering his mistake on his last sweep, instead of cutting up, which seemed open, Kelleybrew stayed wide, and senior cornerback Jordan Carlisle charged into the backfield and dropped Kelleybrew cold at the 5. Central called a time-out with twenty-one seconds left in the game.

On the Catholic sidelines, coach Ellis "Scooter" Register was certain he knew what Central would do: He told his defense to watch for the tight-end dump pass, despite the success Central had had with the run game.

On the Central sidelines, Cox huddled with Callaway, Rankin, and tight end Damien Lee, who insisted that he should be the target. "It's open," he said of the dump pass to him. He was face mask to face mask with Rankin, and he told the quarterback: "Just throw it up, I'll get it." Cox and Callaway agreed they could try.

The Tiger offense lined up in the power I, with Kelleybrew at tailback. Rankin took the snap and faked a dive on the right side to Rollins, which froze the linebacker for a split second. Kelleybrew had sprinted to the right as if on a sweep, drawing wide both the safety and the defensive end lined up over Lee, who faked a block and then cut inside, his right arm waving above his head as a target for Rankin, who put the ball about a foot over Lee's hand. Lee, the self-proclaimed Hands "R" Us, leapt and caught the ball over his head, quickly bringing it into his gut and curling around it as one Rocket hit him low and another high, helicoptering his body as he fell into the end zone. He held onto the ball, bouncing up and striking his bodybuilder's pose again, to tie the game 27–27. Rankin had raised his hands in the touchdown signal as soon as the ball left his hand, almost before the pass had been caught, and he seemed riveted to the ground in that position, a statue while bedlam was breaking loose around him on the field, on the sidelines, and in the stands. Kelleybrew simply said to himself, "Thank you, Jesus." Even as the excitement crested, the extra-point try remained for freshman Walker Hawkins (the only freshman on the roster), and the coaches waved their hands for calm.

A motion penalty before the try moved the ball back five yards, so the kick would be a twenty-five yarder, a yard longer than the earlier field goal attempt that had hit the upright in the second quarter. He'd also had an extra point tipped at the line. Rankin, the holder, knelt and placed his left hand on the spot where the ball would go. He signaled with his right for the snap, but nothing happened. He signaled again more desperately. They couldn't afford a delay-of-game penalty that would move them back another five yards. Rollins finally centered the ball, and Rankin caught it cleanly and planted it. This time the kick was high and true, and Central had the lead by one, 28–27.

Catholic had twenty-one seconds to work with, but three plays later, the game ended with an incompletion, and Central's bench stormed the field. Cheerleaders and fans followed to join the celebration.

After every game, the teams formed two lines on the field and passed each other one by one, slapping hands and repeating "Good game" over and over, but this time the Catholic players were stunned into silence. As every Central player reached the last Rocket in the line, he jumped in the air and ran to join the scrum of black-uniformed teammates.

In the Central locker room, the noisy celebration continued. When Cox came in after talking to reporters on the field, some of the players called for quiet to allow him to address the team. He reminded them that they had an important game, the team's final game, the next Thursday (a scheduling quirk) against the Bryant Hornets, and he then said simply, "As a coaching staff, I can't tell you how proud we are of you." That was it. The players clustered together for the postgame cheer, a call-and-response alternating "Beat Hornets!" and "What!?!" a dozen times before ending in "Tiger Pri-i-i-i-i-i-de!"

Where was Quinton Brown? The nose guard, generously listed at five foot seven in the program, could have been lost in the crowd. He'd had a heck of a game, with three tackles, two assists, and a sack. Here he came down the hall from the weight room, where the visiting team dressed. He'd gone there—on his own, by himself—to congratulate Catholic on the great game.

There was one more player missing, Walker Hawkins. As a freshman, he was assigned a locker down the hall, not with the upperclassmen, so Adam Meeks, the starting quarterback for the game who'd been benched after one series, went to retrieve him, throwing the 150-pounder over his shoulder and bringing him into the main room for another round of applause and cheers.

The coaches collapsed in their respective spots in the office, exhausted but happy. The smallest joke caused peals of laughter. Callaway repeated

Randy's line about Red Bull to those on the staff who hadn't heard it and also said that Catholic coach Scooter Register, one of his best friends in the world, was "speechless," a state he implied didn't happen very often.

One by one, players, after they'd dressed and just before they left the stadium, opened the door, briefly allowing the continuing din of the locker room to enter with them.

Kelleybrew was one of the first. "Way to coach, coaches," he told them.

Aaron Nichols, the senior safety, entered and said, "I just want to tell y'all I love y'all."

The next day, euphoria from the game was still in the air as the coaches met to watch the game film and prepare for the Bryant game.

"I don't care what anybody says, we got some good kids," said Stan Williams as Seward was setting up the tape.

"You betcha," said Siegel.

"I even say that when we lose," said Finley.

The film reached Damien Lee's catch and showed Hawkins lining up for the extra point. As the ball sailed through to give the Tigers the lead, the camera stopped and lingered on Champ, the giant friendly inflatable tiger mascot set up beyond the goalpost.

"That tiger's really smiling now," said Keith Richardson.

"He's so handsome," said Finley.

IIIIIIIIIIIIIIIIIIIIIIIIIIIIIIIIIIIIIIIIII

There was another game to play. In a startling upset on Friday, last place North Little Rock had beaten undefeated Bryant, the No. 1–ranked team in the state, 21–0. That left Bryant and Russellville tied atop the conference standings with 5-1 records. Central came next at 4-2, with Cabot and Catholic following at 3-3. If Central defeated Bryant, they were assured a playoff spot. If they lost, the Tigers were still in a good position, since Cabot had a tough game at Russellville, and Catholic would play Conway. If the Rockets won, which was likely, and ended with the same record as Central, the Tigers would take that playoff spot in the head-to-head. Confusion would reign only if Central lost and Cabot and Catholic both won, which would cause a three-way tie, with no one team who had defeated the other two, or in the parlance of the Arkansas Activities Association, a "perfect triangle." Then the tiebreaker would come down to a point-differential formula.

At the beginning of the week of practice, a short one because of the Thursday game, Cox told the team that several people had called him over the weekend and said to him that, for the first time all season, "we were looking like a bunch of kids and coaches who are becoming a family, people who respect each other and play for each other." They mentioned the excitement on the sidelines, how involved everyone seemed in the fortunes of the others.

As the week progressed, however, the team seemed to regress. It was almost as if in reaching that goal of unity—the one that had eluded them all season until the defense galvanized against Catholic with the blocked punt and the intercepted pass and the offense huddled in their own end zone with a common goal to move ninety-nine yards—they felt free to revert back to their former bad habits. On Tuesday, five players were tardy, so they were assigned five bleachers after practice. On Wednesday, the offense earned five more bleachers for not being organized enough to get a play off on time.

"We've tried to put some urgency in practice today," Cox said on Wednesday. "You guys look up 'urgency' in a dictionary. If you don't have a dictionary, call someone who does. We need to play with urgency tomorrow night." But everything seemed out of whack. That day was Halloween, and there was no school on Thursday (for a teacher in-service day), so their schedule was off. He wondered aloud what his players would do that night, whether the temptation to raise hell on the holiday would be too great to keep them focused on football. He hoped they'd make some good decisions, adding, "This may be your last football game this year." He tried to fire them up by telling them that after the 2006 game at Quigley, which Central had won 23–14 to finish the regular season undefeated, he'd overheard a conversation between two Bryant fans who said that the next year would be better because they'd go 9-0 and for the Central game, "We don't have to go to the 'hood." Now, the next year was here.

Southwest of the city in Saline County, just over the Pulaski County line, Bryant was similar to Cabot in the extravagance of its football facilities and support of its team and the homogeneity of its population, which was only 1.5 percent black (according to the 2000 census). It, too, had an indoor turf practice field in a modern and well-appointed field house, allowing its players to practice no matter the vicissitudes of Arkansas weather. The town had also experienced an exurban boom. On a Little Rock sports-talk radio show, the Bryant coach, Paul Calley, had said that their weight room was "second to none" and had also marveled at the growth of the community. "When I first got here" in the early 1990s, he said, "there was no downtown." Indeed, the population had nearly doubled from 1990 to 2000 (from 5,200 to 9,700), almost all of whom worked in Little Rock, and estimates since then had it increasing by another 4,000. Calley dressed out ninety-five players. Unlike Cabot's nearly exclusive ground game, Bryant ran a spread offense and threw often from a five-wide set, a potential problem for Central's shaky secondary.

Cox and the coaches had believed all season that the Tigers were their own worst enemies, that the talent was there, and as he asked the team on Wednesday, "The challenge is not Bryant, it's who?"

"Us," they answered.

During the defensive meeting before the game, Horton addressed the squad, and though he was happy to be back with the team and had spent hours charting out Bryant's offense from game tapes and though he was recovering well from his injured knee ("I'll tell you what, if we took our football team out there to therapy and put them through what they put me through today, they damn sure would be in shape"), his words had a valedictory tone. Mary Jo worried about him being on the sidelines, had worried before the Russellville game, so perhaps it was time for him to hang it up, and if this was the last game, he didn't want to pass up the chance to say something. After telling them that they needed to be aggressive and that they still had a chance to go all the way, he paused and his eyes began to well. "Fellas," he said, "I've enjoyed working with you this year, and I'd like to have a chance to do it another week." Linebacker Hunter Sinele hugged him.

At the beginning of the year, Cox had told the parents that if their sons didn't hear the coaches preaching about doing the "little things," then they hadn't been to practice that day. At the end of the season, the little things were still of concern to Cox and the staff, were still looming large for Central. Before he sent them onto the field, Cox said he hoped they would make Bryant earn everything they got. "We've been charitable all year," he said. "Play hard, play fast, play smart."

Passing on nearly every play, the Hornets found the seams in the secondary and, with a series of short completions across the middle, jumped out quickly to a 7–0 lead. For their part, Central could not move the ball until the offense went to the power I, with Dunn at tailback behind Rollins and Bennett. Dunn carried all eight times on a sixty-eight-yard drive for the equaling touchdown. Callaway was ecstatic on the sidelines, telling the offense that the Bryant defense was putting "eleven in the box, and we're whipping all eleven."

Seward had moved safety Aaron Nichols to cornerback for this game, precisely because Central had been victimized by Catholic on the wheel route up the sideline for a touchdown, and that move paid off when Bryant tried to run a similar play and Nichols picked off the pass and returned it to the Bryant 9. Dunn scored two plays later to give Central a 13–7 lead (the extra point was no good).

"They've been behind before," Callaway warned at halftime, and Finley echoed him with "They're coming with everything and the kitchen sink in the second half." Bryant's quarterback, Logan Parker, began to find his range in the third quarter, as the Hornets went to a no-huddle offense and hit seven consecutive short passes under the coverage before finding Taylor Masters for a twenty-six-yard score. The extra point gave Bryant the lead, 14–13.

No one thinks much about catching a kickoff. Even if you drop it, the defenders are far away and it rarely results in a turnover. But it's one of the little things. On the ensuing kickoff from Bryant, the ball hit Bo Dillon in the chest and bounced nearby in front of him. He immediately picked it up and started toward the middle of the field, but the brief muff had thrown off the timing of the blocking and the first line of Bryant tacklers converged on him unimpeded. One spun him around and another's helmet landed squarely on the ball, shooting it out of his arms at the 17-yard line, where a Bryant player fell on it. The defense returned to the field, and two plays later, Bryant scored again, making it 21–13.

There would be no comeback this time. The Hornets scored again in the fourth quarter to take a fifteen-point lead, 28–13, with a little more than six minutes left. Even putting Kelleybrew in at tailback didn't seem to make any difference for Central. As Bryant was running out the clock, the PA announcer gave an update of the scores. Catholic had easily defeated Conway, as expected, and Cabot was leading Russellville 48–42 in the final minute, with Russellville in possession and driving near midfield. According to the point-differential tiebreaker, Cabot needed to win by twelve points or more to take the final playoff spot from Central. That seemed highly unlikely in the announced scenario. As the Tigers trudged back to the locker room under the stands, the team at least knew that they'd have a shot in the playoffs to get on a run and perhaps prove that the preseason No. 1 ranking had been justified.

Cox hadn't heard the score of the Cabot-Russellville game. "Guys, we played a good football team," he said. "We knew that going in. . . . We'll get you out of here as soon as we can. What the future holds, I don't know. You'll know as soon as I know. We may not have a game next week. . . . "

"We don't, Coach," said Seward. He had been on his cell phone, hearing a report of the wild end to the Russellville-Cabot game. When Russellville had scored to trail 48–42, 1:40 remained. Cabot fumbled on the next possession and Russellville recovered with forty-three seconds left. That's when the score was announced in Bryant. The Cyclones then threw an interception, which Cabot, needing a touchdown for the point difference to matter, returned to the Russellville 5-yard line with four seconds remaining. On the game's last play, Cabot's fullback, Michael James, bulled in for the score, giving Cabot the margin of victory it needed to knock Central out of the final playoff spot.

The old weight room that served as the visitors' locker room at Bryant began to fill with sobs. Randy Rankin let out a howl. For the seniors, their high school careers were over. For most of them, their football careers were over.

Cox had been more prescient than he wanted to be. Before the first game of the season against West Memphis, he had warned them that he didn't want them to "finish this season 6-4 and play that tenth game and not make the playoffs," but that's exactly what had happened. He left unspoken now what he had told them then he feared he'd have to say: You could have been better.

"Let's go, let's get out of here," he said.

The traffic was bad, and the two buses idled for a long time in the parking lot. Finally, they wove their way through Bryant and onto I-40 toward Little Rock. The route took them up I-430, on which Clarence Finley had worked back in the 1970s as a young man doing summer construction. They merged onto the Wilbur D. Mills Freeway, passing Baptist Hospital, where Clyde Horton had once lay dying in the ICU, and the exit for John Barrow Road, down which John Carter had hung from a telephone pole.

The highway was lightly traveled at that time of night, and the trip went quickly, slicing through the neighborhood along what used to be Eighth Street, now only a historical memory, reduced to a layer of geologic strata impressed upon by the concrete of the interstate. At Woodrow Street, the buses exited and approached the intersection at Twelfth Street, where the four corners held a shuttered funeral home, a liquor store, a beauty-supply shop, and an E-Z Mart, in whose parking lot the whirling lights of four police cars were creating a kaleidoscopic tableau.

As the bus turned left onto Twelfth Street, Stan Williams craned his neck to look at the scene and told the driver, a black woman who was new for the team, "Slow down and let me see what's happening in my 'hood."

"I don't know why they would need *four* police cars," she said.

Six blocks later, she turned right onto Park Street and noticed for the first time the new Central High Museum, dedicated a little more than a month before.

The bus in front of her slowed to a stop before the façade of the school, so she did the same. The building was lit up just as it had been on Halloween night in 1927, eighty years and one night before, when Mary Lewis had returned to her hometown to dedicate its auditorium with the soaring notes of classical arias—and "Dixie."

"Quiet," said one of the boys on the bus. "One . . . two . . . three . . . " And they began to add their own song to the air, a discordant and terribly off-key version of the school's hoary alma mater, the line asserting "Vic-to-ry!" seeming once again to mock the pain of their loss.

During the singing, all heads in the bus, those of students and adults alike, were turned to the impressive structure, taking it in. How many of them were thinking of the nine black students who had ascended those steps, armed soldiers beside them, under the leaning alabaster figures of Ambition, Personality, Opportunity, and Preparation? Probably none. It was their school, too, after all, where their own lives spooled out day by day, and the most important thing in their minds right then was the loss of a game and the end of football, for some just for the fall, for others forever.

THE STORY OF THE "LITTLE ROCK" WAS MISSING. To the right of the Junction Bridge, the former Missouri Pacific railroad bridge recently converted to pedestrian use, and halfway down the steep bank to the water stood a stone podium like an altar from a forgotten ancient sect. It had held a plaque describing the history of the city's namesake outcropping, but the explanatory marker presumably had been removed for safekeeping. The flat surface to which it had been secured now held a strange graffito M, perhaps part of some gang alphabet.

Fences and construction litter surrounded the foot of the bridge, evidence of the city's La Petite Roche Plaza project, a $650,000 effort undertaken in 2009 to spruce up Little Rock's founding site. Besides excavating and revealing more of the geologic formation, the project would eventually set up in the surrounding park interpretive-history displays explaining "a myriad of storylines associated with the rock," according to the city parks department, including those from Indians, settlers, the railroad, and other "commercial enterprises." As part of the beautification, "The rock itself will be exposed with the use of native grasses and shrubs to soften its edges."

In other areas, the edges of Little Rock exposed during 2007 were undergoing some softening.

In January 2008, the *Democrat-Gazette* reported that the Little Rock School Board used a Saturday session "to work on strengthening their interpersonal skills and their ability to work with one another." The primary business of the board in the aftermath of the dismissal of Roy Brooks was finding another superintendent. Linda Watson, a longtime district employee, had been appointed interim superintendent. There had been rumors circulating around the coaches' office that she was a sorority sister of board president Katherine Mitchell and so was assured of being appointed to the position permanently. Some board members objected to investing in a national search firm to fill the position. After all, Roy Brooks, an outsider, had not performed to their liking; maybe a local person who knew the local problems could do a better job.

In March of 2008, the board voted four to three, along racial lines, to hire Linda Watson as the permanent superintendent. In June of 2009, Max Brantley wrote in his column in the *Arkansas Times* that in her year-plus tenure she had managed to unify the school board, but not in a good way: "a shared opinion of black and white board members seems to be that the superintendent isn't getting the job done." The board met in executive session in July and decided not to extend her contract, which had two years to run, and issued some specific objectives for her to meet over her remaining tenure.

Chris Heller, the board's counsel, said in late 2009, "I don't think people see the board today as racially divided." He added that John Walker may have helped get two board members elected, but said that they were "all individuals who have their own ideas about the way things ought to be" and "formed alliances issue by issue." John Walker himself entered electoral politics in the spring of 2010 when he filed to run for the Arkansas House of Representatives in District 34, which includes Central High and neighborhoods just south of I-630.

Central principal Nancy Rousseau admitted that the fiftieth-anniversary commemoration had been "very stressful" as well as exciting, but that it did bring a "closure of sorts": "It was like reading a wonderful book." She added, "I really do have faith that this school will grow—and make choices about opening our minds."

In the Central High football program, things fell apart, shockingly and monumentally. The 2007 game against Catholic High was Bernie Cox's 271st win, the second most of all time among Arkansas high school football coaches, but it would be his last victory as head coach at Central. During

2008 and 2009, the Tigers went 0-20. Along with the loss to Bryant at the end of 2007, the losing streak stood at 21 games, the worst in the 105-year history of the program.

What happened? Part of the reason can be attributed to the cycles of talent in the school. Even in 2007, the lack of strong, powerful players at the running back position had hampered the offense, and Cox's system required a big, durable back to pick up crucial third downs. Bo Dillon, Tim Dunn, and Denzel Harris, not to mention Kaelon Kelleybrew, all had stellar moments at tailback during the year, but none had the day-in, day-out dependability a host of running backs had displayed over the previous two decades: Charles Clay, Mickey Dean, Dedrick Poole, Andre Covington, Corry Adams. In 2008, the Tigers' go-to back was Mayborn Peters, a transfer from Catholic who was quick and fast and almost beat his old Catholic team single-handedly by rushing for two hundred yards, but he stood five foot six, at best. In 2009, Tim "T.T." Campbell and Chris Johnson, while diligent workers, were from the same mold.

Bad luck was also a factor. Before the 2008 season began, three projected starters suffered injuries and missed the entire year. Two other key players transferred—A. J. McCray to Episcopal Collegiate and De'Arius Hudson to North Little Rock.

But other things were at work. Football trends were moving away from Cox's brand of power football. In October of 2008, the sports section of the *Arkansas Democrat-Gazette* ran a front-page story about the offensive scoring explosion in Arkansas high school football, traced to the no-huddle spread offense initiated by northwest Arkansas coach Gus Malzahn, now the offensive coordinator at Auburn. In those schemes, the quarterback often takes the snap in a shotgun formation and has five receivers to choose from. Pine Bluff coach Bobby Bolding commented, "Some people are putting their best athletes on offense. . . . Guys are catching short passes, making that one guy miss and turning it into a touchdown." In Cox's last two state championship seasons, 2003 and 2004, including a decisive victory over Malzahn's Springdale team in the playoffs, the Central coach had proved that his style could still be successful, but it required the proper athletes—conditioned with a punishing work ethic—to execute it. Understandably, high school players might prefer the wide-open, pinball-type football they saw Tom Brady and Peyton Manning executing to the grinding game that Bernie Cox had successfully implemented for nearly four decades.

As Cox once stated, you have to win sometimes, if you have the talent, or you lose the kids. Throughout his career, winning was never the primary goal for Cox, but constant losing can engender a corrosiveness that defeats all good intentions. The winless 2008 season behind them, the Tiger faithful had reason to hope 2009 might produce a better showing.

After a number of years of suffering through invidious comparisons of facilities, Central boosters, led by Walker Hawkins's father, Drake, had initiated a building program called the Q Project to upgrade Quigley Stadium so the school might compete with the Cabots, Bryants, and Texarkanas—or at least not be embarrassed by their own entropic if historic stadium. Future plans called for a field house at the north end, and some progressive ideas knocking around included approaching the National Park Service, which oversaw the visitors' center and the historic district in which the stadium lay, about designating as a permanent empty seat in the stadium the place where Ernest Green had sat as the first black graduate of Central, an event that Martin Luther King Jr. had observed from the bleachers.

In the summer of 2009, the Q Project foundation raised $500,000 to install an artificial surface. The school district, although always determined not to play favorites among its high schools, went along with the seeming benefit to Central because middle school teams also played at Quigley, and during the record-setting rainy season that followed its installation, other district teams were able to schedule games there to save wear and tear on their own grass fields. The first game on the turf, and the rededication of the facility as Quigley-Cox Stadium at Verizon Wireless Field—in "honor" of the corporate partners—saw Central face Van Buren, the league's perennial doormat, and lose, 28–24, after leading by ten points.

Some parents and players had had enough. One starter quit. Discussion boards and talk radio began to buzz with anger, not only complaining that Central *was* losing, but also decrying the *way* the team was losing.

In October of 2009, Cox announced that he was retiring at the end of the season. His last game at Quigley was against Catholic, and many of his former players attended. After the game, Will Rollins, the wide-smiling, mop-haired fullback who had made such a formidable power I blocking tandem with William Bennett to help win the Catholic game two years before, once again descended the stairs to the coaches' office. It looked very familiar to him: Larry Siegel was in the back corner, the plaster tiger behind him still piled with hats; Clarence Finley leaned back in his chair, the DVD player open on his desk; the manila folders and videotapes on Darrell Seward's desk were all squared at the corners, and Stan Williams was off to the side, still needling Seward about the coach's having the rubber bands in his drawer organized by size. Norman Callaway had lost a ton of weight, but still used a pulled-out desk drawer as a footrest. And Bernie Cox was still next to the window, the same sign about not caring who gets the credit on his desk, the same bus forms to be filled out stacked under his pen. It all looked mostly the same, but twenty straight losses (and a probable twenty-first at Bryant the next week) had etched hard lines into every face.

Rollins had been a fullback and linebacker in 2008, so he'd experienced half the losing streak. He wore a blue and red warmup suit, the breast of the jacket stitched with a cursive "Ole Miss." That fall, he had walked on at the University of Mississippi, now coached by Houston Nutt, the quarterback who had given Bernie Cox an undefeated season in his inaugural year as Central's head man. Nutt himself had suffered the scorn of critical fans and left the Razorbacks for the University of Mississippi in late 2007. Rollins was working with the Rebels as a long snapper. He looked around at the characters he'd spent his last two high school seasons with and couldn't help but produce a toothy grin.

"I just wanted to come down and tell you guys I love y'all," he said, and gave hugs all around.

A number of other players from the 2007 team went on to play college football. Kaelon Kelleybrew and Jared Green, who was the Little Rock Metro Defensive Player of the Year as a senior, both received football scholarships to Mississippi Valley State University in Itta Bena, Mississippi, a historically black institution best known for producing Pro Football Hall of Fame receiver Jerry Rice. Kelleybrew intercepted two passes as a freshman and, despite injuries during his sophomore season, returned six kickoffs for an average of 24.2 yards. Green was named to the All-Southwestern Athletic Conference second team as a sophomore and transferred at the beginning of 2010 to the University of Arkansas, where he would have to sit out the following season. Despite having played only two and half games before breaking his leg, A. J. Williams was named to participate in the annual Arkansas high school all-star game, held the following summer. He then matriculated to Ouachita Baptist University in Arkadelphia, Arkansas, where he played in all ten games at defensive back as a sophomore, with four pass breakups and one fumble recovery. Aaron Nichols had initially walked on at Ole Miss, but by early 2010 had transferred to Tyler Junior College in Texas, where he was planning to play in the fall. After finishing his high school football career at North Little Rock, De'Arius Hudson accepted a scholarship to the University of Arkansas at Pine Bluff, where he joined Damien Lee, who had earned a scholarship the year before after graduating from Central in 2009. Kyle Temple, Randy Rankin, Bo Dillon, Joseph Schilling, and others finished their football careers at Central and headed to college at the University of Arkansas at Fayetteville.

Lee, Nichols, Quinton Brown, and other former Tigers met again at a sad reunion in the spring of 2010. Their teammate Tim Dunn, who had made several crucial runs during the final drive to win the Catholic game in 2007 and had been performing well as a walk-on player at Arkansas State University in Jonesboro, was killed in a motorcycle accident there on March 7. Funny, polite, devout, and studious, Dunn was eulogized at a painful and moving two-and-a-half-hour service held at New Hope Baptist Church in North Little Rock. The overflow crowd heard triumphant gospel music and heart-wrenching tributes from his family, fiancée, friends, and pastors.

On the morning of Bernie Cox's final game as Central's head coach at Bryant in 2009, the *Democrat-Gazette* high school football writer, Robert Yates, wrote a story headlined: "Central's Woes at Historic Levels." Yates had been a two-year letterman for Cox in 1980 and 1981 and had edited

Brian Cox's five-hundred-page history of Central football, *Tiger Pride*, writing in the foreword dated June 14, 2005, "I was lucky enough to play on two state championship teams coached by Cox, a man whose blueprint for success hasn't wavered." Apparently, by 2009, Yates thought it should have wavered. His story, leading the sports section, laid the blame for the losing streak entirely at the feet of the coaching staff, whom he accused of gross negligence to duty at worst and detachment at best and quoted disgruntled parents, none of whom chose to go on the record. Nor did he seem to have confronted Cox or the coaching staff with the charges to get their perspective. The athletic director at the school, Jay Pickering, declined to comment. No opposing coach would comment, "out of respect, they said, for Cox." There was certainly something going on in the program and room for a journalistic exploration of that fact, and some of the allegations may have been valid, but this was a nasty piece of work to lay on the breakfast table of a man on the last day he was working at a job he'd already decided to give up after serving the school for so many decades.

Bryant's coach, Paul Calley, brought more empathy to the moment as the game's host team. Before the coin toss, the PA announcer called for Cox to come to the center of the field, which he reluctantly did. There, Calley presented Cox with a plaque honoring his service to the coaching profession on the occasion of his final game as Central's head coach and wished him good luck. Bryant won the game, 34–0.

At first, Bernie Cox thought he might stay on at Central and teach through the 2010–2011 school year without holding any coaching duties, but in the spring of 2010, he decided to leave the school. He took a position as an assistant defensive coach with private Arkansas Baptist High School, where he would also teach history. It would be his forty-fifth fall in a high-school classroom and on a high school football field.

Meanwhile, the search for a new coach had begun, and Internet message boards were burning up with rumors of who might replace Cox. It was still one of the top coaching jobs in the state, though Little Rock School District pay was not great and the teaching requirements might have scared off some successful coaches from other districts who didn't have those responsibilities in their current positions. For most coaches anywhere, the facilities would be a comedown. Many had for years thought of Darrell Seward as the successor coach; he was meticulous, fiery, knowledgeable, and sensitive. After the 2007 season, when Kaelon Kelleybrew's mother, Katrina, called the coaches' office to see if they knew who might help her put together a highlight tape of Kaelon for college recruiters, Seward volunteered to do the job himself. "I called just to ask if they knew anybody that could get me started, point me in the direction," she said. "And he just said, 'I'll do it.' I really thank him for that."

On December 22, 2009, Central called a press conference to announce the new coach, and the name was a surprise to many: Catholic High's Ellis "Scooter" Register. He had coached in the Little Rock public schools before, at Forest Heights Junior High and at McClellan High, where his 1995 team had finished as the state runner-up. He then had moved to the head job at El Dorado High in southern Arkansas, winning the conference title in five of seven years, before moving back to Little Rock and Catholic High in 2003. There, he had brought some excitement and enthusiasm to a program that had lost some of its spark. During the hour-long press conference, no one mentioned Cox's name. The new coach talked about restoring the Tigers to their former glory and said, "I've watched Central closely these past two years and it didn't seem like they were far away from winning, but a little something was missing. We just have to get that back."

ACKNOWLEDGMENTS

This book would not have been possible without the access granted me by Central coach Bernie Cox, who allowed me to observe him and his coaching staff up close from the summer of 2007 to the end of the year and beyond. Cox is a private man, but his belief that he and colleagues had nothing to hide and, in fact, were proud of the way they conducted themselves and ran their program led him to overcome doubts about letting a journalist in their midst. From the end of July 2007 when two-a-days started through the last game of the season, I spent nearly every day on the practice field, at games, and in the coaches' office. I am grateful to the entire coaching staff for the time they spent answering my questions and allowing me into their lives: Adam Acklin, Norman Callaway, Clarence Finley, Clyde Horton, Keith Richardson, Darrell Seward, Larry Siegel, and Stan Williams are all dedicated, selfless educators and good men. In addition, Bernie Cox, Clarence Finley, and Keith Richardson sat for extensive interviews. Special thanks go to Brian Cox (Bernie's son and the team's trainer) and Clyde Horton, both of whose devotion to Tiger football made my experience of spending a year with the team much richer. Brian Cox's comprehensive book, *Tiger Pride: 100 Years of Little Rock Central High Football*, saved me untold hours of research and is as much an indispensable resource for the history of Little Rock and its citizens as it is for Tiger football. Volunteer assistant coach Tommy Walker took the cover photograph, and his photography Web site (arsportspix.com) provided an oft-visited documentary resource for the season as well as a valuable source for photographs in the insert.

Players who agreed to indulge me with extended conversations or interviews included Quinton Brown, Reed Caradine, Bo Dillon, Tim Dunn, Jared Green, Denzel Harris, Rickey Hicks, De'Arius Hudson, Kaelon Kelleybrew, Damien Lee, Aaron Nichols, Dallas Odom, Randy Rankin, Will Rollins, and Hunter Sinele. Parents and other family members of players who sat for interviews, allowed me into their homes, spoke with me at length, or otherwise aided my research were Lori Conley, Johnnie and Wilma Davis, Tony and Janet Dillon, Drake and Melissa Hawkins, Katrina Kelleybrew, Mawmaw Nichols and Tammy Okoli, Randy Rankin Sr., and Ford Sinele.

Others who sat down with me, sometimes on a number of occasions, to discuss Little Rock, Central, and their own lives included Dr. Jay Barth, Max Brantley, Nate Coulter, Bernie Lee Cox, Christopher Heller, Dr. Cal Ledbetter, Antwan Phillips, Nancy Rousseau, and Ken Richardson. I am grateful for their time and cooperation.

I would also like to thank Tiffany Hoffman and Johnny Johnson of the Little Rock School District and Jay Pickering and Chuck West at Central.

Research assistant Sara Thompson diligently helped me track down the most obscure facts and saved me from error a number of times. The Butler Center for Arkansas Studies, headed by David Stricklin, is a treasure for any historian doing work on Arkansas subjects of all kinds and, along with the excellent Central Arkansas Library System, led by Bobby Roberts, makes up one of Little Rock's greatest cultural assets. Rhonda Stewart at the Butler Center was especially helpful.

Chris Parris-Lamb at the Gernert Agency sought me out, helped hone my idea, expertly shepherded it to the right publisher, and provided unerring advice through the publishing process; he, on the other hand, ignored my advice that he not go out too fast in his first marathon. At Rodale, my editor Shannon Welch saw what I was trying to do and then made it better, offering an exit out of dead ends and support throughout. I owe them both a great debt of thanks. Copy editor Nancy Elgin cast a cold eye on my errors but read the book with warmth.

Others who provided various forms of encouragement and help include Garth Battista, Dr. Wesley Burks, Sheila Callaghan, Stephen Chaffin, Chuck

Cliett, Hope Coulter, Stacey Cox, Myrene Cox, Kevin Crass, Lilly Golden, Stephanie Harp, Laura Hendrie, Anna Hubbard, Dara Keithley, Jonathan Mahler, David Margolick, Rhett Miller, Cal Papavasilopoulos, Sophocles Papavasilopoulos, Mary Ellen Richards, Margaret Russell, Skip Rutherford, Becky Spohn, Janet Steen, Warwick Sabin, John Tull, and Scott Walters.

Michelle Kaemmerling put up with a book-length collection of my anxieties and, along with Anna Cay Vernon, gave me with more comfort and joy than I deserved.

My late uncles, Earp Jennings Jr. and Alston Jennings Sr., managers for the Little Rock High School football teams in 1932 and 1933 respectively, went on to become no less than one of the best chemical engineers and one of the best trial lawyers in the country and are a testament to the enduring quality of public education in Little Rock.

This book is dedicated to my father, Walter Jennings, Little Rock High class of '39, and to the memory of my mother, Medora Sifford Jennings, and my brother, Walt Jennings Jr., whose love and pride are with me every day. My sister, Elizabeth Jennings McGee, brother-in-law Sam, and nieces, Grace and Emma, have always provided much love, support, and laughter, but it was never so needed or appreciated during the writing of this book.

If I have inadvertently left out some who should have been acknowledged, I hope they will forgive me, and it goes without saying that no one other than I bears any responsibility for what I have written.

In *Notes of a Native Son*, James Baldwin expressed simply what I also hope to accomplish with my life: "I want to be an honest man and a good writer."

In memoriam: Tim Dunn 1989–2010

SELECTED SOURCES

As the starting point for historical research, I most often turned to the excellent Encyclopedia of Arkansas (encyclopediaofarkansas.net), an online project of the Butler Center for Arkansas Studies and the Central Arkansas Library System. Respected scholars, educators, librarians, and amateur historians have contributed most of the entries. Under the categories below, I have listed those individual entries from the Encyclopedia of Arkansas that I consulted most frequently.

I invariably delved further into topics treated in any depth, searching the considerable holdings of the Butler Center. In addition, for more than a century, Little Rock was blessed with two thorough and often prizewinning daily newspapers, the *Arkansas Democrat* and the *Arkansas Gazette*, whose archives on microfilm were essential to my research. After a bitter newspaper war, in 1991, the *Democrat* bought the assets and ceased publication of the *Gazette*, which five years earlier had been acquired by the Gannett Company, and began publishing its paper as the *Arkansas Democrat-Gazette*. Both the individual papers of the past and the more recent incarnation were searched for almost every topic below.

For contemporary coverage of local education and politics, the *Democrat-Gazette* and the *Arkansas Times* were essential reading. The "Arkansas Blog" of the *Times*, most often manned by editor Max Brantley, supplements the weekly paper's original reporting with notification of breaking news and a freewheeling comments section, which offers both the worst and best of Internet reader reaction: the occasional anonymous, gratuitous attacks and insults, but often thoughtful, eloquent, and well-informed opinions from the full political spectrum.

The most comprehensive book about the 1957 crisis, Elizabeth Jacoway's *Turn Away Thy Son*, published in 2007, is unlikely to be surpassed and was my first and often my last stop for information about that event. The work of historians John Kirk and Ben F. Johnson III provided valuable context around the crisis. I was fortunate that two of the Little Rock Nine published their memoirs in 2009 as I was writing, revealing important insights and details: *A Mighty Long Way*, by Carlotta Walls LaNier, with Lisa Frazier Page; and *Lessons from Little Rock*, by Terrence Roberts.

Books that I turned to again and again for inspiration and sometimes for information were Tracy Kidder's *Home Town*, J. Anthony Lukas's *Common Ground*, and (to state the obvious) Buzz Bissinger's *Friday Night Lights*, all dealing with the idea of community, the "ordinary" citizens who bring it to life, and their various struggles, noble and ignoble.

Following is a list of some sources I used in my research, arranged by subject.

THE EARLY HISTORY OF LITTLE ROCK

Brown, Dee Alexander. *When the Century Was Young*. New York: HarperPerennial, 1994.

Featherstonhaugh, George William. *Excursion through the Slave States, from Washington on the Potomax, to the Frontier of Mexico; with Sketches of Popular Manners and Geological Notices*. New York: Harper, 1844.

Herndon, Dallas T., ed. *Centennial History of Arkansas*. Chicago: The S. J. Clarke Publishing Company, 1922.

Hallum, John. *Biographical and Pictorial History of Arkansas*. Albany: Weed, Parsons and Co., 1887.

"Moving the Rock to City Hall," *Pulaski County Historical Review* (Winter 1988).

Simon, Stephanie. "Arkansas Capital Actually Has a Little Rock—If You Can Find It." *Wall Street Journal*, January 28, 2009.

Worthen, William B. "Little Rock [Geological Formation]." Encyclopedia of Arkansas, www.encyclopediaofarknasas.net.

———. "The 'Little Rock' and the Junction Bridge—The Curious History of a Landmark." *Pulaski County Historical Review* (Spring 2008).

Writers' Program of the Work Projects Administration in the State of Arkansas. *The WPA Guide to the 1930s Arkansas*. Lawrence: University Press of Kansas, 1941.

CENTRAL FOOTBALL

"2007 Little Rock Central Tiger Football Program." Little Rock: Central High School, 2007.

Arkansas Activities Association. *2009–2010 AAA Handbook*. North Little Rock: Arkansas Activities Association, 2009.

Arkansas Activities Association. "Smart Jock" (Flash presentation). www.ahsaa.org/docs/smart%20jock.swf (accessed 3 May 2010).

Brantley, Max. "LR Central: Looking for a Home Game." *Arkansas Times*, December 23, 2004.

Cate, George M. *The Good Ground of Central High*. Little Rock: Butler Center Books, 2008.

Cox, Brian. *Tiger Pride: 100 Years of Little Rock Central High Football*. Little Rock: Arkansas Business Ventures, 2005.

Grimes, David. "Bernie Cox an Icon at LR Central." *The Log Cabin* (Conway, Ark.), September 7, 2007.

Little Rock High School Cage, 1922. In the collection of the Butler Center for Arkansas Studies, Central Arkansas Library System, Little Rock, Ark.

Olson, Nate. "Class 7A Notes." *Hooten's Arkansas Football*, 2007.

Smith, Gary. "Blindsided by History." *Sports Illustrated*, April 9, 2007.

"Tiger Squad Works Hard." *Arkansas Democrat*, September 9, 1927.

Voigt, Kurt. *Year of the Dog: One Year, One Team, One Goal*. Las Vegas: Stephens Press, 2007.

Yates, Robert. "Central's Woes at Historic Level." *Arkansas Democrat-Gazette*, November 5, 2009.

THE 1957 CRISIS

Bartley, Numan V. "Looking Back at Little Rock." *Arkansas Historical Quarterly* (Summer 2007).

Beals, Melba Pattillo. *Warriors Don't Cry: A Searing Memoir of the Battle to Integrate Little Rock's Central High*. New York: Washington Square Press, 1994.

Blossom, Virgil. *It HAS Happened Here*. New York: Harper, 1959.

Brodie, Ralph G., and Marvin Schwartz. *Central in Our Lives: Voices from Little Rock Central High School, 1957–1959*. Little Rock: Butler Center Books, 2007.

Cose, Ellis. "Little Rock: Fifty Years Later." *Newsweek*, September 24, 2007.

"The Current," CAC/Radio-Canada program, interview with Minnijean Brown Trickey, September 2007.

Gordy, Sondra. *Finding the Lost Year: What Happened When Little Rock Closed its Public Schools?* Fayetteville: University of Arkansas Press, 2009.

Jacoway, Elizabeth. *Turn Away Thy Son: Little Rock—The Crisis That Shocked the Nation*. New York: Free Press, 2007.

—— and C. Fred Williams, eds. *Understanding the Little Rock Crisis: An Exercise in Remembrance and Reconciliation*. Fayetteville: University of Arkansas Press, 1999.

Kirk, John A. *Beyond Little Rock: The Origins and Legacies of the Central High Crisis*. Fayetteville: University of Arkansas Press, 2007.

LaNier, Carlotta Walls, with Lisa Frazier Page. *A Mighty Long Way*. New York: One World/Ballantine Books, 2009.

Lewis, Catherine M., and J. Richard Lewis, eds. *Race, Politics and Memory: A Documentary History of the Little Rock School Crisis*. Fayetteville: University of Arkansas Press, 2007.

Margolick, David. "Through a Lens, Darkly." *Vanity Fair* Web exclusive. www.vanityfair.com/politics/features/2007/09/littlerock200709 (accessed May 3, 2010), September 24, 2007.

Roberts, Gene, and Hank Klibanoff. *The Race Beat: The Press, the Civil Rights Struggle, and the Awakening of a Nation*. New York: Knopf, 2006.

Roberts, Terrence. *Lessons from Little Rock*. Little Rock: Butler Center Books, 2009.

DYESS, ARKANSAS

Streissguth, Michael. *Johnny Cash: The Biography*. Cambridge, Mass.: Da Capo Press, 2006.

Hendricks, Nancy. "Dyess Colony Resettlement Area." Encyclopedia of Arkansas, www.encyclopediaofarknasas.net.

MARY LEWIS

Zeman, Alice Fitch. *Mary Lewis: The Golden Haired Beauty with the Golden Voice*. Little Rock: Rose Publishing, 2001.

THE BUILDING OF CENTRAL HIGH

Aikman, W. Russ. "John Parks Almand (1885–1969)." Encyclopedia of Arkansas, www.encyclopediaofarknasas.net.

Almand, A. J. "Pulaski Profiles: John Parks Almand." *Pulaski County Historical Review* (Summer 1989).

Arkansas Historic Preservation Program. "National Historic Landmarks of Arkansas: Little Rock Central High School." Little Rock: Arkansas Historic Preservation Program, n.d.

"Central High History." Little Rock Central High School National Historic Site Visitor Center. www.nps.gov/chsc/historyculture/school-history.htm (accessed May 3, 2010).

Lambert, H. L., ed. "Little Rock High School Building." *Journal of Arkansas Education*, October 27, 1927.

"Little Rock Central High School." Little Rock School District. www.lrsd.org/display.cfm?id=132 (accessed May 3, 2010).

Ross, Frances, and Anne Fulk. *Grand Central: A Short History of Little Rock High School and Little Rock Central High School, 1927–1983*. Little Rock: Little Rock Central High School, 1983.

Smith, Sandra Taylor, and Anne Wagner Speed. "Little Rock's Central High School Neighborhood Historic District." Little Rock: Arkansas Historic Preservation Program, 1999.

ARKANSAS'S REPUTATION

Fulks, Clay. "Arkansas." *American Mercury* (July 1926).

Friedlander, E. J. "'The Misasmatic Jungles': Reactions to H. L. Mencken's 1921 Attack on Arkansas." *Arkansas Historical Quarterly* (Spring 1979).

Jackson, Thomas William. *On a Slow Train Through Arkansas: Funny Railroad Stories, Sayings of the Southern Darkies, All the Latest and Best Minstrel Jokes of the Day.* Chicago: T. W. Jackson Pub. Co., 1903.

Lancaster, Bob. *The Jungles of Arkansas: A Personal History of the Wonder State.* Fayetteville: University of Arkansas Press, 1989.

Mencken, H. L. "The South Begins to Mutter." *The Smart Set* (August 1921).

Schuyler, George S. "Traveling Jim Crow." *American Mercury* (May–August 1930).

SCIPIO JONES AND MIFFLIN GIBBS

Dillard, Tom. "Scipio A. Jones." *Arkansas Historical Quarterly* (Autumn 1972).

Gibbs, Mifflin W. *Shadow and Light: An Autobiography with Reminiscences of the Last and Present Century.* Lincoln: University of Nebraska Press, 1995.

Gordon, Fon Louise. *Caste & Class: The Black Experience in Arkansas, 1880–1920.* Athens: University of Georgia Press, 1995.

Mosaic Templars Cultural Center. "A Building for the Community: The History of the Mosaic Templars of American Building." Little Rock: Mosaic Templars Cultural Center, n.d.

Norrell, Robert J. *Up from History: The Life of Booker T. Washington.* Cambridge, Mass.: Belknap Press of Harvard University Press, 2009.

Stockley, Grif. *Blood in Their Eyes: The Elaine Race Massacres of 1919.* Fayetteville: University of Arkansas Press, 2001.

Teske, Steve. "Scipio Africanus Jones (1863–1943)." Encyclopedia of Arkansas, www.encyclopediaofarknasas.net.

Whitaker, Robert. *On the Laps of Gods: The Red Summer of 1919 and the Struggle for Justice that Remade a Nation.* New York: Crown Publishers, 2008.

THE 1927 FLOOD

Almost all of the information about the immediate effects of the flood on Little Rock was taken from newspaper accounts in the *Arkansas Democrat* and the *Arkansas Gazette.*

Barry, John M. *Rising Tide: The Great Mississippi Flood of 1927 and How It Changed America.* New York: Simon & Schuster, 1997.

Hendricks, Nancy. "Flood of 1927." Encyclopedia of Arkansas, www.encyclopediaof arknasas.net.

JOHN CARTER LYNCHING

The *Arkansas Democrat* and the *Arkansas Gazette* provided extensive coverage daily throughout late May and early June 1927 about the missing children, the Carter lynching, and the aftermath. Most of my narrative is drawn from those accounts and from the Haldeman-Julius below.

Beary, Michael J. *Black Bishop: Edward T. Demby and the Struggle for Racial Equality in the Episcopal Church.* Urbana: University of Illinois Press, 2001.

Chicago Defender (Chicago), May 27, 1927.

Dray, Philip. *At the Hands of Persons Unknown: The Lynching of Black America.* New York: Random House, 2002.

Eison, James Reed. "Dead, But She Was in a Good Place, a Church." *Pulaski County Historical Review* (Summer 1982).

Forman, James. *The Making of Black Revolutionaries.* Seattle: University of Washington Press, 1997.

Greer, Brian D. "John Carter (Lynching of)." Encyclopedia of Arkansas, www.encyclopediaofarknasas.net.

Haldeman-Julius, Marcet. "The Story of a Lynching: An Exploration of Southern Psychology." Girard, Kan.: Haldeman-Julius Publications, 1927.

Harp, Stephanie. "Stories of a Lynching: Reporting on a Mob and Its Victim, 1927." *Kronikos* (2000).

Little Rock Police Department. *Little Rock Police Department: History and Personnel.* Paducah: Turner Publishing Co., 2004.

McClinton, Edith W. *Scars from a Lynching.* Little Rock: Backyard Enterprises, 2000.

Mosaic Templars Cultural Center, Little Rock, Arkansas. Interviews with citizens about the lynching in the permanent exhibit.

Roy, Beth. *Bitters in the Honey: Tales of Hope and Disappointment across Divides of Race and Time.* Fayetteville: University of Arkansas Press, 1999.

"Special Investigation of the John Carter Lynching, Little Rock, Ark." Group I, Series C, Box 349, NAACP Records, Collections of the Manuscript Division, Library of Congress (Washington, DC).

ROOSEVELT THOMPSON

The best starting place for information about Roosevelt Thompson is the Web site for the still-in-progress film *Looking for Rosey* (http://www.lookingforrosey.com), the home page for which (accessed May 3, 2010) contains a trailer including footage I quote from. The producers are still seeking funding to be able to complete the documentary.

"Death of Roosevelt Thompson (The 2nd Obama???); Bill Clinton." Recording on YouTube of *CBS News Sunday Morning* segment from 1984. www.youtube.com/watch?v=QnOiNdnT2c4 (accessed May 3, 2010).

Gupta, Mehak, Abbi Kymer-Davis, and Marinna Wessinger. "Roosevelt Levander Thompson (1962–1984)." Encyclopedia of Arkansas, www.encyclopediaof arknasas.net.

Hoover, Brett. "The Best of Us." The Ivy League. www.ivyleaguesports.com/ article.asp?intID=3960 (accessed May 3, 2007).
Lyons, Gene. "Rosey: He Was the Best of Us." *Newsweek*, April 9, 1984.
"Melancholy Episode at Central High." *Arkansas Gazette*, April 17, 1980.
Thompson, Roosevelt L. Letter to the editor. *Arkansas Gazette*, April 7, 1980.
Wessinger, Marinna. "Remembering Roosevelt Thompson." Little Rock Central High School Memory Project. www.lrchmemory.org/wiki/index. php?title=Remembering_Roosevelt_Thompson (accessed May 3, 2010).

JOHN WALKER AND HOPE

I wrote to John Walker requesting an interview and followed up with phone calls but he failed to answer my correspondence and did not return my calls. I did attend two public speeches he gave and a hearing of the Little Rock desegregation case at which he represented the Joshua intervenors. I also interviewed people, both on- and off-the-record, who know him.

Barnes, Steve. "Federal Supervision of Race in Little Rock Schools Ends." *The New York Times*, February 24, 2007.
"Central High 50th Anniversary Legal Symposium," in partnership with the UALR Bowen School of Law, Little Rock, Ark., September 21, 2007.
Clinton, Bill. *My Life*. New York: Knopf, 2004.
Douglas, Ellen. *Truth: Four Stories I Am Finally Old Enough to Tell*. Chapel Hill, N.C.: Algonquin Books of Chapel Hill, 1998.
Ifill, Sherrilyn A. *On the Courthouse Lawn: Confronting the Legacy of Lynching in the Twenty-First Century*. Boston: Beacon Press, 2007.
Martin, Richard. "Walker Vs. the World." *Arkansas Times*, April 22, 1993.
Mathis, Deborah. "Agitator, Educator, or Both? Perceptions of Prominent Lawyer John Walker Vary Greatly." *Arkansas Gazette*, August 6, 1989.
Schnedler, Jack. "High Profile—John Winfred Walker." *Arkansas Democrat-Gazette*, March 19, 2000.
Smith, C. Calvin, and Linda Walls Joshua, eds. *Educating the Masses: The Unfolding History of Black School Administrators in Arkansas, 1900–2000*. Fayetteville: University of Arkansas Press, 2003.
Walker, John W. "From Civil Wrongs to Civil Rights," speech at the Clinton School of Public Service, Little Rock, Ark., January 18, 2010.
Wiley, Electa Campbell. *Human Resources and Black Elitism in Hope, Arkansas 1900–1935*. Hope, Ark.: E. C. Wiley, 1981.

DESEGREGATION AND RACE RELATIONS

Bazelon, Emily. "The Next Kind of Integration." *The New York Times Magazine*, July 20, 2008.
Clotfelter, Charles T. *After Brown: The Rise and Retreat of School Desegregation*. Princeton: Princeton University Press, 2004.

Garrison, Jerol. "Race and Residence" series. *Arkansas Gazette*, April 8–17, 1966.

Johnson, Ben F. *Arkansas in Modern America: 1930–1999*. Fayetteville: University of Arkansas Press, 2000.

Kirk, John A. *Beyond Little Rock: The Origins and Legacies of the Central High Crisis*. Fayetteville: University of Arkansas Press, 2007.

———. *Redefining the Color Line: Black Activism in Little Rock, Arkansas, 1940–1970*. Gainesville: University Press of Florida, 2002.

Kluger, Richard. *Simple Justice: The History of Brown v. Board of Education and Black America's Struggle for Equality*. New York: Knopf, 1976.

Lukas, J. Anthony. *Common Ground: A Turbulent Decade in the Lives of Three American Families*. New York: Knopf, 1985.

Marovich, Beatrice. "A Divided Central: Student's Essay Gets Wide Play." *Arkansas Times*, May 10, 2007.

Patterson, James T. *Brown v. Board of Education: A Civil Rights Milestone and Its Troubled Legacy*. New York: Oxford University Press, 2001.

Reed, Roy. "Resegregation: A Problem in the Urban South." *The New York Times*, September 28, 1970.

Smith, Griffin, Jr. "Localism and Segregation: Racial Patterns in Little Rock, Arkansas, 1945–1954." Unpublished Masters Thesis, Columbia University, 1965.

Stockley, Grif. *Ruled by Race: Black/White Relations in Arkansas from Slavery to the Present*. Fayetteville: University of Arkansas Press, 2009.

Tushnet, Mark V. *Making Civil Rights Law: Thurgood Marshall and the Supreme Court, 1936–1961*. New York: Oxford University Press, 1994.

US Commission on Civil Rights. *Home Ownership for Lower Income Families*. Washington, DC: US Government Printing Office, 1971.

US Commission on Civil Rights. *School Desegregation in Little Rock, Arkansas*. Washington, DC: US Government Printing Office, 1977.

Vinzant, Gene. "Mirage and Reality: Economic Conditions in Black Little Rock in the 1920s." *Arkansas Historical Quarterly* (Autumn 2004).

Woodward, C. Vann. *The Strange Career of Jim Crow*. New York: Oxford University Press, 2002.

JUDGE RICHARD ARNOLD

Price, Polly J. *Judge Richard S. Arnold: A Legacy of Justice on the Federal Bench*. New York: Prometheus Books, 2009.

Toobin, Jeffrey. *The Nine: Inside the Secret World of the Supreme Court*. New York: Doubleday, 2007.

LITTLE ROCK SCHOOL BOARD AND ELECTIONS

Almost every day during 2007, the machinations of the Little Rock School Board, superintendent Roy Brooks, attorney John Walker, and the various electoral campaigns received some kind of coverage in the press: by the *Arkansas Democrat-*

Gazette's tireless education beat reporter Cynthia Howell and the same paper's editorial page or columnists; or by the *Arkansas Times*, its blog, and the loquacious collection of largely pseudonymous commenters, some of whom may have worked for the competing paper. I read them all regularly and supplemented my knowledge by conducting on- and off-the-record interviews, reviewing board minutes, and watching meetings and campaign events broadcast on local cable television.

The sources that follow provided helpful background, perspective, and facts.

Nitta, Keith, and Joseph Y. Howard. "The Little Rock School District: A Community and School Board Divided." *Electronic Hallway*, Evans School of Public Affairs, University of Washington, 2008.

Nossiter, Adam. "Fifty Years Later, Little Rock Can't Escape Race." *The New York Times*, May 8, 2007.

Arkansas Department of Education. "Average Teacher Salaries for 2007–2008." Excel document, 2008.

Pulaski County Election Commission. "2007 Annual School Election." Pulaski County, Ark., September 18, 2007.

———. "School Runoff." Pulaski County, Ark., October 9, 2007.

University Task Force on the Little Rock School District. *Plain Talk: The Future of Little Rock's Public Schools*. Little Rock: University of Arkansas at Little Rock, 1997.

WHITE FLIGHT, SUBURBS AND EXURBS, AND PRIVATE SCHOOLS

Adams, Russell. "Friday Night Luxe," *Wall Street Journal*, December 9, 2006.

Arkansas Nonpublic School Accrediting Association. *Directory 2009–2010*. Maumelle, Ark.: ANSAA, 2009.

Barth, Jay. "White Flight." Encyclopedia of Arkansas, www.encyclopediaofarknasas.net.

Berube, Allan, Audrey Singer, Jill Wilson, and William Frey. *Finding Exurbia: America's Fast-Growing Communities at the Metropolitan Fringe*. Washington, DC: Brookings Institution Press, 2006.

Butler Center for Arkansas Studies. "Aftermath Collection: Mapping Race & Politics in Central Arkansas, 1957 and Beyond." www.digital.butlercenter.org/cdm-aftermath/index_aftermath.php?CISOROOT=/aftermath (accessed May 3, 2010).

Cabot Panther Education Foundation. www.pantherfoundation.net/aboutus.htm (accessed May 3, 2010).

Hartsell, Heather. "Mayor Removes Graffiti." *The Leader* (Jacksonville, Ark.), January 24, 2007.

Hillier, Michelle. "60 in Cabot." *Arkansas Democrat-Gazette*, October 20, 1995.

Kruse, Kevin M. *White Flight: Atlanta and the Making of Modern Conservatism*. Princeton: Princeton University Press, 2005.

"McClellan High School Crimson Lions: Official Program," Little Rock: McClellan High School, 1981. In the collection of the Butler Center for Arkansas Studies, Central Arkansas Library System, Little Rock, Ark.

Reed, Jennifer Barnett. "Prized Recruits." *Arkansas Times*, September 2, 2004.

Reese, Phillip. "What to Do—Public or Private?" *Arkansas Democrat-Gazette*, October 27, 2003.

Smith, Doug. "The Road to Shiloh." *Arkansas Times*, October 8, 2009.

TEXARKANA

Writers' Program of the Work Projects Administration in the State of Arkansas. *The WPA Guide to the 1930s Arkansas*. Lawrence, Kan.: University Press of Kansas, 1941.

Arkansas High School Alumni. "Hog History, U of A–Texarkana." www.hogalumni.com/memories/pig_stye/pig_stye.html (accessed May 3, 2010).

CENSUS DATA AND EDUCATION STATISTICS

US Bureau of the Census. *Decennial Census of the Population*. Washington, DC, 1920–2000.

US Department of Education, National Center for Education Statistics. Washington, DC.

ARKANSAS POLITICS AND POLITICIANS

Blair, Diane, and Jay Barth. *Arkansas Politics and Government*. 2nd ed. Lincoln: University of Nebraska Press, 2005.

Goss, Kay C. "Wilbur Daigh Mills (1909–1992)." Encyclopedia of Arkansas, encyclopediaofarkansas.net.

Haden, Rebecca, and Randall Bennett Woods. "Bill Fulbright (1905–1995)." Encyclopedia of Arkansas, encyclopediaofarkansas.net.

Johnson, Ben F. *Arkansas in Modern America: 1930–1999*. Fayetteville, University of Arkansas Press: 2000.

Richter, Wendy. "John Little McClellan (1896–1977)." Encyclopedia of Arkansas, encyclopediaofarkansas.net.

"The Senate: Man Behind the Frown." *Time*, May 27, 1957.

Sidey, Hugh. "The Republic of Wilbur Mills." *LIFE*, February 19, 1971.

Williams, Nancy A., ed. *Arkansas Biography: A Collection of Notable Lives*. Fayetteville: University of Arkansas Press, 2000.

INTERSTATE 630

Barth, Jay. *Full-length lecture by Jay Barth*. Butler Center for Arkansas Studies. Online audio clip. July 31, 2007. http://www.digital.butlercenter.org/u?/p1532coll1,1116 (accessed May 3, 2010).

Bowen, William H. *The Boy from Altheimer: From the Depression to the Boardroom*. Fayetteville: University of Arkansas Press, 2006.

Dean, Jerry. "I-630 Seen with Eye of Beholder." *Arkansas Democrat*, July 22, 1973.

"Final Section of 1-630 Opens in Little Rock," *Arkansas Highways* (Winter 1985).

"*Gazette* Project Interview with Jason Rouby." Interview by Jerry McConnell [2003]. Pryor Center for Arkansas Oral and Visual History, Fayetteville, Ark.

"I-630 History: A Dream Becomes a Reality." *Arkansas Highways* (Winter 1985).

"LR Expressway Is Included in Interstate." *Arkansas Gazette*, November 13, 1970.

Nolen, John. *City Plan: Little Rock, Arkansas, 1930.* Cambridge, Mass.: J. Nolen, 1930.

Rebsamen, Raymond. *Little Rock, Poised for Progress.* Little Rock: Urban Progress, 1960.

CRONKHITE-CANADA SYNDROME

Stein, Ernst. *Anorectal and Colon Diseases: Textbook and Color Atlas of Proctology.* Trans. Walter H. C. Burgdorf, MD. Berlin, Heidelberg: Springer-Verlag, 2003.

Yates, Robert. "An Emphasis on Living." *Arkansas Democrat-Gazette*, December 29, 2005.

INDEX